Architectonics of Semiosis

Semaphores and Signs

General Editors: Roberta Kevelson and Marcel Danesi

SENSING SEMIOSIS
Toward the Possibility of Complementary Cultural "Logics"
Floyd Merrell

THE SENSE OF FORM IN
LITERATURE AND LANGUAGE
Michael Shapiro

ARCHITECTONICS OF SEMIOSIS
Edwina Taborsky

Architectonics of Semiosis

Edwina Taborsky

St. Martin's Press
New York

ARCHITECTONICS OF SEMIOSIS

Copyright © Edwina Taborsky, 1998. All rights reserved. Printed in the United States of America. No part of this book may be used or reproduced in any manner whatsoever without written permission except in the case of brief quotations embodied in critical articles or reviews. For information, address St. Martin's Press, 175 Fifth Avenue, New York, N.Y. 10010.

ISBN 0–312–21657–2

Library of Congress Cataloging-in-Publication Data
Taborsky, Edwina, 1940-
  Architectonics of semiosis / Edwina Taborsky.
    p. cm. – (Semaphores and signs)
  Includes bibliographical references and indexes.
  ISBN 0–312–21657–2
  1. Semiotics—Philosophy. I. Title. II. Series.
P99.T22 1998
302.2—DC 21   98–25745
                                                                                                   CIP

Internal design and typesetting by Letra Libre

First edition: November, 1998
10 9 8 7 6 5 4 3 2 1

CONTENTS

Part I
The Structure

1 The Levels of Reality   3
2 Purity and Power   15

Part II
Codification

3 Codification as Transformation   49
4 The Metanarrative   71

Part III
Interaction

5 Codal Regimes   91
6 Rituals and Regimes of Knowledge   117

Part IV
Evolution

7 Evolution of the Metanarrative   137

Notes   183
Bibliography   196
Index   201

To the memory of Louis and Malcolm

PART I

The Structure

1

THE LEVELS OF REALITY

In this book, I am attempting to explore the *architectonics* of semiosis. Peirce used this word in the development of his philosophy (Peirce CP: 1.176–179; 6.7–34)[1] to promote the cosmic or generalist perspective. The dictionary definition is "the scientific arrangement and construction of systems of knowledge." Importantly, architectonics should be understood not as a structure but as an action—an action of organization of knowledge—and therefore ongoing and transformative.[2]

All of life is organized energy. That includes not simply atoms and molecules - the merest specks of matter before us—but also all the more complex forms of energy, such as plants and animals, human beings and their societies. Energy is the basis of all life, energy is the power to make work, it is the power to "make something." There is only one thing that energy desires, and that is to exist, in any form whatsoever. In order to exist, energy must be organized into a "packet" of finite energy; it must be a sign. Signs are spatiotemporally closed codifications of energy; any and all existential realities are signs—a molecule, a proton, a bird, a human being, a word, a thought, a gesture, a society. Semiosis is the transformation of energy into these organized forms of matter. Semiosis is not "words about reality," but is reality itself; and it takes place within architectures, which are organized regimes of knowledge.

THE MOUNTAIN AND THE RIVER: TWO LEVELS OF CODIFICATION

To begin this exploration of semiosic architecture and architectonics, I would like to examine two seemingly contradictory forces of existential reality: the continuative and the transitory.

The concept of a force of infinite and continuous power has played and always will play an important role in the human idea of reality. The truths or powers of this force are understood to exist *per se esse:* separate and, indeed, unaffected by any of the immediate particularities of life. This essentialist purity provides the continuity of life and is more expansive, more enduring, and more powerful than any single articulation. It has been imagized in countless tales, among many peoples, as a mountain. We read that

> They that trust in the Lord shall be as mount Zion which cannot be removed, but abideth forever (Ps. 125:1);

and also

> He set above them
> Granite of high mountains—and a king
> Empowered at command to rein them in
> Or let them go (Virgil 1990: Bk. I. Lines 86–89);

as well as

> On the face of the mountain, the cedar lifts its seed.
> Its shade is good, full of comfort (*Gilgamesh* 1984, 133).

Another common image is that of water—the rain, the rivers, the streams. We read that "a mist went up from the earth/and watered the whole face of the ground" (Gen. 2:4); and "A river flowed out of Eden to water the garden, and there it divided and became four rivers" (Gen. 2:10). Water, in the boundless polyphonic plurality of its forms, is the image of renewal of the immediate, the multiple individual experiences of life. "Blessed are ye that sow beside all waters" (Isa. 32:20); life can begin again.

Semiosic actions within the architecture of a regime of knowledge consist of these two seemingly contradictory forces of stability and change. The individual sign, unfettered as these waters, must always, however one defines it, "dwell in the shelter of the Most High" (Ps. 91) and operate within the bonds of another force, for "In the Lord I take refuge . . . [I] flee like a bird to the mountains" (Ps. 11). What is the relationship of these two disparate forces, which operate within a single regime and, therefore, must interact? What of other relationships and other interactions that must be dealt with by a regime of knowledge?

SELF AND OTHER

S'an ist une goute de sanc
Do fer de la lance an somet,
Et jusqu'a la main au vallet (Chretien de Troyes [c.1181] 1990, lines 3136–3139)

Un graal entre ses deux meins
Une demoisele tenoit (lines 3158–3159)[3]

Reality exists; it is "Other" to us. We fall over, bump into, meet with the brutality of its basic existentiality; as Peirce described, "the real is that which insists upon forcing its way to recognition as something *other* than the mind's creation.... The real is active; we acknowledge it, in calling it the *actual*" (1.325). We generally admit that we experience the realities of this otherness within the particular nature of ourselves as individuals, "for all men begin, as we said, by wondering that things are as they are" (Aristotle *Metaphysics* Bk.I:Ch.2.983a15).[4]

Therefore, I am bringing to this analysis a premise that the Self and the Other(s)—we and whatever we experience in external reality—both exist. A key question is, do we have direct or indirect access to the verities of this experienced reality? Is our understanding *dyadic* and direct between these two focal points, the Self and the Other, or is it *triadic*, with a mediate action inserted between these two nodes? These two cognitive frames, the dyadic and triadic, are as ancient as human thought. I consider this debate, over the existence of a *mediate metanarrative* that plays a role in cognition, the basis of all human inquiry. There seem to have been only these two answers, both of which have their followers: a dyadic cognitive frame, which is to say, direct and lacking mediation; and a triadic, which includes a mediative action. The dyadic interaction operates within a *unileveled*, or one-dimensional, architecture; the triadic operates within a *bileveled*, or multidimensional, architecture. A unilevel architecture involves codal or semiosic actions operative only as particular or single-fact existences; a bilevel architecture adds codal actions of generalization and commonality to those of the particular sign.

Most of the time our reflections about the codal operations of the universal and the particular forces consider one of the two as dominant. Indeed, the history of analytic theories within both the sciences and the humanities is a pendulum swing of exploring, promoting, privileging, denying, or rejecting one or the other as the basis of our reality. However, it is the thesis of this book that the most strategically adaptive semiosis is operative within a bilevel architecture. One level, the group-based line of continuity, permits stability. The other level, the individual-based line of finite specificity, permits heterogeneity and diversity. The transformative organization and interaction of these two levels of reality, neither of which can be reduced to the other, and yet both of which are necessarily constantly interactive, is the basic architectonics of life, permitting a transformative semiosis capable of flexible yet constructive evolution. A bilevel architecture provides a schematic structure of interactions that includes *both* a level of behavior that promotes homogeneity of particular instances; restraint and rejection of deviation, and, therefore, an assurance of continuity—and *also* a level of behavior that promotes the diversity of pluralism, chance, and uncertainty. Let us take a first look at the nature of these two levels.

A FIRST DESCRIPTION OF THE UNIVERSAL AS THE METANARRATIVE

Repetition, for a god, is a sign of majesty, necessity's seal (Calasso 1993, 33).

Among nonhuman forms of reality, both inorganic and organic, the laws of stability are, for the most part, innate; in the human species, these laws are not merely innate (physical, chemical, biological codalities), but developed through human experience; they are conceptual or textual constructs.[5] For Aristotle, the universal is also the community, for "that is called universal which is such as to belong to more than one thing" (*Metaphysics* Bk.VII.Ch.13:1038b20). As such, it is also a provisory of continuity, and Peirce states that "belief is not a momentary state of consciousness; it is a habit of mind essentially enduring for some time, and mostly (at least) unconscious; and like other habits (until it meets with some surprise that begins its dissolution) perfectly self-satisfied (5.417). Furthermore, the idea that "mere individual existence or actuality without any regularity whatever is a nullity" (5.431) is the necessity of Laws. As Peirce's term of Thirdness, it is " that which is what it is by virtue of imparting a quality to reactions in the future" (1.343).

The communitas—this "metanarrative"—is the text within which individuals author, read, and act out their lives. I should point out that this metanarrative is not a narrative in the structuralist sense; it is not an articulated and authored text, something that we might consider a formal "metalanguage," a "metatext." Rather, the metanarrative is a discourse of axiomatic habits that have been developed by its users over a long period of time; its codes are general, adaptive, and highly pragmatic interactions with the multiple forces of their reality. These codes permit the development of a network of consistent interactions with the environment, but by their generality (also called universality) they permit differences of specification in these interactions.

The metanarrative is not Truth—as essence, as pure intentionality to exist, (or as formal articulation)—but is a means of encoding energy that is operative as a particular regime of knowledge functional within spatial and temporal horizons. Within its own general codalities, it mediates multiple codal impulses—those at the sensual node,[6] those at the conceptual node—and transforms these particularities into contextually based meaning. Organically, the metanarrative can be considered the DNA codal format of a species, the cytoskeleton of an organism; socially, it is the habits of belief and behavior of a particular group. It provides the continuity, the verification of being, within which actual individual-coded forms emerge and exist within its horizons of operation. As texts of axiomatic premises, developed by experience, these "habits of behavior" are durable by virtue of what we will discuss under "legitimacy" and "fixation of beliefs." As a construct, however, the metanarrative is reflexive, which is to say, it operates in a dialogic and interactive manner with surrounding forms of energy; it is itself, necessarily amenable to changes asked of it by those other codal forces. If the individual members of a particular species begin to die out because of changes in the environment, then that species' metanarrative will *itself* recognize that it is less successful in encoding energy, and will *self-organize* a change in its codal format, to permit more encoded "signs" (individual members of the species) to exist.[7] The enormous adaptive value of one's behavior being a social rather than only innate construct has meant that the human species has the capacity to change its codes and interact with multiple and changing environments far faster and more powerfully than other species. This has resulted in the ability of the human species to spread to all ecological parts of the world and develop its interactions with the environment in complex and increasingly powerful forms. It is also for this reason that we have been warned, again and again, to be wary of hubris, the arrogance that springs from this enormous power that we, alone of all species, have.

In this sense, a regime of knowledge, as developed by the architectonic forces, is a gradually developed construction, developed by human beings over time; it should be viewed as a complex, unconscious, diverse, often contradictory system of habitual beliefs and subsequent behavior. It can be considered a set of *uninterpreted* or metaphorically expressed axioms and rules of inference. This text, this construct, can be termed the *metanarrative*. I am considering the development of a metanarrative as basic, as fundamental to human existence, as the chemical and molecular elements of the natural world. Its codes operate with the force of what Peirce defined as synechism, the "coalescence, the becoming continuous, the becoming governed by laws, the becoming instructed with general ideas" (5.4). Chomsky has spoken of "an approach to the mind that considers language and similar phenomena to be elements of the natural world, to be studied by ordinary methods of empirical inquiry" (1995, 1). He hopes for a "naturalistic approach to linguistic and mental aspects of the world . . . hoping for eventual unification with the 'core' natural sciences: unification, not necessarily reduction" (1). I am considering the metanarrative—that foundation of thought—as a natural, which means a *necessary* rather than sufficient, characteristic of not merely human but all existence.

The architectonic form of the metanarrative is not conscious imagery; indeed, idolatry brought disaster to the Israelites, and they were roughly cursed by God for so doing: "You shall be a reproach and a taunt, a warning and a horror, to the nations about you" (Ez. 5.15). To formalize or transform this set of uninterpreted axioms into an articulated body of given knowledge rather than the experience of the consequences of those unconscious axioms is the error that we will discuss under "commodification" and "structuralism."[8] The metanarrative should rather be considered the infrastructural general will of a people, loosely bound to those particular habits of those particular people in that particular geographic area and permitting the expression, in belief and behavior, of a particular way of life. "Stories never live alone: they are the branches of a family that we have to trace back, and forward" (Calasso 1993, 10). The stories, the texts, are developments of an ability and awareness of living, articulated in diverse metaphors of thought and action, meant to be told and retold, changed, adapted, and most certainly never sealed (as they would be if formalized) from such ongoing dialogue.

The codal force of this deep level of existence, this "desire for continuity of being," which I will discuss under the theme of dynamic codification, is a basis of all life. The development of the human form of this is a vital part of human existence. Because it is human, it is conceptual—a construction of the individual intellect, or rather, of the society within which the individual exists. This means that the metanarrative is accessible to change, for the human mind, operative in signs rather than instinct, can create and assign a variety of meanings to these signs. "We must suppose that there is an original, elemental, tendency of things to acquire determinate properties, to take habits . . . [and] the tendency to take habits is something essentially finite in amount, an infinitely strong tendency of this sort (unlike an absolute conformity to law) is inconceivable and self-contradictory. Consequently, this tendency must itself have been gradually evolved; and it would evidently tend to strengthen itself" (Peirce W 5.293)[9]. In other words, this making of conceptual habits is infinite in process, but not in experienced form. The actual narrative developed by the architectonic forces of a society is both closed *and* open; the two factors must coexist. This necessarily stable text must be open to the particular variations of unstable everyday life; indeed, this conjunction of the two, the infinite and the finite, has been imagized as the Fall from Grace. Every society has its tales of the Fall from the mountain site of that direct bond with the stability of an endless purity into the blinding waters of chaotic pluralism. Every society operates within the echo of God, who said, "cursed is the ground in your works, in sorrow you shall eat from it all the days of your life . . . in the sweat of your face you shall eat bread, until you return to the earth" (Gen. 3:17–19). The fact that human beings must actually author their own text—must develop their own patterns of belief and behavior, their own habits of interaction with Otherness—is a terrifying future; who knows the viability of such actions? What if our "habits of behavior" are wrong? "I hold it to be an impious and detestable maxim, that, politically speaking, the people have a right to do anything; and yet I have asserted that all authority rests in the will of the majority. . . . If it be admitted that a man possessing absolute power may misuse that power by wronging his adversaries, why should not a majority be liable to the same reproach?" (de Tocqueville 1956, 114). No matter how much we continuously reject and deny our involvement in such a task—no matter how often we insist our behavior is innate and therefore, essentialist—there is not only no proof that this "easy way out" from the responsibilities for our actions has any logical or empirical validity but such a direct bond would nullify the strategic value of the metanarrative to the human species.

Lyotard's famous analysis (1984) on the postmodern condition considers the gradual development of metanarratives. He understands them in the Hegelian/Cartesian nominalist sense of a *totality*, an articulated monolithic and monologic "text" that stood over the individual as an authoritative force inhibiting individual thought.[10] White (1973) has described these texts as "authoritative" in the sense that they have no human—which is to say, vulnerable and finite—narrator. For the postmodernists, the metanarrative as a monologic mountain had been developed, possibly quite consciously, by the modernists and was part of a degenerate political agenda. Jameson (1981) refers to these master narratives as our "political unconscious." The coupling of the theme of "political" to the narrative suggests a subversive agenda and defines the metanarrative as an agential and conscious power. This view, incidentally, is exactly similar to the view of the modernists several centuries earlier, who campaigned against the smothering of the individual mind within the monologic agenda of scholasticism. Lyotard begins his critique with a seemingly unconscious acceptance of the actual viability of a direct (dyadic)—or what I will call pure—access to nature, for "science has always been in conflict with narratives. . . . I will use the term *modern* to designate any science that legitimates itself with reference to a metadiscourse of this kind making an explicit appeal to some grand narrative, such as the dialectics of Spirit, the hermeneutics of meaning, the emancipation of the rational or working subject, or the creation of wealth" (1984, xxiii). And he writes "I define *postmodern* as incredulity toward metanarratives." His idea of the future or best-operative (I won't use the term "ideal") society is that it will be fully conscious of its entrapment within the metanarrative's language. It will operate less "within the province of a Newtonian anthropology (such as structuralism or systems theory) than [within] a pragmatics of language particles. There are many different language games—a heterogeneity of elements. They only give rise to institutions in patches—local determinism" (xxiv). His analysis of the modernist framework within which cognition develops, is that the metanarrative is *owned* by "the decision makers," "who allocate our lives for the growth of power" (xxiv). This perspective of the metanarrative as a commodity—in this instance, language that is employed in political control—is an error made by those who argue against metanarratives. The mistake is the reification and commodification of that which should never be so transformed; the metanarrative must remain subconscious and must never be articulated into a finite "set of laws."

However, Lyotard correctly asks, Without the metanarrative, where is legitimacy? What ensures continuity of semiosis? An existential entity is a particular sign, a spatiotemporally closed and finite codification of energy; it lasts for one minute. How does one move from one sign into another? Is it simply a linear step-by-step action, with, as some have noted, an infinitesimal "gap" in between? Such an unmediated semiosis, such a Darwinian gradual evolutionism, is, as I will explain, too dangerous for the continuity, not merely of the particular sign, but of energy. What we must consider is the nature of energy—it desires only to exist; are there different types of continuity, and are some actually harmful to this desire?

There can be different degrees of the health of a semiotic architecture, ranging from a degenerate and dissipative form to a robust and adaptive form. A degenerate semiosis will only express iconic copies of itself and will, as such a machine, without the constant input of more energy and the authoritative energy required to prevent deviant interference, gradually "run down" and dissipate its codal operations—this type of continuity, in which semiosis can only replicate itself, dissipates energy. A robust semiosis will be able to absorb energy from various sources and, unlike a machine, transform all of that variety of energy into new codal forms—this type of continuity is beneficial to energy. A robust semiosis operates within a bilevel architecture; the codal generality of the metanarrative permits an action of "communion," and a deeper, less-than-superficial contact is set up between diverse codifications; this action permits a codal reflexion—an awareness of both commonality and differences—and a subsequent recodification that includes both the commonality and the differences such that all of the total energy is semiotically articulated, and within not iconic but indexical transformations.

Essentially, the bilevel architecture permits mediation, a vibrant phase of codal communion and transformation between separate nodal points, an activity that Aristotle referred to as the mediation of *mundus imaginabilis*. Two differently coded entities cannot interact until a "mediation zone" is established; this is a commonality of generalizations that is broad enough to permit the different specifications of the two entities to find some common ground and so develop shared signs or meanings. Just so can two people, each speaking a completely different language, gradually communicate by agreeing on the meaning of their gestures. They must move from a complex and highly specific codification (their languages) to a more general and loose codal level that can permit their gestures to then develop common specific meanings, and therefore, the development of a new, shared, complex language. If, let us say, we were to conduct an experiment and forbid each participant to learn the language of the other, but insist on their common habitation and the necessity of their working together, then the mediation level with its codal generalities would permit them to find a common conceptual ground and thus develop a new language that would become increasingly complex such that they would be able to fully communicate the specialization of their lifestyle. Mediation is Peircean Thirdness: "The beginning is first, the end second, the middle third. The end is second, the means third. The thread of life is a third; the fate that snips it, its second.... Continuity represents Thirdness almost to perfection.... Law as an active force is second, but order and legislation are third" (1.337).

Mediation permits semiosis. Plato's soul has three parts: appetite, reason and spirit (see the "Three Parts of the Soul" in *Republic* Book IV). The third part, spirit, is a force that may mediate between the desires of appetite and reason, for "in the factions of the soul, it much rather marshals itself on the side of the reason" (1937, Bk. IV, 403); it is associated with reason and moral behavior but should not be thought of as a true codal mediation. Plato's three parts of the soul can be metaphorically compared with the Vichian triad of gods, heroes, and men (appetite, spirit, and reason).[11] Think of the sword of Roland, which mediated between him and the Other: "Ah, Durendal, how fair and white you shine,/And with what fire you glitter in the sun!" (1972, lines 2316–7). Roland tried to destroy it, to prevent its falling into pagan (asocial or, more accurately, "a different social") hands, but the destruction of a mediative force, because it is so general and therefore broadly based rather than specific and vulnerable, cannot be done that easily. Think of oxygen, which is harder to destroy as a basic chemical than a cube of ice. And so it was:

> Roland strikes hard upon a swarthy stone
> Cuts more of it away than I could tell
> Loud grates the sword, but does not break or snap;
> Instead it flies rebounding to the sky.
> When the count sees he cannot shatter it,
> In soft tones to himself he makes lament;
> Ah, Durandel, holy and fair you are!
> Relics in plenty fill your gilded hilt
> For infidels to wield you would be wrong' (1972, lines 2338–2349).

We must remember this: A metanarrative permits a species to exist because each "sign-unit" is also a member of its commonality.

The metanarrative—the sword of interaction between different codifications—must still be understood to operate from a host-site of a specific or distinct semiosic organism. The metanarrative may exist within a simple or complex organization: a single species and also an ecological biome, a single tribe and also a conglomerate of global societies. In other words, the metanarrative, which provides the capacity for both general continuity of its organism and also interaction with other organisms, may itself be simple or complex; it may have the capacity to permit only a limited amount of different codal realities or may be broad enough to permit multiple and diverse codal realities that are able to interact because they share a deeper commonality within the generalizing codal actions of their metanarrative. The metanarrative exists as such generalities and cannot be "dismembered" (or commodified) into bits and pieces. Each society, for example, will have a different metanarrative; the colonists tried to spread their way of life by transforming their metanarrative into an ideology and marketing it throughout the world.[12] If two societies wish to develop economic ties, they must develop a new, *shared* metanarrative general enough so that semiosis can permit both groups to interact their meanings and activities.

As we will see in later chapters, as the basic grammars of the metanarrative become more complex over time, they build up spider-like webs of interaction with other narratives over many experiences. Such a network provides a framework of continuity amongst different codifications and thus, as it did for Odysseus, inserts the requirement for analysis, reflexion [13] and decision making. Cognition, as Aristotle insisted, cannot take place by the addition of distinct nominalist particles.[14] Without the reflexions and analysis provided within the comparative and generalizing capacities offered by metanarrative, we could not "think." "It would be a sharp one, and a stealthy one, who would ever get past you in any contriving; even if it were a god against you. You wretch, so devious, never weary of tricks, then you would not even in your own country give over your ways of deceiving and your thievish tales. They are near to you in your very nature" (Homer 1965, Book XIII, lines 291–295). So is Odysseus, the hero of reflexive wile, described by Athena.

There are only two models to use in considering the relation between the Self and the Other. One uses either a unilevel model, which is based around the existentiality of the particular entity and is thus a nominalist model, or a bilevel model that considers the habits of the group communitas or metanarrative as a generalizing force. The two forces of continuity and diversity operate, in very different styles, within both models. The mountain, with its unchanging enormity, stabilizes us, and the diversity and openness of all those rivers and streams and brooks that carve their lives in the mountain, provides us with the freshness of regeneration. "One woman struck her thyrus against a rock and a fountain of cool water came bubbling up. Another drove her fennel in the ground, and where it struck the earth, at the touch of god, a spring of wine poured out. Those who wanted milk scratched at the soil with bare fingers and the white milk came welling up. Pure honey spurted up, streaming, from their wands" (Euripides 1959, *The Bacchae,* lines 702–711). Together, the mountain and the flowing liquids provide life. In contrast to what will be outlined as the unileveled frame of modernism and postmodernism, the architectural frame of the most strategically adaptive society is bileveled; interaction is not simply and only between two versions of existence on one level—which was the dyadic error of the Marxist analysis of two classes[15]—but is between two completely different forms of organization, necessarily understood as existential on two levels that can never merge under any circumstances.

First, a warning. We may be part of a group, we may become so bonded to the multitude, our beliefs and behavior may become so homogenous that it may seem as if the group "thinks," but despite this seeming uniformity of thought, there is no such thing as a group that "thinks" or "feels." Only the individual can do either; the fact that this individual can do so only within a group semiosis—is something that we will explore throughout this book.

2

PURITY AND POWER

MODERNIST/NOMINALIST REJECTION OF THE UNIVERSAL

The unilevel architecture of the nominalist or modernist cognitive frame, like that of the bilevel architecture, is as old as the human species. In our times, Descartes is merely one of its most famous residents. Experience and knowledge are confined to codal operations at only two nodal sites: the sensual and conceptual actions, which both operate within the singular referentiality of the individual. The knowledge base of the *sensus communis,* Aristotle's communal knowledge, the realm of *nous,* and the mediating role of *mundus imaginabilis* is rejected for the subjective perceptions of the "enlightened" individual. The three key concepts of nominalists are their sense of the ultimate purity or essential completeness of the Other (external reality) in its nature as a single continuous force of truth; their conclusion that the knowledge/truth of this Other can be accessed by another single entity, the Self; and their idea that this knowledge is direct and unmediated.

The unilevel or nominalist cognition rests on this idea of purity, which implies that external reality is "as itself" fully accessible, whether existent in god or in matter. It is the impurity of "prejudice," an impurity found only within the individual intentionality, which prevents one from full access to this pure reality. The more perfect the result, defined by that famed feeling of certainty,[1] the more perfect the agential abilities of the one who feels such certainty.

> Blessed are they who have kept the flesh pure, for they shall become a temple of God (Cor.2 6:16).

> Who shall ascend the hill of the Lord?
> And who shall stand in his holy place?
> He who has clean hands and a pure heart (Ps. 24).

The nominalist experience, whether Platonic, Cartesian, or Christian, is understood to be made up of these two forms of discrete "things-in-themselves": sensual matter and conceptual ideas. One is transitory, the other is eternal; their identities will vary depending on the particular brand of nominalism. The sensual matter is separate from the knowing Self and any problems of interaction between these two nodes or codification sites are due to "pollution" or the mingling of these nodes with each other. This is the standard dualism between the mind and the body, or "between a thinking and corporeal thing." Descartes, when he says that "I, (that is to say, my mind, by which I am what I am), is entirely and truly distinct from my body, and may exist without it" (1962, 91), has acknowledged the distinction between the sensual and the conceptual nodes of individual experience; he has, however, separated them into two different existentialities rather than two codal operations within the one body.[2] His next two assumptions give the conceptual mind immense powers over the sensual body, which is reduced to a fixed result of an a priori codification—a mechanical commodity—rather than an ongoing and generative semiosic codification. With this method of analysis, the individual loses two means of codification of energy—a simplification that is reductionist rather than scientific. The selection of a unileveled direct frame of interaction between the sensual and the conceptual means that the transformative codal generalities of a third codal action, that of a mediative level, are lost. The rejection of both the sensual and conceptual codifications as ongoing codal *actions*, their transformation into *static* forms whose codal identity was a priori fixed, and the actual existential separation of these two nodal sites into two self-existent realities, meant that only one codal phase was available to the individual—the conceptual, "cogito ergo sum"—and its task was simple mnemonic "perception" of that external and eternal truth. This loss of complexity of codification within both the Self and the Other, means that knowledge, or what I would rather call "life," is reduced to mechanical and non-generative codification. Semiotic complexity, ongoing diversification, and all potentiality of codal development—which is to say, evolution—cannot be part of this semiosic architecture.

The next assumption can be defined as the principle of *Purity,* by which I mean the belief in the "fullness of truth" of the data accessed by the conceptual node. That is, the essential truth of the corporeal/conceptual Other is understood to exist, in itself, and is fully transparent and completely accessible to the "correct" human mind via reason, which is understood to be not a means of codification but a means of decodification of sensual/conceptual pollutants, in order to access the essentiality of this reality. Therefore, quite logically following this acceptance of a fullness of truth and its nature as a transparent or fully accessible reality, is the third assumption, which postulates that the human mind has a *direct linear access* to this pure truth.

Let me first consider the purity of truth. Descartes' assertion was that "I have no ground for believing that Deity is deceitful" (1962, 44), and "I discover that it is impossible for him ever to deceive me, for in all fraud and deceit there is a certain imperfection" (64). Without any evidence, and with only a desire for the comfortable state of certainty, we are further assumed to have the capacity for direct access to these Platonic truths. Descartes then establishes his general rule that "every clear and distinct conception is doubtless something . . . and every such conception (or judgment) is true" (74).[3] This ability is innate, not communally acquired, for "I will assuredly reach truth if I only fix my attention sufficiently on all the things I conceive perfectly, and separate these from others which I conceive more confusedly and obscurely" (74). There are no restrictive or expansive biologic or social bonds to the community; the individual, alone, has direct access to God, to Purity. The individual, with his tremendous freedom of thought, "the power of free choice" (69), is "the measure of all things" for "I possess in myself the means of arriving at the truth" (93). And what does man possess? A mind, capable of a Superman-like gaze into the essential truth of things. What is the source of error in humans? Their sensual reality, placed as they are, between God the perfect (and non-sensual) and "nothingness" or "that which is at an infinite distance from every sort of perfection." This Platonic idealism suggests that any error of understanding is due to a defect of understanding within the individual. To further this sense of the individual origin of truth, human beings have the "faculty of will," that freedom to do and think whatever they so wish, and if there is error of thought, it is because their will "muddied up" the clear faculty of understanding. To thus restrain the will (which is somehow associated with communal or universal pressures of the species because it is related to emotional, sensual or innate susceptibility), will lead to a clear knowledge of reality. Cartesian nominalism operates within the same ideology of the culpability of the sinful individual as Christian nominalism. The principal property or essence of existence, whose origin is in God, is expressed in natural matter, which is perfect in that it is unsocialized and so moves directly into the mind of the individual. Any "stops" along the way are attributable entirely to the socialized impurities of the individual.

That which is social is corrupt; a priori reason is, above all, free—which is to say, asocial. What can one say of such heroic linearity? As de Tocqueville wryly comments on the egalitarianism of America, the "equality of conditions leads men to entertain a sort of instinctive incredulity of the supernatural, and a very lofty and often exaggerated opinion of the human understanding" (1956, 147).

The Platonic Ruler; the Cartesian reason; the steely-eyed stringency of Ockham; and the sensualist essentiality of the twelfth-century goliards and, later, Rousseau—these seemingly innate rational or sensual powers of the individual define the heroes of nominalism, who all operate within the unilevel architecture of direct confrontation. This form of semiosis privileges individual agential powers. The "truths" of the divine/natural force are understood by those who are human, but human in a very special way. In this regime, heroes rather than gods are the source of truth—they who are both mortal and directly in contact with the gods; they who are, in the words of Vico, "from this same lack of reflective capacity . . . bluff, touchy, magnanimous and generous" with what they have discovered (1948, 708). All our heroes must fit this image, whether they are Achilles, Lancelot, Gilgamesh, or Schwartzkoff.

> The hero born of Uruk, the goring wild bull.
> He walks out in front, the leader,
> and walks at the rear, trusted by his companions.
> Mighty net, protector of his people,
> raging flood-wave who destroys even walls of stone! (*Gilgamesh* 1985, 4)

Indeed, Cartesian reason developed as a reaction to the stultifying reification of yet another unilevel frame, that of Christianity and its monological truths. Descartes' analytic frame rejected its blatant commodification of purity, and considered its conceptual vagueness and arbitrary hierarchies indicative of ignorance and confusion. Cartesian conceptual knowledge is a "form of" corporeal existence; it actually exists in itself—and not in some bishop's mind. Therefore, the better the innate individual abilities of accessing this "body" of knowledge, the purer the resultant stock of knowledge. It was a brave attempt at de-commodification of a former purity, a purity that had become invested within the isolate authority of a debased Church, an attempt to "recontact" that essential purity of life that existed outside the theistic "logos." However, semiotically, it operated within the same unilevel frame as the degenerate scholastic regime and therefore, was doomed to fall into the same isolationist trap.[4]

It has been argued that modernism with its insistence on a unileveled interaction, a direct contact between the individual and the Other, is not bound to the past, interacting, as it were, with objects existent only in the "current-now." Such an asocial frame considers that the individual understands knowledge intuitively and rejects the past as an historical or group-based development,[5] which becomes understood as an articulated sign—what we will later call a "metalanguage," something that operates as a degenerate form of control over that individual. The idea of the group, or social order, becomes reduced to an authoritarian and alienated set of rules to prevent juvenile pranks; this ideology equally reduces the individual to an innately dissentive force that must at some time be calmed. In this view, the conflict is between the sensual and the rational—understood as the communal (whether sins of our common flesh or common beliefs)—and the individual; the conflict is between the "socialized" and the "unsocialized," the restrained and the free, the elders and the juveniles—that old opposition of *sapienta* and *fortitudo:* the wise and the valiant, the past and the present. Modernism, in all its forms, whether Cartesian or Marxist, rejects a textual or social past and retains a belief in an essentialist purity of origin. The goal of modernism is that bond with original purity—which goal is to be extended to all people, all individuals who have the particular capacity to so access it: "Blessed are the pure in heart, for they shall see God" (Matt. 5:8).

There is a price to pay for such a direct contact. Despite the century-long flush of success of this campaign of heroic individuals, such an architecture of knowledge is, as a unileveled frame, degenerate—by which I mean that it can only replicate a finite set of truths—which was exactly the state of affairs of the medieval church. This direct bonding of Self and Other, mind and purity, leads almost inevitably to the *commodification* and ownership of that which has been so cleverly, so readily accessed—that "pure knowledge." Such a semiotic regime has no ability to access or codify energy in any form other than that iconic echo—which must be shouted ever louder in order to be heard. In this regime, our beliefs are stabilized not by an external authority, but via our own people—our heroes who have, in their capacity as leaders, selected our truths for us. When it is we ourselves who have set up this mountain, its authority is even more tenacious than that set up by the gods.

Nominalism, whether operative within the faith of St. Augustine or the reason of Descartes, sets up walls against dialogue. For "the mass of mankind . . . if it is their highest impulse to be intellectual slaves, then slaves they ought to remain" (Peirce 5.380).

THE POWER OF COMMODIFICATION

> Usury is the commodification of purity.
> And because the usurer takes another way,
> Treating nature and what follows from her
> Contemptuously, he puts his hopes elsewhere (Dante 1993. *Inferno* Bk.
>   XI, lines 109–111).

The classical understanding of *misthos* "wages" began with the understanding of something won in competition, or an "honorific compensation for deed performed," and therefore, "a deed worthy of praise by poetry is incompatible with wages suitable for artisans" (Nagy 1990b,190). However, within a conceptual architecture that sees reality as essentialist, and promotes the human ability to access this purity, an insidious transition takes place. Pure energy moves from being an abstract potentiality, infinite in its offering of itself to semiosis, to being a mechanical actuality and finite in its reality. The human individual, as the sole being deemed fit to access this purity—by his intellect, by his skills—is understood as a source of power for the world. Purity is always linked to power; the power of accessing and providing a continuity of accessibility to this purity becomes the definition of the civilized man. The natives who do not till the soil are denigrated as not carrying out their human task of transforming potentiality to actuality; peoples are judged by their actions in transforming potentiality to actuality. Whatever and whoever provides the most commodities, the most articulations of energy, is the most powerful.

The only possible reason why the human species, almost alone of all species, has little capacity for innate and therefore unchanging habits of behavior and belief and instead must develop them within social experiences is to permit a highly flexible adaptive response to the environment. To transform a metanarrative—with its powers of generalization and therefore expansion of relationships—into a commodity, to move the unconscious to the conscious, is powerful: highly successful in the immediate range for fixing and stabilizing beliefs, but in the long run, completely disastrous. It provides a first flush of wealth but that transformation has rendered its semiosic articulations inflexible and authoritarian. Inflexibility will destroy any species, and in the case of Homo sapiens, with its need for constant adaptation, inflexibility will destroy a society within one generation. This commodification of the essence of generality is one means of depriving the metanarrative of the power of generative adaptation; the commodification of the methods used to articulate the general laws of the metanarrative is another means. These two techniques are the basis of structuralism, which understands continuity to be provided by group-run systems that are static and fully articulated structures. The individual is understood to be dominated by these systems and must struggle for their dissolution, setting up a society in internal dyadic conflict. Where "the power of individualism becomes extinct; the organization alone has life" (Peirce, note 1,5.380). Lyotard considers "two basic representational models for society: either society forms a functional whole, or it is divided in two. An illustration of the first model is suggested by Talcott Parsons . . . and his school, and of the second, by the Marxist current (all of its component schools, whatever differences they may have, accept both the principle of class struggle and dialectics as a duality, operating within society)" (1984, 11). I am not commenting here on the image of a complete versus an incomplete and developing society but on the nature of his rejection of the complete or whole society and his support for a conflictual society.

Certainly, Lyotard's rejection of the unified totality is quite correct: nothing could survive in such homogeneity; this is as valid in organic as it is in social formations. The reification or specification of the metanarrative, whether it is expressed within particular artifacts or in the means of artifactuality, is a degenerate act and should actually be considered a means of self-destruction. Lyotard points out that "society does not form an integrated whole, but remains haunted by a principle of opposition. The alternative seems clear: it is a choice between the homogeneity and the intrinsic duality of the social, between functional and critical knowledge" (1984, 13). Knowledge "coincides with an extensive array of competence-building measures and is the only form embodied in a subject constituted by the various areas of competence composing it" (19). It is social, for the "consensus that permits such knowledge . . . is what constitutes the culture of a people" (19). These commodified metanarratives, these "created objects-in-themselves . . . allow the society in which they are told . . . to define its criteria of competence and . . . to evaluate according to those criteria what is performed or can be performed within it" (20). That is, the narrative establishes horizons of existential performance; despite this criticism, this is exactly what a metanarrative, genetic or social, must do.

"Narratives . . . determine criteria of competence . . . [and] define what has the right to be said and done in the culture in question, and since they are themselves a part of that culture, they are legitimated by the simple fact that they do what they do" (23). What is missing from this analysis is the "reflexivity" of the metanarrative: the fact that a metanarrative must never be concrete, must never be articulated into an artifact, but must remain a generalizing, reflexive and dialogic action-of-ordering. To ignore this basic aspect of the metanarrative leads one to consider that this knowledge, this narrative, is an existential entity; a *structured* commodity; and therefore, a political tool. As such a nominalist, Lyotard is swept within the postmodern fear of stable structures, viewing such as the site at which the "assassins, or followers of the Old Man of the Mountain, used to rush into death at his least command, because they believe that obedience to him would ensure everlasting felicity" (Peirce 5.371). So it is with every perception of the Mountain as either the artifact or the artifactual agent.

The Marxist analysis of potential energy, in which purity of being is accessed by a particular class and transformed into its actual state, also operates on a unilevel model. It is not simply a commodification into money—as in "all commodities are perishable money; money is the imperishable commodity" (Marx 1971, 67). It is rather the commodification—the transformation—of an infinite energy into a finite form of that energy that is, in its finite form, infinite in power. It is to have brought Zeus to bay, to not merely covet his power, but to imagize it and also keep it without also destroying oneself. That is power. Access to such powers may be devious and stealthy; one moves toward it in stages: "deprive the object of its social power and this power will have to be exercised by people over people" (75), which really means: deprive the object of its power by transforming it from actual to potential, and then give people this power/right to make it "actual" and you will have them at each other's throats. Marx's stages move from a first "primitive" existence, which he saw within a unileveled frame in which people were involved in direct "relations of personal dependence" within a direct contact with the "reality/purity" of the object, rather than a contact with a finite or commodified sign.[6] When energy has been bonded, trapped within a closed sign, as within Marx's idea of money, then the energy of the work of codification is equally trapped. But a sign is always codified energy; there is no such thing as free energy floating in a void outside the sign. Equally, that sign may increase its codal complexity within semiosic contacts: the statue increases its semiosic complexity when transformed into an expression of an artistic or social era; money, as a sign of value, increases its complexity within trading transactions. The codification of work-energy within the artifact is an increase in the complexity of the resultant sign but is not a degenerate act. It is only degenerate if the sign becomes a metalanguage, if it assumes a formal order whose authority is non-reflexive and abstracted from contextual reality. The final stage—and we must compare this with the Cartesian ideal—is "free individuality—based on the universal development of individuals, on their mastery of their communal and social productivity, and on their control of their social capacities" (75). Consider his words: free, individual, mastery, and control. This is a unilevel frame, convinced that the individual can indeed be a master; can own all forms of Others, and can thereby prevent chance, with its indifferent denigrations from purity, from ever disrupting the comfort of stasis.

If we accept this unilevel frame, and define Otherness within the context of its mastery and control, then potential energy (which Marx called "value") would be transformable by us into actual energy ("use value"). This means that we are both the owners and the articulators of potential energy. We become, in a word, gods. As a true unilevel modernist, Marx refused to accept our limitations of access: any problems were due to our "pollution" by our group socialization. "First of all there is a limit, which is inherent not in production generally but in production founded on capital" (318). The idea that the limit "exists in nature and in the mind is something Marx refuses to consider" (Calasso 1994, 238). We, agents for actual energy, must so develop ourselves that potential energy and its forces can never evade us. "Marx is a prisoner of the Enemy he attacks.... What offended him was not so much and not only the iniquity which capital engendered, but the fact that capital was preparing to become an *obstacle* to production, an antiquated and sclerotic form compared with the immensity of what was possible"(1994, 237). "Capital had become his Madame de Beauseant. From her he had learned manners; it was she who had introduced him into society. But now she seemed to him withered, a bit ridiculous, doomed. He turned his gaze elsewhere, to the *debutantes* of the proletariat" (237). Marx has swallowed—no, *is* swallowed by—the traps of the unilevel frame. Purity has no limits. Escape from the strictures/structures of capitalism, and purity—which has always belonged to the gods—is yours.

As Calasso notes, "Ricardo and Marx were rival theologians, but both were 'honestly' and 'scientifically' devoted to the same God" (1994, 241). Both were unilevelists, both believed in purity and power; it is immaterial whose purity, whose power. The point is, it was accessible—whether by force of body or mind.

MODERNISM AS PURITY

Modernism, by virtue of its unilevel frame, is an insistence on "purity of existence," a belief that objective reality as "pure essence" exists, and that, in our nature as individuals, both our sensual and conceptual access to it is direct and uncorrupted. In this sense, the nominalist frame, like that of the angels, is the simplest; the purest; the most sublime; the most hopeful; and, equally, the most disastrous architecture—resulting almost inevitably in racism, ethnocentrism, and totalitarianism, in essentially impure forms of society. The fact that such a regime does not work—that the human species, if it continuously operated within such a direct interaction would lose what is most quintessential to its nature (namely, conceptual semiosis and the adaptive diversity of interactions based on this codal trope)—is an unfortunate and usually completely ignored reality.

The politicization of the unilevel nodal points of contact with this purity is a logical step of nominalism/modernism. It is based around the commodification of the power provided by pure truth as owned by the individual agent who has accessed its essence. Lyotard commented that "legitimation is the process by which a 'legislator' dealing with scientific discourse is authorized to prescribe the stated conditions (in general, conditions of internal consistency and experimental verification)[7] determining whether a statement is to be included in that discourse for consideration by the scientific community" (1984, 8). This is a clear statement of the "proprietorship" of knowledge. Lyotard immediately affirms this, with his statement that "the question of the legitimacy of science has been indissociably linked to that of the legitimation of the legislator since the time of Plato" (8)—who was, it should be pointed out, another great nominalist. To continue, "the right to decide what is true is not independent of the right to decide what is just" (8)[8]. By this statement, I understand that the true (the essential) has merged with the particular (the existential). Lyotard points out their similarity; "there is a strict interlinkage between the kind of language called science and the kind called ethics and politics: they both stem from the same perspective" (8); and we see that "knowledge and power are simply two sides of the same question: who decides what knowledge is, and who knows what needs to be decided?" (9).

Commodification of purity is a source of power. "The *state of sweetness* is not stable; it is occasional perfection, fleeting and insidious, the *dulcedo* of the mystics. When it becomes stable, sweetness demands to be devoured. Sweetness ends in the knife of sacrifice; sensual pleasure ends in spasms" (Calasso 1994,60). The sweetness of purity, bonded to reality, devoured as such, may seem to provide the potency of power, but it leads, inevitably, to destruction. It is a small and necessary second step to that ingestion that sets up identifiable status groups to control this "truth," as did Plato with his rulers, as do all totalitarian regimes, as any godfather well knows. This results in what Lyotard says is "a thorough exteriorisation of knowledge"(1984, 4) which is to say, a separation of it, in the Marxist sense, from the polyphonic and heterogeneous actions of a diversity of human beings. Knowledge, like labor, becomes a commodity, and the "relationship of the suppliers and users of knowledge to the knowledge they supply and use is now tending, and will increasingly tend, to assume the form already taken by the relationship of commodity producers and consumers to the commodities they produce and consume—that is, the form of value. Knowledge is and will be produced in order to be sold, it is and will be consumed in order to be valorized in a new production: in both cases, the goal is exchange. Knowledge ceases to be an end in itself, it loses its 'use-value'" (4–5). This "mercantilisation of knowledge" is based on a key idea of nominalism, the transparency and, therefore, accessibility of truth by individual agential actions. "Wherever there is no initiation, we find the autodidact. Wherever knowledge is not wisdom transmitted through experience, everyone is enrolled in correspondence courses" (Calasso 1994,222). Nominalism, with its belief in "free individuality—based on the universal development of individuals, on their mastery of their communal and social productivity" (234) can only end with the commodification not merely of the "Other," the material world, but also of the individual; human beings will become "as 'human material'" (234). Equally, de Tocqueville comments; "I perceive how, under the dominion of certain laws, democracy would extinguish that liberty of the mind to which a democratic social condition is favorable; so that, after having broken all the bondage once imposed on it by ranks or by men, the human mind would be closely fettered to the general will of the greatest number" (1956,149). Human beings, with the commodification of their conceptual ability will "be a parody of Anthropos—a progressive Anthropos, a ghastly hybrid of Monsieur Homais and the Homunculus of alchemy, produced by the application of a model (productivity as infinite growth) to the increasingly "universal" subjects of society. They will be the only subjects that *improve themselves* perpetually! And we must remember that 'improvement' was the word Adam Smith used to mean 'development'" (Calasso 1994, 234).

To the unileveled nominalist, reality is directly accessible. The "truth," the "reality" is existential "in itself" and one simply has to develop the skills or ability to access it. Peirce refers to this a priori essentialism as "infallibility," and points out that the "infallibilist naturally thinks that everything always was substantially as it is now" (1.175). Are we able to, "by the simple contemplation of a cognition, independently of any previous knowledge and without reasoning from signs . . . enabled rightly to judge whether that cognition has been determined by a previous cognition or whether it refers immediately to its object" (5.213)? We have no capacity to distinguish "intuitive from mediate cognition" (5.224). Nominalism, "the chief burden of Hegel's song," is based on an architectural simplicity of direct linearity, and Peirce comments that in "that strangely influential hodge-podge, the salad of Cartesianism, the doctrine stands out very emphatically that the only force is the force of impact, which clearly belongs to the category of Reaction" (5.63).

Modernists, who developed in the heady reactionary freedom of that escape from the degenerate unileveled architecture of the scholastics, actually set themselves up to be at the same time, colonists and colonized. "The men who live at a period of social equality . . . commonly seek for the sources of truth in themselves, or in those who are like themselves . . . they will seek to discover the chief arbiter of their belief within, and not beyond, the limits of their kind"(de Tocqueville 1956,148). As the unilevel architecture develops, it transforms the energy it accesses into signs that rapidly become commodified. Within such a self-referential validation process, the codes and their artifacts at first become authoritative and exclusionary, and then disintegrate into meaningless rhetoric. This is because no semiosic process can deal with an infinite production of signs, which is to say, with the full materialization of the potentiality of god, as Semele so tragically learned. To consider that one is actually performing such a transformation of the infinite into the finite denigrates the resultant artifacts into empty rhetoric.

A semiosis that is based within artifacts, within the closure of the sign rather than the discourse of the action, must operate within a process that does not permit deviation, and "not only is common opinion the only guide which private judgment retains among a democratic people. . . . The public . . . does not persuade to certain opinions, but it enforces them, and infuses them into the intellect by a sort of enormous pressure of the minds of all upon the reason of each" (de Tocqueville 1956, 149). This is a succinct description of the results of the "glued bond" of the Sender-Other and the Receiver in a unileveled architectonic society. The violence we feel, both for and against the unileveled frame—that longing for its purity; that comfort of having an ultimate source of truth; and still, our fear of its simplicity and its directness, its total disregard and indifference to our part in the matter—is evidence of both its attraction for us and its danger to our sanity. To remove oneself from the reflexive accountability that is a requirement of a bilevel architecture inserts a state of constant and disturbing uncertainty, and that is why we will always remain attracted to the blind securities and enveloping warmth of the unilevel frame.

A unileveled frame, made up of single sign-units, has no capacity for interaction between the source of knowledge and the individual except via force. It must resort to the idea of the hero, some individual with innate superhuman purity or extraordinary skills of accessing truth for that society, whether as king, scientist, international businessman, or Mafia leader. As noted, the unilevel frame, with its direct access to pure truth and the private ownership of this truth promotes ideologies of different levels of genetic and social evolution. A mediatory framework[9] cannot operate within these themes of the priority of individualism; direct accessibility of truth; existence of this truth as pure and transparent; and private ownership of the resultant commodified truths, or the structural means of its access and storage. Here, Peirce's comment on power applies to the modernist frame, wherein it "is hard for man to understand this, because he persists in identifying himself with his will, his power over the animal organism, with brute force" (5.315). He continues, "The heart of the dispute lies in this. The modern philosophers . . . recognize but one mode of being, the being of an individual thing or fact, the being which consists in the object's crowding out a place for itself in the universe, so to speak, and reacting by brute force of fact, against all other things. I call that existence" (1.21). Peirce's three modes of being—Firstness, Secondness, and Thirdness (1.24–26); of possibility, actuality, and the law of potentiality, with the latter understood as a "rule to which future events have a tendency to conform" (1.26)—brings in the mediate process operative in a bileveled architectonics. Whether the access to knowledge begins with the external material object, as in Positivism, or in an ideological concept, as in Platonism, it is the same type of interaction, based as it is on a unileveled plane of existence.[10] Whether nominalism considers that the semiosic action between the object and the mind to be direct (as in Cartesianism and Platonism), or aided by a socially developed framework (as in Saussurian-based structuralism and framework analysis),[11] it is an action operative on a unileveled plane of existence. This is the key error: in an adaptive semiosis, the transformation of energy into signs or existential entities must function on at least two levels of energy—two completely different systems of organizing and encoding energy, no matter how many nodal points, or points of reorganization of energy/knowledge. The statement that "we live in two worlds, a world of fact and a world of fancy" (Peirce:1.321) does not mean two nodal points within the *same* world, as the nominalists understood, but two quite different; conflictual;

and necessarily *dialogic* parallel fields of energy. Again, Peirce points out that "the nominalist metaphysics [is] the most blinding of all systems, as metaphysics generally is the most powerful of all causes of mental cecity, because it deprives the mind of the power to ask itself certain questions" (5.499). The ability to question signification can only occur within a reflexive, mediative, semiosis.

"Who dares climb the mountain of the Lord or who will stand in His holy place? . . . Only the humble man can safely climb the mountain, because only the humble man has nothing to trip him up" (St. Bernard). It is the man without hubris who, as Socrates pointed out again and again, will admit ignorance and dare to reveal it, within the question.

> Que tu ne pois demander
> Por coi cele gote de sanc
> Saut par la pointe do fer blanc?
> Et do traal que tu veis
> Ne demande ne n'enqueis
> Quel riche home an en servoit (Chretien de Troyes, 1990, lines 4588–4592)[12]

POPPER'S PURE BUCKET AND OTHER COMMENTS

Popper's "bucket" analysis describes the nominalist/modernist architecture very well, with "its emphasis on the perfect emptiness of the mind at birth" and its belief that "all experience consists of information received through the senses" (1972, 61). This is also De Man's "false model:" "it accounts for the metaphorical model of literature as a kind of box that separates an inside from an outside, and the reader or critic as the person who opens the lid in order to release in the open what was secreted but inaccessible inside" (1979, 5). Certainly, all our cognition begins in sensual data. Peirce states unequivocally that we have no power of intuition, and "that there is no reason for supposing a power of introspection; and, consequently, the only way of investigating a psychological question is by inference from external facts" (5.249). But, equally, this inference is not unilinear, with "the infant's mind [considered] to be a *tabula rasa* and the adult's a school slate" (5.519). In such a unilevel framework, cognition is misunderstood as communication; the key operations are the movement of an intact object, in conceptual sign form, from the sensual, as carried by its media systems (transparent in a "pure" world and obscure in a "degenerate" one) from one spatial site to another. Bateson too, in his critique of cumulative evolution, comments that "if evolution proceeded in accordance with conventional theory, its process would be blocked. The finite nature of somatic change indicates that no ongoing process of evolution can result only from successive externally adaptive genotype changes since these must, in combination, become lethal, demanding combinations of internal somatic adjustments of which the soma is incapable" (1972, 350). Popper continues his critique that "our mind is an empty slate upon which the senses engrave their messages" (1972, 61). Here, the mind is considered empty at birth, and is, over time, filled up with these objects-in-themselves. He writes, "Knowledge is conceived of as consisting of things, or thing-like entities in our bucket" and "knowledge is, first of all, *in* us: it consists of information which has reached us, and which we have managed to absorb" (62). This "immediate or direct" knowledge is similar to Peirce's examination of the unilevel framework of nominalism in "The Spirit of Cartesianism" (1868) wherein he denigrates this process, pointing out that we "cannot begin with complete doubt," an empty mind, but rather, "must begin with all the prejudices which we actually have" (5.265). He rejects completely the privileged role of the individual as repository of truth, for "to make single individuals absolute judges of truth is most pernicious" (5.265). De Tocqueville remarks that "the practice which obtains amongst the Americans, of fixing the standard of their judgment in themselves alone, leads them to other habits of mind . . . they readily conclude that everything in the world may be explained, and that nothing in it transcends the limits of the understanding. Thus they fall to denying what they cannot comprehend" (1956,144).

The unilevel architecture permits a cognitive format that begins with an individual's empty mind and ends with the "full mind" of that same individual. Popper's comments on this linearity are that it means that "all error, all mistaken knowledge . . . comes from bad intellectual digestion which adulterates these ultimate or 'given' elements of information by misinterpreting them, or by wrongly linking them with other elements; the sources of error are our subjective admixtures to the pure or given elements of information, which in their turn are not only free from error, but are the standards of all truth" (1972, 62). And again, arguing against this privileging of the individual acquisition of knowledge, de Tocqueville writes "if man were forced to demonstrate for himself all the truths of which he makes daily use, his task would never end" (1956,146).

Peirce presents us with a definition of the functionality of pragmaticism, which consists "in that process of evolution whereby the existent becomes more and more to embody those generals which were just now said to be *destined,* which is what we strive to express in calling them *reasonable*. In its higher stages, evolution takes place more and more largely through self-control, and this gives the pragmaticist a sort of justification for making the rational purport to be general" (5.433). We will return to the concept of "self-control," which is a necessary factor of the interactions within the bileveled architecture in later chapters. The point to consider here, is the gradual development of an architectural frame, of "reasonable" and "general" stable planes of contact between nodal points of the members of that society and others. This forms that deeper level of the bilevel architecture, the "communitas," the architectural construct of habitual themes, wherein specific semiotic interactions or the transformation of energy into signs, can take place. Such common frames must develop, for "without such common belief no society can prosper—say, rather, no society can exist; for without ideas held in common, there is no common action, and without common action there may still be men, but there is no social body. In order that society should exist, and *a fortiori,* that a society should prosper, it is required that all the minds of the citizens should be rallied and held together by certain predominant ideas; and this cannot be the case unless each of them sometimes draws his opinions from the common source, and consents to accept certain matters of belief already formed" (de Tocqueville 1956, 146).

If we use the unilevel model—with its two tactical nodal sites of essence and existence—with knowledge understood as moving from one site to the other, mimetically or via cumulative linearity, two things can result. First, these two nodal points can merge, with a subsequent "essentialism" of individual existence as the only active force of semiosis. This is the authority of Cartesian certainty and the Saussurian sign. This essential/existential nominalist bond will translate, in a social sense, into a narcissistic self-absorption of the individual as the sole source of power, to the exclusion of the group, permitting an ideology legitimizing the individual will to power and rejecting accountability. The "honeyed trap" of this bond will display itself in a constant and even desperate accumulation of signs that have become artifacts, static commodities. The only semiosic interactions available will be monologic dyads of confrontation with Otherness. No dialogical interaction is possible without the bileveled architectural framework. A sign that chances to come into existence without such constructs will never last beyond its first breath—except by the authoritative force of its new owner. Based on this merger of the "pure" with the "actual," one will see the commodification of the resultant existentiality, that Saussurian sign. This is absolutely inevitable; what other means of stability can there be in a society whose semantic images are produced without the ongoing dialogical and transformative input of "habitual codes"—other than crystallizing that single product into static immobility? The commodification of this marketable form of purity/value, and the subsequent politicization of its ownership, is equally inevitable. Modernism is a concern with both purity and power. This will manifest itself in structures of elitism and racism. The society may resort to violence because any "state of Secondness" is violent[13] and most certainly has nothing to do with semiosis, with the production of meaning.[14] "The image of rape . . . is no longer the contact of a shared meal; rather it is the sudden, obsessive invasion that plucks away the flower of thought" (Calasso 1993, 52). A merged codification is an admission of loss: a deep and terrible loss of the basic architecture of generative semiosis, a loss of the means of dialogical interaction.

Attempts to prevent the nodal merger and maintain the two nodes by affirming their distinction, and thus prevent the value of the essential from merging with the form of the existential, are doomed to failure within a unilevel framework of existence. One attempted method has been to define the process of interaction with either node as different. This acknowledgment of difference (the sensual and conceptual require different approaches) is also an acknowledgment of similarity (both operate on a unilevel, and are thus amenable to being mistaken for the other, as Saussure warned with his separation of the synchronic and the diachronic). The academic world has been at great pains to maintain the distinction between the humanities and the sciences (sensual and rational) and has been on the watch for "bad science," as might happen if the humanities or social "sciences" stepped beyond their boundaries and attempted to deal with "objective reality." Modernists/nominalists have defined reality as basically rational, and, therefore, completely accessible "in its totality" via mechanical methods; they have defined sensuality as "historic," "social" or "narrative," which is to say, socially constructed.[15] Lyotard's comment that "Science has always been in conflict with narratives" (1984, xxiii), is a clear acknowledgment of the separation. A third aspect of the unilevel frame is the development of "megastructures," which are commodified codes that "sit" as static metalanguages, perspectival frameworks between the nodes of the unilevel, and that guide/structure the concepts formed within the interactions with reality.

Lyotard's definition of the "modern" (nominalist) approach to science is that it legitimizes itself "with reference to a metadiscourse . . . making an explicit appeal to some grand narrative, such as the dialectics of Spirit, the hermeneutics of meaning, the emancipation of the rational or working subject, or the creation of wealth" (xxiii). The grand narrative of Lyotard is that stultifying structure that blocks interaction and yet provides a much-needed stability for the unileveled society. What happens when it goes too far, when its order freezes all life?

> The reckless fools, ignorant of the vengeance of the gods. . . . Justice will be decided by force, and there will be no honour. . . . And then Respect and just Retribution, wrapping their beautiful shapes in white robes, will leave the wide-pathed earth, and forsake mankind to go to Olympus and join the race of the deathless gods, and bitter sorrows will be left for mortal men" (Hesiod. In Trypanis 1971, 105).

THE POSTMODERN REACTION

Why are the mountains black? Why do they stand covered in cloud? Is the wind fighting with them? Is the rain beating on them? Neither does the wind fight with them, nor does the rain beat upon them; it is Death who strides across them carrying away the dead . . . The old implore him, the young kneel before him, and the little children, with crossed arms, cry: 'Death, pass through a village, stop at a cool fountain'"

—Anonymous folk song, eighteenth century (Trypanis 1971, 479)

The ultimately disastrous results of this architecture led to postmodernism, which can be understood as emerging within both a total revulsion against such a political usurpation of the potentialities of knowledge and a deep awareness of the impoverishment of modernism. Modernism had "used up" its energy and had taken to devouring its own signs, its own people, its own identities. The postmodernist recognizes the frailty of the unilevel frame, and postmodernism has exactly the same goal as did modernism: the rejection of the past—in this case, the rejection of the modernist's heroic and ultimately pathological goal of daring to package purity. "The postmodern reply to the modern consists of recognizing that the past, since it cannot really be destroyed, because its destruction leads to silence, must be revisited: but with irony, not innocently. . . . [Postmodernism exists] in an age of lost innocence" (Eco 1992, 227). What postmodernism quite rightly rejects is the belief in the accessibility of purity, the belief that one could—directly, immediately, by one's own powers—dare to touch it. We deceived ourselves, and so we are yet deceived.

The themes of postmodernism are, interestingly enough, similar to those of modernism: the focus on the individual and the rejection of the group. Postmodernism, however, reverses the identity of the individual. The modernist individual is innately pure, if potentially fallible; the postmodern individual is a borderline degenerate. Postmodernists are highly aware of the logical framework of the unileveled architecture and its commodification of the essence of reality into a material form. This merger of essence into existence is the crux of the unileveled architecture; the merger leaves the sign with no place to go but forward or back,[16] at which point it is trapped by its commodification and removed from temporality, whether as an artifact of the past or a commodity of the next market. Lyotard felt that there was "a kind of flight of reality out of the metaphysical, religious, and political certainties that the mind believed it held. This withdrawal is absolutely necessary to the emergence of science and capitalism" (1984, 77). Here we see modernist thinking; that separation of the codal nodes of the sensual and the conceptual, that denigration of the former for the latter, that belief in the transparent accessibility of reality by the individual. Saussure's bonded sign is also Marx's bonded labor. Lyotard's "vision of nonhegemonic Greek philosophy (the Stoics, the Cynics, the Sophists), as the guerilla war of the marginals, the foreigners, the non-Greeks, against the massive and repressive Order of Aristotle and his successors" (in Forward by F. Jameson, 1981, xix) can be understood as a reaction against this power. Postmodernism in its rage, its despair over the results of this bonding of purity with power, deconstructs the codal factories; but then, like Orpheus, looks back at what it has done, and turns all that it has freed into an endless murmuring babble—bats that "have formed by holding one on another [and] so gibbering . . . go on their way together" (Homer 1965, Bk. XXIV, lines 8–10).

Postmodernism is fear: a fear of power; of Otherness; of the self; and, ultimately, of codification. In its rejection of the ultimately depraved modernist bond between the essential and the existential, postmodernism does not offer us an architectonics—the bileveled frame—that would prevent the formation of yet another blind arrogance by an insistence that habit or stability act in a constant dialogical pragmatic interaction with the current experience. Instead, the postmodern fear of contact between essence (referent, object, external reality, body) and existence (image, meaning, concept, mind)—its fear of that essence's power over our minds, particularly when elevated to deism or commodified; and, importantly, its assumption of the basic fallibility of human beings—leads to a rejection of the effective power of any relationships. Postmodernism leaves us completely backed up against the wall. It retains that single unilevel frame of modernism but cuts off all contacts—a rather simple, desperate and ultimately foolish action, like the dog that bites off the leg caught in a trap. We are left unsteady, wavering, isolated from any reference, any ground. We, as fallible, weak, and inherently evil, cannot participate in anything that has meaning. We, and any thoughts we might have, "vanish like water that runs away" (Ps. 58)—such is Derrida's endless slippery deconstructionism, and so are we, as usurers, punished.

Lyotard concludes that the postmodern "is undoubtedly a part of the modern" and a "work can become modern only if it is first postmodern. Postmodernism thus understood is not modernism at its end but in the nascent state, and this state is constant" (1984, 79). We see here an acknowledgment of their relationship, with the postmodern understood as a liminal between two stable regimes—whether that stability is derived from a unileveled or bileveled architecture. Postmodernism is a regime in which only the current existence is actual; it is thus in a first, Hegelian phase of a "thesis," a state of being in which existence is proposed but only as a signifier, and is without its essentiality or stability. Therefore, a postmodern regime is condemned to endless interpretation, which is to say, non-interpretation. "Dionysus is not a useful god who helps weave or knot things together, but a god who loosens and unties. . . . Dionysus is the river we hear flowing by in the distance, an incessant booming from far away; then one day it rises and floods everything, as if the normal above-water state of things, the sober delimitation of our existence, were but a brief parenthesis overwhelmed in an instant" (Calasso 1993, 45). So it is with the rivers of deconstruction; they wash away the stabilization of our mountains.

Derrida writes that Levi-Strauss commented that "if my hypothesis is correct, the primary function of writing, as a means of communication, is to facilitate the enslavement of other human beings" (1976, 130). Derrida adds that "this hypothesis is so quickly confirmed that it hardly merits its name" (130). This is a clear statement, I suggest, of modernism, with its belief in the purity (of knowledge) as a holistic power, of structuralism with its commodification of the systemic codification of that knowledge, and of postmodernism, with its fear of both purity and power, its concerns that access to this purity would become politicized and so, as "touched" by impure humans, degenerate. I am not saying that postmodernism denies the reality of purity or power; to the contrary—it is obsessed with both. However, its denigration, its despair, of the human species is such that any individual contact with these forces is considered to empower the essential evil in humanity. Derrida continues that it "has long been known that the power of writing, in the hands of a small number, caste, or class, is always contemporaneous with hierarchization, let us say with political differance;

it is at the same time distinction into groups, classes, and levels of economico-politico-technical power, and delegation of authority, power deferred and abandoned to an organ of capitalization" (130). But is it writing itself that causes hierarchies? Is writing an existential form of essential purity and thus, as so bonded, tainted? Rather, it is the commodification of essentialism via a unileveled frame that is the problem.

What is wrong with hierarchies? Certainly Derrida admits that complexity (which is to say, hierarchies) is "produced well before the appearance of writing" (131). Derrida quotes Rousseau, with the concept that writing "may well have been indispensable to the consolidation of dominions.... The struggle against illiteracy is thus indistinguishable from the increased powers over the individual citizen by the central authority" (132). Derrida is against this form of structuralism, with its definition of the structure as a social construct; he points out that such a logic necessarily suggests that "liberty and the like 'go hand in hand' . . . with illiteracy and the absence of compulsory military service, public instruction or law in general" (132). Derrida attempts to de-commodify writing; however, his Writing is still a monologic force, in its a priori "essence," in its nature as "the name of these two absences" (41)[17]. Derrida separates the two nodal points of the sensual and the conceptual by deconstructing their bonds. He then destroys the codal structures that developed between them, that dominated their—and our—existence and controlled the individual. He leaves us with essence and existence, forever separated (signifier and signified elusively sliding, in their Lacanian fashion, from each other), and sets up an untouchable purity of Writing as demiurge, as the agency to move, isolate, in the gap between these two nodal points and so, somehow, in an asemiotic and equally essentialist manner, to permit "meaning" to exist. Writing thus assumes the causal force of Cartesian reason; it can produce signs in our consciousness. The difference between Cartesian Modernism and Derridian Postmodernism is that the former rests on a belief that pure truth *can* be accessed and that the signs that result are, or should be, iconic copies of this truth. Derridian postmodernism admits that such a truth may exist, but denies its access to any individual and inserts the cave-like amorphous shadows of Writing as our only reality. This same retreat from a structuralist metalanguage into mysticism can also be found in the liminal antirational phase of the fourteenth and fifteenth centuries that promoted such anti-Aristotelians[18] as Eckhart and Nicolas of Cusa.

Hassan has outlined some key aspects of the postmodern perspective: namely, that it aims to decanonize current metanarratives, for its goals are "indeterminacy" or rather, indeterminacies which includes "all manner of ambiguities, ruptures, and displacements affecting knowledge and society" (1987, 168) There is fragmentation, for the "postmodern only disconnects, fragments are all he pretends to trust. His ultimate opprobrium is 'totalisation'—any synthesis whatever, social epistemic, even poetic" (168). We are witnessing, Lyotard argues again, a massive "delegitimation" of the mastercodes in society, "favouring instead '*les petites histoires*' which preserve the heterogeneity of language games" (169). Then, there is "Self-less-ness and Depth-less-ness," for "Postmodernism vacates the traditional self, stimulating self-effacement—a fake flatness, without inside/outside—or its opposite, self multiplation, self-reflection" (169). We should note this next comment, that postmodernism "suppresses or disperses and sometimes tries to recover the 'deep' romantic ego, which remains under dire suspicion in post-structuralist circles as a 'totalising principle'"(169).

Purity, in the full idealism of its flavors, is therefore an integral part of the postmodern theme. The difference is in its power over us, and our power over it. The fact that one could access purity, that one could actually masquerade as a god, as a hero, is a strictly modernist theme.

> Proud of his wonderful achievements, civilized man looks down upon the humbler members of mankind. He has conquered the forces of nature and compelled them to serve him. He has transformed inhospitable forests into fertile fields. The mountain fastnesses are yielding their treasures to his demands. The fierce animals which are obstructing his progress are being exterminated, while others which are useful to him are made to increase a thousand-fold. The waves of the ocean carry him from land to land, and towering mountain-ranges set him no bounds. His genius has moulded inert matter into powerful machines which await a touch of his hand to serve his manifold demands (Boas 1919,1).

This is Boas's sardonic critique of the self-glorification of an ego-centered society. Here, we have the powers of stasis as well as diversity within the control of the human individual, who thereby quite naturally sees himself as all-powerful and believes "the king must rule." Can finite beings handle such infinite powers—or will they instead "take up arms" and use these powers against each other? Machiavelli was cautious and repeatedly warned his prince to include the people in decisions; Lincoln wrote that "Men are not flattered by being shown that there is a difference between the Almighty and them" (March 15, 1865). Perhaps we too should hesitate. And on another level, is such a discourse infinite and therefore abstract, or finite and therefore commodified?

Postmodernism firmly believes in gods, but imprisons all forces: they from us, and we from them. We have fallen too far, and the gods have turned their backs on us. What is degenerate, even enraging, to postmodernism is the structuralist, capitalist action, which, by its flagrant commodification of purity, lured the individual into a belief that one could walk hand-in-hand with pure essence. "There was an age when the gods would sit down alongside mortals . . . At this point gods and men had no difficulty recognizing each other; sometimes they were even companions in adventure . . . gods and men met simply to share some feast before returning each to his own business" (Calasso 1993, 53). For the postmodernist, purity and the gods may exist—but there will never be, again, any contact; and "the third regime, the modern one, is that of indifference, but with the implication that the gods have already withdrawn, and, hence, if they are indifferent in our regard, we can be indifferent as to their existence or otherwise" (53).

The key distinguishing factor of postmodernism is its concern with the degenerate relationship between purity and power. "A few hours of mountain climbing turn a villain and a saint into two rather equal creatures" (Nietzsche 1969, 184). Certainly, postmodernism has been identified with fragmentation, relativism, and an elitist snobbery against wholeness and completeness, but all of this is simply an attempt to deny the reality of power, to deny that there is anything "out there" that has control, that has a means of power over anyone. Hassan speaks of power as something that "profoundly engages knowledge" (1987,176), and moves onto Foucault, whose whole work was the examination of the means of power. There is Barthes, who insists on "the 'truth of desire' which discovers itself in the multiplicity of discourse" (Hassan 1987, 179). I use the term "power over," for it is understood on a unileveled and therefore dyadic and oppositional frame. It is observed, covertly, operating in the political and economic arenas, as capital, something that is the focus of the individual, who is already defined by the postmodernists as inherently degenerate. This capital is coveted, owned, marketed, blatantly copied; whoever observes this capital is transformed into another commodity, each set against the other, each engaged in devouring the other. Such is the postmodern perspective.

In the late, "mature" stage of nominalism, whether it is that of the scholastics or the modernists, the truth is owned and obscured by the State, by a hierarchy of commodified power rather than the reflexive communitas as originally intended. The "ideology of communicational 'transparency', which goes hand in hand with the commercialisation of knowledge, will begin to perceive the State as a factor of opacity and 'noise'" (Lyotard 1984, 5). Reactions to such commodification and ownership can move from the narcissistic self-absorption of the surrealists to the equally isolate mysticism of an historic search for that essential purity. Or, purity can be understood as lost, beyond reach of our mechanical and spiritual abilities: "modern aesthetics is an aesthetic of the sublime, though a nostalgic one. It allows the unpresentable to be put forward only as the missing contents" (81). The form of this "something which does not allow itself to be made present" (80) will be multiple, for "let us be witnesses to the unpresentable; let us activate the differences and save the honor of the name" (82), for "there are no rules, there is no game" (10). Our acceptance of legitimacy as essentiality, beyond our reach, "allows us to believe only in what we choose, in what we agree to choose. Here there is no consistent meaning: the meaning is given each time. And as it is given, so is it taken" (Calasso 1994, 168). The painter and novelist will work with "the rules of the art of painting or of narrative . . . as a means to deceive, to seduce, and to reassure, which makes it impossible for them to be 'true'" (Lyotard 1984, 75).

In the postmodern phase, truth is achievable, if at all, by a constant harvesting of haphazardly floating, disconnected signs. Although Hassan accepts these results of deconstruction, he still promotes an objective reality that is beyond "the Text," such that his limiting factor on unimpeded relativism is "a different kind of 'authority' [lower case], pragmatic, empirical, permitting pluralist beliefs. Between these beliefs there can be only continual negotiations of reason and interest, mediations of desire, transactions of power or hope"(1987, 181). This seems to be a critical or reflexive regime, but Hassan does not inform us of the locus of our reflexivity, unless it is to suggest that it is in the objectivity of the environment. To "prevent critical pluralism from slipping into monism or relativism," he can only "call for pragmatic constituencies of knowledge that would share values, traditions, expectancies, goals" (182). This is a commodification again—of the codal systems of the communitas. We are no further ahead with this analysis, because its reflexions are based not on generalities but on specifics, which are thereby static and non-adaptive.

Baudrillard regrets the transparency of modernism, the hope and actuality that everything can/will be articulated. His metanarrative is, however, a set of articulated rules; a commodity in itself; a "tactic of potentialities linked to usage: master, control and command" (1992, 152). This system of articulated rules, which becomes a degenerate metanarrative, and Baudrillard's key loss, is also a metaphor of the "unreal," "what used to be lived out on earth as metaphor, as mental or metaphorical scene, is henceforth projected into reality, without any metaphor at all" (152). Again, we see that hope for a pure reality, that anger against the seemingly impure results of mixing metaphor and reality. It is the "private sphere" that has become externalized; "it signifies as a whole the passage into orbit as orbital and environmental model, of our private sphere itself" (152). The metanarrative is seen not as an internalized cognitive logic but as an articulated force/power. What Baudrillard is mourning is the loss of a system of rules that is hidden; and in this, he is exactly correct. Furthermore, the articulation of this "attempted-metanarrative" is not by the individual, but by the group—whether it be the State or the media.[19] "Obscenity begins . . . when all becomes transparence and immediate visibility, when everything is exposed to the harsh and inexorable light of information and communication" (154). When the metanarrative moves from its bileveled architectonic form of habit-process into articulated laws, Baudrillard writes that it "is no longer the traditional obscenity of what is hidden, repressed, forbidden or obscure,"[20] but instead, the power over us of the structures, "of the all-too-visible . . . of what dissolves completely in information and communication" (154).

The postmodern escape from articulated power into an inarticulated and, therefore, mystical power, defined incorrectly as the aesthetic (Baudrillard, Lyotard, Derrida, Heidegger)[21] is, I suggest, an invalid and incomplete attempt to escape the problems of modernism. This sense of "that which cannot be said" (Hassan's "aesthetics of silence," Lyotard's aesthetic, Derrida's Writing) and the emphasis, then, on metaphor, irony, parody—all the codal tropes that slide meaning away from any direct and forbidden contact with this force of stasis—is simply an admission of a failure to deal with our relationships with reality. This "aesthetics of silence" is not similar to the Aristotelian *dunamis,* the Peircean Firstness, the Vichian muteness—which are not "that which cannot be said" but are rather "the potentiality to speak." The unilevel god is holistic, stern, and aloof; the bilevel god is desire, *eros,* which is related to *erotesis,* the action of questioning. It is this action, *erotesis,* which we must maintain within the architecture of the metanarrative.

The commodification of the encoding systems, which are the means of transforming energy into signs, turns them into static authoritarian structures—Plato's Laws, Derrida's Logos, Lyotard's metanarratives. A codal system must permit context-specific agreements, heterogeneity, and pragmaticism; such actions are not external to the code, but are part of its architectural operation. The point of a bileveled framework is that it develops an architectural frame of multiple dyadic planes that are set into "actions of contact" by triadic or mediate interactions. The bileveled frame, like the postmodern, prevents direct contact—that intuitive lock dismissed by Peirce—not out of despair and grief, but out of Desire, which is understood as an acceptance of energy as a force of infinite potentiality to exist in as-yet-undefined semiosic forms. The bilevel architecture functions within a reflexive, interactive level of mediation that understands energy as pure potentiality, and current actualities as reflexive and variational catalysts of this energy. It is this transformative involvement that is important, for this is the basis of semiosis. "It is not always easy to be a man, still less to be a pure man. But being pure is recovering that spiritual home where one can feel the world's relationship, where one's pulse-beats coincide with the violent throbbing of the two-o'clock sun" (Camus 1955, 121).

Peirce said, "every genuine triadic relation involves meaning, as meaning is obviously a triadic relation. . . . A triadic relation is inexpressible by means of dyadic relations alone" (1.345). A dyadic plane is set up between two points of contact, for "all physical forces appear to subsist between pairs of particles" (1.345). However, the interaction between these nodal points can only produce an existential particle that is capable of contact with other particles *if* such interaction is triadic, rather than dyadic—which is to say, if it includes the reflexive interactions of a true metanarrative. With a direct dyadic interaction, the resultant particle of energy is crystallized into a static and isolated Saussurian sign, a state of Peircean Secondness, Derrida's logocentric word. It can only exist as an isolate particle, and, following the second law of thermodynamics, will immediately begin an entropic decay. Within a triadic interaction, which sets up a mediative grid of communal and shared networks (to be discussed in later chapters) the interaction becomes both determinate and indeterminate, and as a result, flexible and productive of energy in a variety of interactions, rather than restrictive and monologic. Reflexion, multiple perspectives, and decisions based on that multiplicity are all possible. Without such a mediatory plane—material particles or signs come into being only as a result of "brute force," that Saussurian hammer of arbitrary bonding, and can be interacted with, not by thought but "lacking thought," with a fixed acceptance—whether it be via a force of authority; tenacity; or sheer, a priori chance.

Again, postmodernism is really a form of modernism; it is the grief of modernism over what it did to us. Its anger against nominalism is an anger against the metastructures that developed from this inevitable transformation of the essential to the existential; this has led to its refusal to be interpreted, its refusal of any hint of continuity. However, with no habitual ties within the "communitas," signs, released from their stasis, flash heatedly around our heads in an endless, unattached, and alienated diachronics. The emphasis is on "play," on deviance, on hiding, on being "there but not there," using all tropic parodic forms—which is to say, the postmodern existence is cut off from the skeptical eye of reality, from the accountability of the communitas, and from the stabilizing forces of its generalities. The existential reality of the postmodern unileveled frame is completely entropic and, as we will discuss in the next chapter, so dissipates energy that it is as degenerate as the modernist frame. Hassan speaks of the fragmentation, deconstruction, "gay relativity," "immanence of laughter," that he sees as elements of postmodernism (and that I see as impossible in a unileveled frame without an underlying metanarrative of reflexivity) and suggests that their role is to provide "ludic and subversive elements that promise renewal" (1987, 171). Certainly, the collapse of one form of stability, especially one that has become degenerate, is absolutely vital. Some do indeed consider postmodernism as a deconstructive phase before construction; others, however, have elevated it to a theory, a way of life, without realizing that its transitoriness is the opposite of life. Here, we have a key problem: postmodernism believes in purity but never in human regeneration and the evolutionary capacities of semiosis, by which I mean a generative and lyric semiosis. Its evangelistic message promises us, that by "deconstructing" the degenerate texts, we, as modernists, developed; by tearing down the walls, the prisons; it will permit us a release from the guilt of their construction and thus, somehow, an existence in the freedom of our existentiality—which may be, and quite possibly is—that purity we have lost. But how can we exist only as signifiers? Will we have lost, with the narrative structure, the results of its existence, "its great hero, its great dangers, its great voyages, its great goal" (Lyotard 1984, xxiv) and will we become lost in the sudden downpour? Postmodernism is doing exactly what the nominalists of the fourteenth and fifteenth centuries did, in their reaction against the decayed and degenerate metanarratives of the scholastics. As Richard Poirier warns, the postmodernists too may "also veer towards solipsism, lapse into narcissism" (1971, 198) and deprive us of our abilities of semiosis just as readily as did modernism.

Postmodernism operates as a conscious rejection of any codal continuity—whether it be that of the degenerate unileveled form or that of the bileveled form. It exists, as Peirce commented on the tenacious style of establishing belief, by "taking as answer to a question any we may fancy, and constantly reiterating it to ourselves, dwelling on all which may conduce to that belief and learning to turn with contempt and hatred from anything that might disturb it" (5.377). This type of belief rests within a sense of temporal fragility, which will quite easily slip into a feeling of constant conspiracy against this *fantasia* identity. The "instinctive dislike of an undecided state of mind, exaggerated into a vague dread of doubt, makes men cling spasmodically to the views they already take" (5.377). Postmodernism is the foolishness and pride of a drowning man refusing the life raft because it came from the ship that sank. But it was the revolt of postmodernism against slavery that sank the ship, and the only thing to do now is to pick up its flotsam and jetsam and build, in the manner of a bricoleur, a new vessel, a new metanarrative wherein we may all be sailors rather than slaves. But postmodernism does not trust humanity: it is too close in time to the bonds that so indifferently linked it to the oars, and it cannot distinguish between the slave-owners and the slaves.

It is essential that there come a time when we must, as did Priam, look death in the face, and ask for the return of our bodies to our souls, of Hector to our home. "Your son is given back to you, aged sir, as you asked it. He lies on a bier. When dawn shows you yourself shall see him as you take him away" (Homer 1951, Bk 24, lines 599–601). It is then that we may begin to live again.

THE QUESTION AND THE REALITY OF THE METANARRATIVE

Do graal cui l'en an servoit.
...
De la lance por coi el saigne . . .
Et do graal ou l'an le porte

—Chretien de Troyes (lines 3231, 3337–3339)[22]

The key to the search for the Grail should be understood as a commitment, an accountability to a dialogic interaction with the generative forces of semiosis via *erotesis,* the desire/action of the question. The key is therefore not the answer, the *sema,* for signs are finite and entropic; the key is the question—which is to say, the interaction with the desire for semiosis, for the constant transformation of sensual data into conceptual meaning.

The Grail or the mountain; the lance or the waters are trapped in their metaphors; the people who use these metaphors are equally trapped, longing for release, which comes about with the interaction, the question that breaks up these metaphors and permits the generation of new meaning. "De quoi li Graaus sert?"—who is served from the grail? "Et demandates vos por coi/Elle saignoit?"—did you ask why it bled?

Why have a metanarrative? First, because the human experience is dyadic, not merely between Self and Other but between Self and Community. The human being's "body" is finite but the knowledge base within which this body operates must exist as a continuity before and after this finiteness. Within homo sapiens, this knowledge is not simply a biological, chemical, or physical codality, but is above all a conceptual knowledge; it is a communal and acquired, rather than innate, regime of knowledge. Therefore, the material body must become a social body; the only way it can do so is within a continuity of a knowledge base. This dualism of body and mind forms, as I have said, the unique infrastructure of the adaptive capacities of the human species.[23] The true metanarrative, the basis within which questions exist, the only one that does not ultimately lead to a degenerate society, exists within a two-leveled architecture. It operates within a reflexive and contextual, ongoing interaction that links reality with the communal habits of behavior and belief. Its communal dialogue mediates between the sensual and the conceptual experiences of the individual; relates them into a signification that is actual, pragmatic, accountable to reality. Speaking of the Vichean triad, Verene compares it with the Aristotelian syllogism. "The verum-factum is the middle term . . . [which] makes possible any particular line of reasoning. The middle term is the term held in common by the two premises of a syllogism; it is the basis for the connection between the other two terms of the syllogism asserted in the conclusion. The middle term is a product of the fact that the Aristotelian syllogism is built on the notion of threes—three terms, one being the middle term, contained within three propositions, one of which being the conclusion" (1981, 47). The middle term is "the element necessary to bring a syllogism into existence" (48) and thus, "refers to the self-coherence of thought, the ability to connect thoughts conceptually. The syllogism is not just a framework for the reiteration of truths, but a process through which probable truths can be formed. Produced by ingenuity, the middle term is a conception of the mind's ability to make a thought intelligible by placing it into a proper or new arrangement with other thoughts" (48). Therefore, this active mediation, this Peircean Thirdness "is a manifestation of the verum-factum principle . . ."the ability of thought to connect itself to itself, to create intelligibility" (48). The unileveled architecture, as we have discussed, rejects mediative interactions as pollutive.

The bileveled architecture has given human beings the ability to pragmatically mould and adapt their own metanarrative; it has given them the power of reflexive thought, and permitted them to live within an adaptive and evolving relationship with the environment. What did Prometheus do? He gave human beings the power of semiosis, that fire that breaks open the *sema,* the tomb of the sign; he gave them both the power of transforming energy into meaning and a self-conscious awareness of this action; he mingled them with the gods. The gods were furious and told Zeus that he must be nailed "to the high craggy rocks in fetters unbreakable of adamantine chain. For it was your flower, the brightness of fire that devises all, that he stole and gave to mortal men; this is the sin for which he must pay the Gods the penalty—that he may learn to endure and like the sovereignty of Zeus and quit his man-loving disposition." Prometheus would be "fixed" into an artifact. "I shall nail you in bonds of indissoluble bronze on this crag far from men . . . such is the reward you reap of your man-loving disposition. For you, a God, feared not the anger of the Gods, but gave honors to mortals beyond what was just" (Aeschylus 1959 *Prometheus Bound,* lines 19–28). So Might mocks Prometheus, as he is bound to the rock: "The Gods named you wrongly when they called you Forethought; you yourself *need* Forethought to extricate yourself from this contrivance" (lines 84–85). But the name is correct; and his own forethought is a matter of indifference to him: "What am I saying? I have known all before, all that shall be, and clearly known" (lines 100–101). He knows that even the gods themselves cannot last for long within their own self-absorption of Firstness, that a relationship between potentiality and actuality must, for the sake of the continuity of energy, be established; and that this relationship must not be direct and finite, but reflexive, a constant shrug and debate and decision-taking.

The fixation of belief, the means of social stability in the bileveled frame, is a communal force, whether that community is of physical, chemical, biological, or conceptual codal regimes. "To satisfy our doubts, therefore, it is necessary that a method be found by which our beliefs may be determined by nothing human, but by some external permanency—by something upon which our thinking has no effect" (Peirce 5.384). This is not that essence so affirmed by Tenacity or Authority; it cannot be restricted to individuals, but must "affect every man." It is based on a belief in external reality, "whose characters are entirely independent of our opinions about them; those Reals affect our senses according to regular laws, and, though our sensations are as different as are our relations to the objects, yet, by taking advantage of the laws of perception, we can ascertain by reasoning how things really and truly are. . . . The new conception here involved is that of Reality" (5.384). Peirce's scientific method is an awareness that we think and understand via a communal or social "habit" of belief; this "communitas" is not a structure but a mediation between the external reality and our conception of that reality. As such, it is reflexive, dialogic, constantly subject to reformulation and testing for its ability to inform us of that world. The metanarrative is the force of equalization, of generalization—a hostility towards divisiveness, an attachment to continuity. The metanarrative gathers energy into a powerful focus of shared desire whose architectonic codes of stabilization and continuity are the basis of life; just so are "the highest mountains, where the river's strength gushes from the very temples" (Aeschylus 1959, lines 720–721).

"The basis of sacrifice lies in the fact that each one of us is two, not one. We are not a dense and uniform brick. Each of us consists of the two birds of the *Upanishads,* on the same branch of the cosmic tree: one eats and the other watches the one that is eating. The revelation of the sacrificial stratagem—that sacrificer and victim are two persons, not one—is a dazzling, ultimate revelation concerning our selves, concerning our double eye" (Calasso 1994,134). One self is active, the other is reflexive. The architectonics of a textual society is bileveled; one level is that of the metanarrative, understood neither as the a priori essentialism nor the existential structure of the unileveled frame, but as a generalized, amorphous, and reflexive habit of being of a communitas; the other level is the level of the sensual and conceptual nodes of being within the conscious experience of the individual. The importance of two levels of codification—of their distinctiveness, their eternal separation; and also of the persevering dialogue between the two—cannot be underestimated. Among human societies, the acceptance or rejection of this architecture becomes an ethical choice. "But now my spirit in turn has driven me to stand and face you. I must take you now, or I must be taken. Come then, shall we swear before the gods?" (Homer 1951, Bk.22, lines.252–254). The unilevel architecture of modernism and postmodernism meant that all objective (and subjective) reality was understood to exist only in the current or potential perceptual/conceptual domain of the individual human being. There is yet another reason for this dyadic interaction. Life is an organized form of energy, and there are two, rather than one, codal formats by which energy conserves and expresses itself on this earth. Following Prigogine (1984), I am defining these two forms as *dynamic* and *thermodynamic,* but a valid comparison could be made with *potential* energy, understood as the energy within stasis; and *kinetic* energy, understood as the energy due to motion.

PART II

Codification

3

CODIFICATION AS TRANSFORMATION

Ce ies tu, li malaureus,
Quant veis qu'il fu tans et leus
De parler, et si te taus!

—Chretien de Troyes (lines 4597–4599)[1]

There is one key theme in life: energy desires to exist, and it is *order* that permits that existence. Energy can only exist within the confinement of organization, which is to say, within codification into a spatiotemporally closed entity, which I will refer to as a sign or artifact. "Entities that evolve must exhibit spatiotemporal continuity and some intrinsic boundary conditions. In short, they must be individualized" (Brooks and Wiley 1988, 104). A sign is something that is "sealed" into a specific time and space; it is "at rest" as itself and only itself, even if only for a millisecond. The Greek *sema* means not only "sign" but also "tomb." "In order to produce equilibrium, a system must be "protected" from the fluxes that compose nature. It must be "canned," so to speak, or put in a bottle, like the homunculus in Goethe's *Faust*, who addresses the alchemist who created him: "Come, press me tenderly to your breast, but not too hard, for fear the glass might break" (Prigogine and Stengers 1984, 128). Energy is "canned" by its being encoded or organized into a particular pattern of order, operative within a particular spatiotemporal frame. A "sign [is] anything such that when it is another thing is, or when it has come into being the other has come into being before or after, is a sign of the other's being or having come into being" (Aristotle *Prior Analytics,* Bk.II:Ch.26.70a5). Semiosis sets up particularities and therefore permits the existential.

A code system exists to make signs. To function, to survive as a practicing code system, a codal system must carry out this transformative action by producing signs that are able to exist and interact with other signs. If a codal system organizes energy into signs that cannot interact with other signs—that dissipate quickly, that haphazardly lose and scatter their energy—then, as far as energy is concerned, this is an extremely impractical and ultimately dangerous system. Therefore, codal systems must be not merely continuously but repetitively productive. They must produce signs that can, without trials or tests, immediately interact with each other. This means that the codal systems will regulate themselves into the most productive, which is to say, habit-forming, networks of organization. "Matter near equilibrium behaves in a 'repetitive' way" (Prigogine and Stengers 1984,13).

One form of organizing or encoding energy can be called *dynamic*. Prigogine's definition of the dynamic form of organization is that it permits states in which a "moment, whether in the present, past or future, was assumed to be exactly like any other moment." Events "can, in principle, go either backward or forward in time without altering the basics of the system. For this reason, scientists refer to time in Newtonian systems as 'reversible'" (1984, xix). In physics, this force has been studied within the so-called classical theories, which were understood as "deterministic," "so the future is always completely fixed by the past" while quantum theories dealt with the theories of "uncertainty, indeterminism, and mystery" (Penrose 1990, 194). Aristotle wrote that "there are two parts of the soul—that which grasps a rule or rational principle, and the irrational," and further, "let it be assumed that there are two parts which grasp a rational principle—one by which we contemplate the kind of things whose originative causes are invariable, and one by which we contemplate variable things" (*Nicomachean Ethics* Bk.VI:Ch.1.1139a1–10). What if the differences in these two descriptions are not two different theories about energy but actually two different codal formations of energy? That is, there is not only a form of codification that is *continuous* but also a form of codification that forms *discrete processes*. This other means by which energy organizes itself is the *thermodynamic* codal format. Such codes concern themselves with pluralistic, random, irreversible, fluctuating events. Thermodynamic "systems are inherently random and have no 'memory' of initial conditions" (Brooks and Wiley 1988, 356). Both codes exist; are they opponents or partners? Let us first consider dynamic codification.

DYNAMIC ENCODING OF ENERGY

If we could define dynamic energy, simply, what could we say? One word—continuity. "The desire in seeking to attach the one to the other" (1.342) is a "synthetic consciousness"(1.390): the "tendency to take habits" of generalization (1.390), a form of codal behavior that Peirce referred to as Thirdness. "Mythical figures live many lives, die many deaths, and in this they differ from the characters we find in novels, who never go beyond the single gesture" (Calasso 1993, 22). Mythical figures and Vichean heroes are metaphors of dynamic energy. They and their deeds are reversible, transformable, completely indifferent to the ravages of time, and also intensely communal, intensely interested in each other—for—they are each other. "In each of these lives and deaths all the others are present, and we can hear their echo" (22). Dynamic energy is energy produced by codes that are seemingly immune to Otherness. Any contact by other forces, other codes, are flicked off like errant flies; their autistic indifference to any attempt of contact has bewildered and grieved human beings for centuries:

My god, my god, why hast thou forsaken me? (Matt. 27:46)

I cry unto Thee, and Thou dost not hear me;
I stand up, and Thou regardest me not (Job 30:20)

The image of dynamic codification is Anake, goddess of necessity, living within a blind singularity of purpose—to provide a stable means of encoding energy. Dynamic encoding is non-random, and "non-randomness, or macroscopic order, which is transmitted to the next generation as initial conditions, *constrains, burdens* (Riedl 1978), *instructs* (Waddington 1977), or *informs* the system as to possible energy dissipation" (Brooks and Wiley 1988, 361). This codal format permits deterministic and reversible experiences that are bonded to a memory of an initial condition or even a number of initial conditions. The basic characteristics of dynamic codification are its commitment to those initial conditions; its observance of those original laws; and thus, deterministic and mimetic actions. Prigogine writes that "the remarkable feature is that once the forces are known, any single state is sufficient to define the system completely, not only its future, but also its past. At each instant, therefore, everything is given. Dynamics defines all states as equivalent" (1984, 60).

Dynamic codification is predictable; Peirce notes that "all operations governed by mechanical laws are reversible" (6.14), and "the future determines the past in precisely the same way in which the past determines the future" (6.69). We can recall de Tocqueville's caution about democracy, with its stress on "equivalency," its insistence on "sameness"—which processes actually set up a monologic authoritarian force, "the same equality which renders him independent of each of his fellow-citizens, taken severally, exposed him alone and unprotected to the influence of the greater number. The public has therefore, among a democratic people, a singular power . . . for it does not persuade to certain opinions, but it enforces them, and infuses them into the intellect by a sort of enormous pressure of the minds of all upon the reason of each" (1956, 148). That simile, "the enormous pressure of all upon each" well describes the force of dynamic codification. "For myself, when I feel the hand of power lie heavy on my brow, I care but little to know who oppresses me; and I am not the more disposed to pass beneath the yoke because it is held out to me by the arms of a million of men" (149).

Dynamic codification sets up processes within a regime that stabilize its processes, conserve its energy, and provide it with its laws of continuity. Prigogine commented that "once the particular state of a system has been measured, the reversible laws of classical science are supposed to determine its future, just as they had determined its past" (1984, 3).[2] This codification provides us (and energy) with the assurance of predictable future encoding processes. We are safe within the assurance that "whatever is god is strong/ whatever long time has sanctioned/that is a law forever/the law tradition makes/ is the law of nature" (Euripides, 1959 *The Bacchae,* lines 892–895). Dynamic codification sets up a regime in which "everything is given," values are fixed, determined, defined, each part integrated with each other; everyone, so to speak, "knows their own place." Whether we view such "noblesse oblige" with disdain or not, it provides us with a feeling of great security. Dynamic codes are understood to "speak the truth."

Dynamic codes are vital to all continuity. "In ancient literature, it is memory, and not knowledge, that serves as the source and power . . . that is how it was, it is impossible to change it: the tradition of the past is sacred" (Nagy 1990a, 14). Nagy provides Burkhert's definition of ritual: "Ritual, in its outward aspect, is a programme of demonstrative acts to be performed in set sequence and often at a set place and time—sacred insofar as every omission or deviation arouses deep anxiety and calls forth sanctions. As communication and social imprinting, ritual establishes and secures the solidarity of the closed group" (Nagy 1990a,10). Rituals are a specific description of a society's deeper axiomatic laws; they articulate its codal stability. Myths and rituals express the activities of the gods; our heroes are always related to, or in constant discourse with, the gods and, therefore, with the ultimate sources of our realities.

How does dynamic codification operate within regimes of knowledge? Within a unilevel architecture, dynamic codification acts as an isolate and self-referential mechanism of duplication; it sets up codal laws that replicate an original in as simple and clear a format as insisted on by Ockham. Within biological codification, such laws will be the hereditary codes, governed by the necessitarian hand of Natural Selection, operating as an external power of judgment that decides the "preservation of favourable individual differences and variations, and the destruction of those which are injurious. . . . Some have imagined that natural selection induces variability, whereas it implies only the preservation of such variations as arise and are beneficial to the being" (Darwin 1963, 64). Darwin asserted that natural selection is not "intentional," is not an "active power or Deity," but such an ego-centered consciousness is not the only definition of a necessitarian or theistic intentionality. The fact that the only type of code allowed to "be semiosic" is the dynamic code of hereditary replication means that Darwinian biology operates on a unileveled framework. "Darwin was himself inheritor of the tradition of Natural Theology, a tradition in which organisms were considered to have been constructed by the agency of God. This tradition focused on the design of organisms, their intimate meeting, and the matching of their traits to their environments, all as evidence of a higher purpose and intelligence. . . . Powerfully inimical to the theological consequences, Darwin's notion of natural selection can be enthroned in God's stead as the creative agency" (Kauffman 1993, 11). Within a conceptual codification, dynamic codes operate within the structural frames of Levi-Strauss and Barthes, the codified frames of Jakobson and Greimas, the inherent meaning of New Criticism, the reactivity of Behaviorism, most of sociology and anthropology—the list is endless. Leibniz's teleological monads, Lucretius's atoms, and Dawkin's memes—can all be seen as mimetic codal actions operating within a unileveled, non-interactional architecture.

A unileveled architecture using only dynamic codification, understands change as a predictable development of an initial state. That is why phylogenetic evolution has so frequently been imagized as ontogenous; it is thereby seen as driven by the ego-centered intentionality of an a priori necessity. The Kantian, Hegelian, and Marxist themes of social change are dynamic in that they are not irreversible[3] and not unpredictable, but are instead an aspect of an inherent and universal monologic intentionality of life. The goal of human intelligence is to find and control these basic laws. "The dynamic object could be controlled through its initial conditions" (Prigogine and Stengers 1984, 120) and "the future determines the past in precisely the same way in which the past determines the future" (Peirce 6.69). This assumption of an ability to control all nodal points of existence from origin to end is the key flaw in a nominalist or unileveled approach to reality. Prigogine continues, "in dynamics, a system changes according to a trajectory that is given once and for all, whose starting point is never forgotten (since initial conditions determine the trajectory all the time)" (121). The dynamic codes are completely stable; whatever happens is not by chance but a direct result of the single gaze of the code. Whether this gaze was directed at the energy mass "in the beginning" (God) or "in the end" (natural selection) is irrelevant.

Irreversible and uncontrollable processes, which we will explore as the codification processes of thermodynamics are considered "noise," nuisance factors to be regulated out by increased knowledge.[4] To someone working only within a unilevel architecture, dealing only with dynamic energy[5]—whether accessible as with the modernists, or inaccessible as with the postmodernists—unpredictable or uncontrolled change is understood as a dissipation of energy, a "forgetting of initial conditions" (Prigogine and Stengers 1984, 129). This can mean, socially, a movement away from an original historic purity and moral purity, and therefore, an inevitable and tragic "fall" into social disorder and decay. Indeed, the term *stasis,* in its normative, balanced sense, is derived from the verb *histemi,* which means to "set up, establish, take a stand." Therefore, *stasis* provides a sense of the permanency of an "establishment, station, status." But, like the particle to the wave, every sign has its Otherness, and *stasis* also means "division, conflict, strife." When one is establishing a *stasis,* one must also conflict with the intentionalities of Otherness that hinder such a focused determinism. Purity is always about power.[6] Nemesis, the goddess of necessity, is raped by Zeus, a god of necessity; dynamic energy curling into itself. Out of such a union arises our idea of purity: the image of a cyclic, entwined, infinite source of intentionality, of an eternal commitment to "initial conditions." Forever unattainable lest we destroy it, forever desirable lest we forget our need for it. The Greeks called it Helen. Can we access such a force? The modernists—who believe only in the life of the unilevel—say "yes indeed," and set up all sorts of structures for both the meeting and, even, her ultimate housing. The postmodernists admit her existence, but say it is impossible to keep, let alone mate with, such a one.

"Homer did not want to reveal the secret about the nature of Helen, the fact that she was a phantom" (Calasso 1993, 130). Gods and men have fought for centuries, in every society on earth; they have fought, not over the idea of the existence of purity, which no one has ever doubted, but whether it could be accessed, could be touched by human hands, could be transformed into something within the sensual or conceptual experience and ownership, of "hapless mortal men." To even hint at the possibility of direct contact was considered an affront. And so Haemon warns his father Creon, who took upon himself the powers of an ultimate authority: "Do not have one mind, and one alone/that only your opinion can be right" (Sophocles *Antigone,* lines 705–6); Teiresias also warns him: "You've confused the upper and lower worlds . . . all gods will even you with their victims" (lines 1068, 1077).

Dynamic codification is necessary for the continuity of energy. It is represented, within a bilevel architecture as the laws of order and habits of behavior. But there are also fluctuations and disorder that cannot be accessed and controlled, and these forms of organizing energy are equally vital for the continued existence of energy. The adaptive or "robust" architectural frame is bileveled, operating with two codifications of energy. Prigogine points out that the "biological structure thus combines order and activity" (1984, 131). Order as expressed by dynamic codificiation; action, as expressed by thermodynamic codification. He continues, "we are now confronted with two basically different descriptions: dynamics, which applies to the world of motion, and thermodynamics, the science of complex systems with its intrinsic direction of evolution toward increasing entropy. This dichotomy immediately raises the question of how these descriptions are related" (122). They are related within an architectonics that permits the establishment of multiple and differential semiotic nodes or sites of codification. These sites develop to deal with the interactions of different codes, and, using the axioms of the metanarrative and its developed complex layers, they construct interlocked networks, planes of "binary decisions," rules of semiotic order, that guide a prismatic semiosis. Without different codes, semiosis becomes a mimetic description rather than a reflexive and dialogic transformation. We may describe life, but that description is neither life nor knowledge of that life; "sense perception is common to all, and therefore easy and no mark of Wisdom" (Aristotle *Metaphysics* Bk.I:Ch.2.982a12).

When Alexander the Great was proposing to build a city that should rebound to his credit, Deinocrates, the architect, came to him and suggested that he should build it on Mount Athos, for, besides being a strong place, it could be so fashioned as to give the city a human form, which would be a remarkable thing, a rare thing, and worthy of his greatness. And on what, Alexander asked, would the inhabitants live? Deinocrates replied that he had not thought of this. Whereupon Alexander laughed, and, leaving the mountain alone, built Alexandria where inhabitants would be glad to live owing to the richness of the land and to the conveniences afforded by the sea and by the Nile (Machiavelli 1983, Book I.1, 103).

Dynamic codification is an absolutely vital codal format and is the basis for the development of the "communitas," that group nodal area, operative on the deeper (unconscious) level of the bileveled frame. Bateson comments on what he calls the "defense in depth," which is to say, that the means of preserving energy is via the development of a deeper reactive system, and "when we encounter a new problem for the first time, we deal with it either by trial and error or possibly by insight. Later, and more or less gradually, we form the 'habit' of acting in the way which earlier experience rewarded. To continue to use insight or trial and error upon this class of problem would be wasteful. These mechanisms can now be saved for *other* problems. Both in acclimation and in habit formation the economy of flexibility is achieved by substituting a deeper and more enduring change for a more superficial and more reversible one" (1972, 352). The codification of energy in the dynamic format provides an ethics of the way life "ought to be" within a society. Equally, it views history, the past, within the same contiguity, the same sense of indexical bonds and ongoing responsibility, and so "I bear, as lightly as I can, the destiny that fate has given me; for I know well against necessity, against its strength, no one can fight and win" (Aeschylus 1956, lines 103–105). Dynamic energy operates within codal forms that express energy in states of order that are *necessary* rather than ad hoc and variable; it is a vital means of conserving energy, setting up what Prigogine and Stengers define as "the entropy barrier" (1984).[7] It permits the establishment of universal or general codal sentences of order.

I am going to consider dynamic codification as the "wave-function" of the quantum packet of energy. Penrose explains that "we have seen that the wave-function does not merely provide a probability distribution for different positions; it provides an *amplitude* distribution for different positions. . . . We must come to terms with this picture of a particle which can be spread out over large regions of space, and which is likely to remain spread out until the next position measurement is carried out" (Penrose

1990, 326). In other words, the momentum or dynamic codal formats are generalizing; they are expansive; they are recursive algorithms that function as "general calculations" of commonality; they are "the same *finite* set of instructions no matter how big the numbers" (46). What about the particle, the immediate and transitory?

THERMODYNAMIC ENCODING OF ENERGY

Tourists "climb mountains like animals, stupid and sweating; one has forgotten to tell them that there are beautiful views on the way up" (Nietzsche 1969, 183). There is something else other than the mountain.

Thermodynamic codification is the domain of the particular particle, the currently "now." The codes of thermodynamics are not bonded to the past or future; each particular sign may be quite different from—and, equally, quite indifferent to—any other entity. If left entirely on its own, detached from any links with the restraints and habits of dynamic codes, the energy within these units will quickly dissipate, as in the sudden explosion and death of a star, or the rapid rise and fall of a media star. "Chance is a thing absolutely unintelligible" (Peirce: 6.63), which means that thermodynamic codification itself cannot form signs or units-of-meaning. As Aristotle pointed out, "the accidental is obviously akin to non-being" (*Metaphysics* Bk.VI:Ch.2.1026b20). However, if linked by semiosic interaction with the stable forces of dynamic codes, then this particular organization of energy can last for much longer; it can even recode itself and generate more versions of itself—the reproduction of offspring, the expanded usage of an invention. Thermodynamic articulations are not recursive copies; they are accidents that provide an enormous expansion of adaptive potentialities.

It is love of the unknown; the nature of thermodynamics is a wild Dionysian love of flowing, tumbling, sparkling randomness.

> The enormous strength of Ocean with his deep-running waters,
> Ocean, from whom all rivers are and the entire sea
> and all springs and all deep wells have their waters of him (Homer 1951,
> XXI, lines 195–197).

Peirce writes that "there is probably in nature some agency by which the complexity and diversity of things can be increased; and that consequently the rule of mechanical necessity meets in some way with interference" (6.58). "By thus admitting pure spontaneity or life as a character of the universe, acting always and everywhere though restrained within narrow bounds by law, producing infinitesimal departures from law continually, and great ones with infinite infrequency I account for all the variety and diversity of the universe, in the only sense in which the really *sui generis* and new can be said to be accounted for" (6.59). Besides continuity, besides the repetitive and thus indifferent assurances of the gods, energy encodes itself in a completely different format—that of randomness. We have to "admit the inexhaustible multitudinous variety of the world . . . admit that its mechanical law cannot account for this in the least, that variety can only spring from spontaneity" (6.29). That is the definition of thermodynamic encoding: spontaneity—what Monod refers to as "essential uncertainty." It is whatever was not before; it leaves the observer stunned by its irreverent rejection of law. "That a pitched coin should sometimes turn up heads and sometimes tails calls for no particular explanation; but if it shows heads every time, we wish to know how this result has been brought about. Law is *par excellence* the thing that wants a reason" (6.12). Law is dynamic encoding, but chance is not; it is an interaction that is *hic et nunc,* without a thought for the past or the future. It is Aristotle's accidental, "which is neither always nor for the most part," and furthermore, it is obvious that "there is no science of the accidental" (*Metaphysics* Bk.VI: Ch.2). That is why Einstein so opposed it; it carries the stigma of *ate,* of behavior without accountability.

Prigogine says that "irreversibility plays an essential role in nature and lies at the origin of most processes of self-organization" (1984, 8). He adds that we "find ourselves in a world in which reversibility and determinism apply only to limiting, simple cases, while irreversiblity and randomness are the rules" (8). Thermodynamics provides the capacity to explore, adapt, and expand; while dynamic codification provides the capacity to retain the benefits of these actions. The Dionysian is the image of the thermodynamic: "Saying Yes to life even in its strangest and hardest problems, the will to life rejoicing over its own inexhaustibility. . . . Not in order to get rid of terror and pity, not in order to purge oneself of a dangerous affect by its vehement discharge . . . but in order to be oneself the eternal joy of becoming, beyond all terror and pity—that joy which includes even joy in destroying" (Nietzsche 1969, 273). It is "*becoming,* along with a radical repudiation of the very concept of *being*" (ibid). "I ask of absurd creation what I required from thought—revolt, freedom, and diversity" (Camus 1955, 94). The "Thousand and One Goals" referred to in Zarathustra suggest the plurality and randomness of the thermodynamic codal actions. But a thermodynamic codal act is by its very nature unable to bond with any other codal system; all it can do is generate one particular artifact/sign that must be "grabbed" by other networks if the result of that codification is to survive.⁸ Therefore, the will to power, which I understand as the will of energy to exist (which it can do only in signs), means that the single thermodynamic codal action must interact and link with dynamic codal formats;⁹ randomness must interact with non-randomness to set up "ensembles" of interlocking networks of relationships. Semiosis is a double-action; the sign exists as a closed, self-referential unit while, at the same time, it must establish interactions with Otherness. That is why the adaptive semiosis is bileveled; the two processes of immediacy and continuity operate within parallel, separate, and yet interactive levels. This is an action of great power as well as restraint, for it means that semiosis, must overcome, but not obliterate, the monologues of both codal levels; it must *force* the two codal levels into a dialogic interaction.¹⁰ "If there are energy fluxes of sufficient magnitude flowing through the system, it can be 'perturbed' from its inherently random state to a nonrandom state. Prigogine and Stengers referred to such production of nonrandom states as 'self-organization', but we will call it *imposed organization*" (Brooks and Wiley 1988, 357).

Semiosis is the fire of transformation, that force that codifies energy, and consistently and infinitely produces new signs, new indexical expressions of its will or force. The father of Servius Tullius was Vulcan (Hephaestus), the god of fire. His conception was a semiosic act, an interaction of dynamic (infinite) and thermodynamic (finite) forces at a nodal catalytic point: the hearth, the *focus,* the sacrificial fireplace.

> When the sacred rites were enacted, according to tradition,
> Tanaquil ordered her to pour wine into the ornate *focus*.
> At this point, among the ashes, there was, or seemed to be,
> the male form of something indecent. More likely there was one.
> Ordered to do so, the slave girl sat at the *focus*. Conceived
> by her, Servius has the seeds of his *gens* from the sky.
> His father gave a sign, at the time when he touched his head
> with flashing fire, and a flame lit up in his hair"
> (Ovid *Fasti* 6.625–634; in Nagy 1990a, 173).

Two codifications—dynamic and thermodynamic—and so Servius began his life, which means he became a sign.

What is the nature of thermodynamic encoding? A chance, quite random formation; a quick tumble of energy rolled together; a sense of irresponsibility, unanswerability; that Dionysian "sweetness upon the mountains." After all, something that cannot even exist except as a potentiality, that must rely on that potentiality's being seen, being grabbed by another codal act, need consider no one other than itself. Thermodynamic forms can be only "partially controlled" (Prigogine 1984, 120). Thermodynamic encoding is irreversible, a "change towards states of increasing probability" (122); its behavior cannot be reduced to "mechanical trajectories, to the calm domination of dynamic laws" (136). "The irreducible plurality of perspective on the same reality" means that "the real lesson to be learned from the principle of complementarity . . . consists in emphasizing the wealth of reality, which overflows any single language, any single logical structure" (225). There are several key terms—chance, randomness, irreversibility, increasing probability—that all focus on the increased potentiality to the uniqueness of specificity. Thermodynamic coding limits the mechanical repetitiousness of the dynamic code, limits "the possible initial conditions available to a dynamic system" (123). This means that it blocks and weakens the monologic force of essentialism, adds its particularities to that "calm domination of dynamic laws" (136), and thereby produces the genuinely specific and individual sign. Life, semiosis, exists within a "tendency to form habits . . . which produced all regularities" (6.63). It is almost blissfully easy, as Peirce has commented in "Fixation of Belief" (1877) to live within such monologues of habit, without "the irritation of doubt," but a monologic society rapidly becomes, in turn, totalitarian and chaotic. It will happen very quickly that one no longer hears the voice, which is then forced to make itself louder, more enveloping, totalizing—and thus is born the tyrant, whether as prince or mob. Thermodynamics is the spark that permits the sacred forces of pure potentiality to come to life. "Whatever fosters [*fouet*] a fire is called a *focus*, whether it be an *ara* or anything else in which fire is fostered [*fouetur*]." (Servius on Virgil's *Aeneid* 12.118; in Nagy 1990a, 163). Thermodynamics *focuses* the codal formations. It "sets, puts, places" dynamic energy, that sacred energy of the gods, into specific signs.[11] However, in that fire-of-immediacy, it changes and transforms the dynamic code, and so permits an expansive flexibility of semiosis.

TWO CODES AND THE INTERACTION

There is a rock streaming with water,
whose source, men say, is Ocean,
and it pours from the heart of its stone a spring
where pitchers may dip and be filled.

—Euripides, *Hippolytus* (lines 121–124; in Grene and Lattimore)

Dynamic codification is not "old science"; it should not be understood as the "Newtonian mistake" and discarded. Rather, *both* Newtonian and

Copenhagen physics are right; they are both necessary; they should be understood as a very clever way of energy organizing itself to ensure its existence. Energy has set up a system of codification that limits the ongoing expense of the energy that is required to set up a basic codal format by establishing a semiosis based around the replication of forms that ensure the steady transformation of energy into signs. This stability also ensures the development of inter-networks of more complex codification, which in turn, permit more energy to be encoded, in more complex fashions. *And,* it has also developed codal formats that permit chance adaptation, that permit free or more loosely encoded energy to be "grabbed" and encoded, and saved from dissipation and ultimate extinction. Life does not exist within one *or* the other method of encodement, but both. That there are these two formats is nothing new; that they are confrontatively different is not new. "The care of god for us is a great thing. . . . So I have a secret hope of someone, a god, who is wise and plans;/but my hopes grow dim when I see the actions of men and their destinies. For fortune is ever veering and the currents of life are shifting, shifting, wandering forever" (Euripides. *Hippolytus,* lines 1109–1110). What we must understand is that these two forces of encodement must be permitted; indeed, we must insist on their constant dialogic interaction with each other. "Biological systems [are] . . . both deterministic (history; initial conditions constraints) and stochastic (inheritance is imperfect, and hence entropic; boundary conditions can affect evolution)" (Brooks and Wiley 1988, 363). Life is "the double imperative of flexibility and security" (Prigogine and Stengers 1984, 172).

The Epicurean philosophy involved two forms of energy; there was stability, which was a property of compounds; and a minimal random movement, known as "the swerve," which was a force that initiated new patterns of motion and blocked the danger of determinism. How did the two relate? Indeed, how do the two forces—that of the axiomatic grammar of dynamic and that of the randomness of thermodynamic—relate? "How can concrete reality become abstract and mathematical? . . . Perhaps, in some sense, the two worlds are actually the *same?*" (Penrose 1990, 557). They are not the same, and must never be so considered; rather, the transformative interaction of their codes within the current action of semiosis is the means by which energy makes itself existent and thereby permits us to "dip and fill our pitchers." The linear or serial model of semiosis, the unilevel architecture of a one-dimensional reality, sets up these two codal actions as sequential rather than dialogically parallel. Current models of Darwinian evolution operate in a serialistic framework, for "Darwin's theory begins with an assumption of the spontaneous fluctuations of species; then selection leads to irreversible biological evolution" (128). In this serial model, random codes appear and merge with current dynamic codes; this produces specific forms that must then pass through an "immigration review board" that judges and selects whether these codal forms may take up permanent residence.[12]

Sema is related to the Indic *dhyama,* which has the meaning of "thought." Nagy explains that "the semantics of *sema* are indeed connected with the semantics of thinking" (1990a, 202); that is, *sema* has a "working relationship" with two other words connected with mental activity, *noos* (mind, sense, perception) and *noeo* (perceive, take note, think, think through). The two actions taken as an interaction, that of the sensual "signing" (which could be random and therefore meaningless) and "thinking through" (referring to a memory and therefore meaningful), are the true semiosic process. These two codes operate within the quantum infrastructure as the wave and the particle. Dynamic codification provides the wave momentum of spatial expansion; thermodynamic codification temporalizes this spatial energy and thus "sets it" into a particle, a particular sign. Spatial codal formats are long-term, homogenizing, expansionist; they are Peircean Thirdness; they are syncretic continuity. Temporal formats, with their immediacy, their random closure, operate within thermodynamic codification. Both dynamic and thermodynamic methods must coexist, or energy will entropically dissipate to absolute zero. In a society, we may understand this to mean that there will be a communitas of axioms of belief and behavior that operates within a constant reflexive and dialogical flexibility in interaction with the variances of individual actions of codification.

Multiple and/or hierarchical, rather than single, nodal sites permit a wide-ranging and enormous flexibility of codification and ultimately, increase the conservation of energy. Multiple codal sites permit energy to quickly adapt; to organize itself into a variety of forms; to change its abilities of interaction with otherness; to grab loose energy close by, incorporate it, and so reorganize its nature. There are two nodal sites for the codification of thermodynamic energy: the sensual and the conceptual nodes. The sensual nodal site organizes energy in a variety of ways, according to the varieties of sensual codification; the conceptual adds more organization—much as it adds a telescope to the eye, a laser tool to the surgeon's fingers, an airplane to the traveler's feet. The conceptual node expands the codifications of energy by its metaphoric actions, and increases the complexity and therefore the total codification powers of the semiosic process.

What we have seen over the years is that these two architectural codal processes, and the three nodal sites of codification,[13] have been incorrectly isolated from interaction with each other, and one or more have been denied viability of operation. Modernism and postmodernism ignore the metanarrative and its nodal site of generalization. The nodal sites of sensual and conceptual codification have been reified; Cartesianism reifies the conceptual and sets it up as essentiality; structuralism reifies the mediative process and sets it up as a conceptual artifact-structure of monologic authority. The nodal sites have been merged into a cumulative algorithm in Hegelianism. Each of the three codal nodes has been denigrated within various competing philosophies as a "pollutant" to pure knowledge. As I have said, I am in complete agreement with the dyadic frame of the body and mind (codification at both the sensual and conceptual nodes); the increase (up to a point) of different methods of codifying energy increases the ability of energy to adapt and so conserve itself. However, the mistake has been to keep all these nodal sites for encoding energy semiotically isolated from each other, rather than understanding them as each distinct parts of an entire interactive architecture of codification.[14] An equal mistake, within this same unilevel architecture, is to merge the nodal sites together; "If the profane—that is to say, the profaner—devours what is sacred, then sacred and profane will merge in an unprecedented blend that will make it impossible ever to separate them" (Calasso 1994, 311). Nodal sites can never exist as single modalities; they must establish dyadic or interactional horizons. This sets up geometric planes of contact, enlarged horizons within which semiosis as the exchange and reorganization of energy can take place. It is within these geometric planes that the triadic interaction of semiosis, the encoding of energy into spatiotemporal signs, can take place.[15] Both modernism and postmodernism have maintained a strict arithmetic and linear separation of these nodal sites of the thermodynamic level—as well as moving the metanarrative nodal site of dynamic mediation to the same level as the sensual/conceptual nodes,[16] and making it a self-referential and isolate authority.[17] As discussed in chapter one, this formalization of "uninterpreted axioms" whether within an essentialist or mechanical form reifies this force into a commodity.

In this perspective, traditional science has been understood as the study of the "coding devices" that access pure truth; true science deals only with dynamic forces—with the stable, provable actions of experimental, mechanical interactions. "In the classical view the basic processes of nature were considered to be deterministic and reversible. Processes involving randomness or irreversibility were considered only exceptions" (Prigogine and Stengers 1984, xxvii). This dichotomy was expressed by confining each codal typology (stasis and randomness) to a different domain; the atemporal sciences, and the time-oriented and fluctuating humanities. Or, we had "classical" studies, which expressed the seemingly innate and universal "laws of life," versus the seemingly ad hoc and unpredictable "popular" studies. However, with the advent of quantum physics, we have found that material processes do not always behave within a dynamic mechanical order, but may also behave in quite random, fluctuating and unpredictable ways. That is, the two forms by which energy exists on this planet—dynamic and thermodynamic—are indeed separate and distinct from each other, but they exist within the same concrete matter—and are constantly interactive. "Thought is a thread of melody running through the succession of our sensations" (Peirce: 5.395). De Tocqueville wrote, "I am of the opinion that, at all times, one great portion of the events of this world is attributable to very general facts and another to special influences. These two kinds of cause are always in operation; their proportion only varies" (1956, 186).

Besides the bilevel architecture, networks[18] are a further means for the expansion and stabilization of both forms of semiosic codification. Over time, semiosis develops networks that relate different codal regimes and permit them to work together. These bonds increase the spread of a particular codality's influence, for it can use not merely its own networks but can also move rapidly along these "friendly" interlinked networks. A single artifact will develop multiple uses; a word will acquire different tropic meanings dependent upon the contextual situation. These networks, by encouraging multiple and diverse codifications, increase the power of semiosis, and a particular semiosic biome or regime of knowledge becomes more secure in its capacity to store and use energy. Networks also establish horizons of semiosis that restrict the nature of the codifications that are possible within these networks; this also acts as an immune barrier against deconstructive influences—mutant signs will not be able to reproduce themselves. A network that produces zebra sign-units cannot produce camel sign-units. Networks further inhibit the debilitating influence of "rival" codalities because they increase the codal capabilities of a particular semiosic regime. As Penrose states, "different 'alternative possibilities' open to a system must always be able to co-exist . . . all alternatives must somehow be combined together (1990, 314) to create "an evolving quantum linear superposition of many different alternative arrangements of attaching atoms" (565). Therefore, to use the well-known example, a moth with white wings can alternatively have black, soot-like wings—and birds will eat both types.

These two forms of codification, and the codal networks they develop within their semiotic interactions, are vital to semiosis. We must insist on their interaction. It is not that the dynamic level is the norm, with deviations understood as polluted or irresponsible rejections of these homogenous ideals. Boltzmann had thought that the nature of reality was a one-way increase in complexity; this is the dynamic model of basic social evolutionism, with its serial linearity, its cumulative order, its goal-oriented gradual and progressive development. Rather, there is one "level,"[19] the dynamic, which concerns itself with stability; another level, the thermodynamic, concerns itself with instability. "For a long time turbulence was identified with disorder or noise. Today we know that this is not the case. Indeed, while turbulent motion appears as irregular or chaotic on the macroscopic scale, it is, on the contrary, highly organized on the microscopic scale" (Prigogine and Stengers 1984, 141). The codal interaction of the two processes is a combining of coded energies, and a recodification of these energies into a new sign. This new sign may be a near duplicate of the previous sign, or be completely different. In either case it is not a disintegration of an "original identity," which is a purist and serial analysis. Semiosis gives energy the capacity to adapt, to free itself from being an iconic clone of its past; semiosis is the basis of the organization of energy; the world comes alive with its contact, "like the leaves that the many-blossomed season of spring brings forth"(Minnermus, 630BC; in Trypanis 1971, 135). "This mixture of necessity and chance constitutes the history of the system" (Prigogine and Stengers 1984, 170); the interaction between the two codalities and their energies establishes not simply the particular nominalist sign-unit, but also an organizational architecture, that secondary codal network, that functions as a metaphoric trope, permitting ever more semiosic expressions. The interaction between the two codal forces—dynamic and thermodynamic—creates a complex network within which necessary, probable, and alternative signs can exist. "One must consider an evolving quantum linear superposition of many different alternative arrangements of attaching atoms.... There is not just one thing that happens; many alternative atomic arrangements must co-exist in complex linear superposition" (Penrose 1990, 565).

Lukacs, as a Marxist, operates within a unilevel and serial architectonics; he speaks of "opposed views of the world—dynamic and developmental on the one hand, static and sensational on the other" (1963, 19). He does not speak of these as two separate, yet interactive codification formats, but as two perspectives, understood as that of the Self and that of the social. This is a unileveled model of the two nodal sites of thermodynamics: the sensual (or individual, which is seen as static because its codes are innate), and the conceptual (or social, which is seen as developmental).[20] He insists that man is not simply "in himself," but is also for others, a social being. I see this as an attempt to deal with the monologic stasis of a unileveled frame by forcing the static units (the individuals) into interaction with a supposed force of change—the society, which is invested with an essentialist Hegelian-style intentionality of progress. This is not a mediative semiosis, which must be understood as an interactive transformation of energy within two different codifications of energy. To simply bump one sign into another leads nowhere, except to increase the dissipation of energy and the actual degeneration of the single sign-units. Heidegger's concept, according to Lukacs, that man is an ahistoric being (and therefore unileveled) is an example of this Saussurian isolation of the sign-unit, which becomes an essentialist force, a "pre-existent reality beyond his own self, acting upon him or being acted upon by him" (1963, 21). And, "by destroying the complex tissue of man's relations with his environment, it furthered the dissolution of personality. For it is just the opposition between a man and his environment that determines the development of his personality" (28). A unileveled frame traps one into an oppositional, rather than a dialogic interaction. The two forces of codification exist; they are indeed, operationally different; they must never merge; they must remain "different from," but they have no possibility of self-existence and, therefore, no ego-centered intentionality of ultimate domination of the other. "Note that thermodynamics does not enter into conflict with dynamics at any point. It adds an additional, essential element to our understanding of the physical world" (Prigogine and Stengers 1984, 285). Indeed, as I have pointed out, neither can exist for very long without the other.

Two levels: one with rules, the other entirely lacking such stability. To reify the one into the other, as in nominalist modernism, is to prevent either from functioning correctly—to crystallize society into a mindless, decontextualized atomic mass that is governable only by authoritarian force. Monod describes such a state as "animism," wherein all actualities are a result of an a priori intentionality. All unilevel architectures commodify dynamic energy. The dialectic concepts of Hegel and Marx attempted to mobilize the force of this pure intentionality, to historicize its energy, provide it with a unilinear motion denied, not by the stability of its initial condition restraints, but by the entropic decay of those codal formats, when abstracted from interaction with randomness. Poincare "proved that every closed dynamic system reverts in time to its previous state" (253);[21]

but we should understand this not as a mimetic return, but a return to an early, simple, state of openness to semiosis.

Along this line, we could briefly consider here whether the metanarrative, or the codal architecture of dynamic codification, can be owned. To suggest so is to consider it as already commodified, and removed from a state of potentiality into the specifics of the unilevel architecture. Foucault was almost obsessed with the private ownership of the metanarrative—quite rightly so, as he had seen it used in exactly that form in both fascist and communist governments. The metanarrative, as the force of the potential to articulate, must never be the property of any single group; to have it as such is always the mark of a totalitarian regime—whether that fundamental certainty be vested within a church, a government, a group, or an individual. "It is necessary for a prince to have the friendship of the people; otherwise he has no remedy in times of adversity" (Machiavelli 1995, Bk. IX, 41). Machiavelli repeats this again and again: the prince must respect the people; "above all, a prince must abstain from the property of others;" a prince should always "win the people over." The reflexive dialogue with the metanarrative provides the "ethics of being" of all semiosic regimes, and to reify it and prevent such dialogue can only be defined as immoral.

The dynamic codal format is based on repetition and reversibility: it is the "physics of being;" the thermodynamic on arbitrariness, randomness, and irreversibility: It is the "physics of becoming." The dialogic interaction between dynamic and thermodynamic codification cannot be carried out in the linear, arithmetic actions of the unileveled frame. The correct architectural interaction is geometric, prismatic, moving within multiple dyadic planes of contact that set up pluralistic "horizons of association" within which semiotic actions can take place. The architectural frame can be thought of as "a web of regulatory circuitry which orchestrates the . . . system into coherent order" (Kauffman 1993, xvii). Indeed, "we must accept a pluralistic world in which reversible and irreversible processes coexist" (Prigogine and Stengers 1984, 257). In this sense, our world involves not merely the rational and the habitual, but the irrational and the uncertain—even the impossible.

No wonder the game is so beloved of men over time. "There is no greater glory that can befall a man living than what he achieves by speed of his feet or strength of his hands. So come then and try it, and scatter those cares that are on your spirit" (Homer 1965, Bk. VIII, lines 147–149). The game involves rituals of strict rules of behavior, a watchful attentiveness to see that these codes are followed. But within this ritual, thermodynamic chance is brought to the forefront—is groomed, oiled, and placed, shining with the heat of the moment, before everyone—as "he who wins," he whose actions have triumphed not over, but with, the rules. It has become art. "It is Theseus and Heracles who first use force to a different end than that of merely crushing their opponents. They become 'athletes on behalf of men.' And, rather than strength itself, what they care about is the art of applying it" (Calasso 1993, 62).

Alexander Koyre writes that "there is something for which Newton—or better to say not Newton alone, but modern science in general—can still be made responsible: it is the splitting of our world in two . . . by substituting for our world of quality and sense perception, the world in which we live, and love, and die, another world—the world of quantity, of reified geometry, a world in which, though there is a place for everything, there is no place for man. Thus the world of science—the real world—became estranged and utterly divorced from the world of life, which science has been unable to explain—not even to explain it away by calling it 'subjective' . . . Two worlds: this means two truths. Or no truth at all" (In Prigogine and Stengers 1984, 35–36). It is not really a "substitution" of one nodal site for the other (the rational for the sensual); again, this is a unileveled response. Rather, this is what happens when we—and it is only humans who make this error—reify the two codal formats, consider them similar, merge them into one—such that they become, completely, the products of our hands, our minds. Again and again, the gods have warned us against such an abrogation of power: "I will stop the music of your songs, and the sound of your lyres shall be heard no more" (Ezek. 26:13).

Order is what law, on its own, cannot achieve. "Order is law plus sacrifice, the perpetual supplement, the perpetual extra that must be destroyed so that order may exist. The world cannot live by law alone, because it needs an order that law alone is unable to provide. The world needs to destroy something to make order; and it must destroy it outside the law, with pleasure, with hatred, with indifference" (Calasso 1994, 148). The law is blind necessity; order is the relativity of the contextualized situation. To have only the monologue of necessity cannot be permitted. "The habit of all loose thinkers is immensely to exaggerate the universality of what they believe" (Peirce: 2.148).[22] The world has always rebelled against tyranny.

> Do not have one mind, and one alone
> that only your opinion can be right . . .

Have you not seen the trees beside the torrent,
the ones that bend them saving every leaf,
while the resistant perish root and branch? (Sophocles, *Antigone,* lines 705–714).

Generous father of rivers
and famed for his lovely waters
that fatten a land of good horses (Euripides, *The Bacchae,* lines 572–575).

4

THE METANARRATIVE

THE METANARRATIVE AS A SOCIAL CONSTRUCT

The interaction of these two forms of energy are not found only in chemical, biological, and physical processes—that is, in the fields of the "natural sciences"—but also in social formations. Societies are enormous ensembles of energy, made up of vast numbers of diverse, interlocking, and hierarchical networks of semiotic codal formats. A society operating within both dynamics and thermodynamics is not "balanced" in the sense that it is at peace and restful. A complex system that is able to adapt is one that can "achieve a 'poised' state near the boundary between order and chaos, a state which optimizes the complexity of tasks the systems can perform and simultaneously optimizes evolvability" (Kauffman 1993, 173). This requires alertness, decisions, constant reflexion, and debate. "To me those who condemn the quarrels between the nobles and the plebs, seem to be cavilling at the very things that were the primary cause of Rome's retaining her freedom. . . . In every republic there are two different dispositions, that of the populace and that of the upper class and that all legislation favourable to liberty is brought about by the clash between them" (Machiavelli 1993, Bk.I.4, 113). Peirce stated that the nonscientific or nondialogic methods of fixing belief by authority, tenacity, and a priori certainty were common among human beings because they were so comfortable. "Doubt is an uneasy and dissatisfied state from which we struggle to free ourselves and pass into a state of belief; while the latter is a calm and satisfactory state which we do not wish to avoid, or to change to a belief in anything else" (5.372). *Mens sana in corpore sano,* the new barbarian, "the passionate man who is the master of his passions" (Kaufmann 1974, 363); that is the ubermensche, a being who is in a state of "constant self-overcoming."

Like other organic beings, we operate within codal formats that follow the strictures of physics, chemistry, and biology. We cannot escape these axiomatic rules. However, as social beings, we—almost alone of all life forms on earth—have developed dynamic code formations that *we create and control.* It is not simply that these codes are social, in that they operate by networks of communication that develop within the group rather than only within the individual. There are many other social organisms on earth—such as ants, bees, and herd animals. However, our codes are not only set up in social networks; they are also of our own construction. Peirce defined these complex systems in his description of phaneroscopy and the phaneron, which is "the collective total of all that is in any way or in any sense present to the mind, quite regardless of whether it corresponds to any real thing or not" (1.284). We have actually constructed our own grammars of behavior, we are the authors of our mythic tales. It is our heroes, the heroes we nurture and select to mold our metanarratives, which tell us not only what we do but also why we do it.

Heroes are related to gods; they lead "parallel lives." Indeed, in most cases, they are the result of some coupling of a god with a mortal, of the infinite with the finite. Heroes live many lives and die many deaths. That is the nature of a hero: to show us how to live and how to die. An ordinary man has only one life and one death, and cannot tell us anything. "You who go across the wide earth and over the whole sea upon swift horses, and who with ease save men from freezing death, brilliant from afar as you run up the forestays of the well-benched ships, bringing light to the black ship in the cruel night" (Alcaeus, 600 BC; in Trypanis 1971, 143): These are heroes. All societies must have heroes; you have only to enter a village or city anywhere on earth to begin to learn their names—the names of streets, buildings, children, the names of special days, the names of ceremonies, laws, even actual objects. "Glorious is the fate of those who died at Thermoplylae, and beautiful their death; their tomb is an altar; for lamentation they have remembrance, for sorrow praise. Mould will never darken such a winding sheet, nor all-conquering time" (Simonides, 556–467BC; in Trypanis 1971, 163).

The reality that has been validated by these heroes is locked within hierarchical and interlocked codal networks: ritual behavior within the group is linked to role behavior within the family, which is linked with the judicial laws of the community, which are linked to the ordered "truths" within their science and technology, which are linked to the beliefs within their religion—and so on. Peirce comments that "all knowledge rests either on authority or reason" (5.359), which means that the community accepts these architectural constraints and operates within its total codal organization. Popper states that *"theories, or propositions, or statements are the most important third-world linguistic entities"* (1972, 157; italics in original). Aristotle's definition of the universal is "that which is of such a nature as to be predicated of many subjects" (*De Int.* Ch.7.17a38), and the universal is the communitas.

The point of having an "aesthetic"[1] as well as a genetic metanarrative is that it is an immensely adaptive system. It can transform itself rapidly and with little loss of energy—that is, without destroying the whole species. A zebra cannot adjust to a different climate or different diet, but human societies are found in a variety of environments all over the world. A hyena pack cannot adjust to a change in population but human societies can change their metanarrative and therefore their technology, and increase the carrying capacity of their environment to support larger populations. The song of a bird defines its relational horizons; a human society can develop different songs and different voices, create spatial satellites and instantaneous translation systems, and—seemingly without horizons—expand its relational capacities. The metanarrative is formed within the actions of synechism, "on the notion that the coalescence, the becoming continuous, the becoming governed by laws, the becoming instinct with general ideas, are but phases of one and the same process of the growth of reasonableness" (5.4). The mediation of the metanarrative, as the element of reflexive interaction, provides for an expansive generalization of semiosis. Peirce's triadic semiosic interaction says that a sign, the conceptualized (spatiotemporally existent) entity, "is related to its object only in consequence of a mental association, and depends upon a habit.... Habits are general rules to which the organism has become subjected. They are, for the most part, conventional or arbitrary. They include all general words, the main body of speech, and any mode of conveying a judgment. For the sake of brevity, I will call them *tokens*" (M 5.296). These tokens are not self-sufficient memes or Platonic Forms, for "it would seem impossible that the substance and that of which it is the substance should exist apart" (Aristotle *Metaphysics* Bk.I:Ch.9 991b1). We should note Peirce's words—that these habits, these general rules are "conventional or arbitrary." They are aesthetic constructs, acting within their dialogic development, as authoritative codifiers; the individual organism is subjected to their rules. Thirdness, which is Peirce's term for these habits, is a mediative action; within its reflexions sensual data is transformed into conceptual signs. In contrast to the unilevel and mechanical architectural actions, we do not move directly from the sensual to the conceptual; the sensual input of Firstness is transformed via the codal networks of Thirdness, into the sign-unit of Secondness. The formation of a habit, this Thirdness, "produces a belief, or opinion . . . a habit" (2.148), which need not be conscious; and "every habit has, or is, a general law" (2.148). As such, it ensures a potentiality of behavior, its "mode of being is *esse in futuro*" (2.148).

Popper quite correctly sees the dualistic world of the single-level architecture as entropic; and replaces this deadlock with the pluralistic potentiality of the triad, with his "three worlds"—which are comparable to the Peircean three categories. "There are three worlds: the first is the physical world or the world of physical states; the second is the mental world or the world of mental states; and the third is the world of intelligibles, or of *ideas in the objective sense;* it is the world of possible objects of thought: the world of theories in themselves, and their logical relations; of arguments in themselves; and of problem situations in themselves" (1972, 154). This follows the Peircean categories of Firstness, Secondness, and Thirdness, in similar order. The "three worlds are so related that the first two can interact, and that the last two can interact. Thus the second world, the world of subjective or personal experiences, interacts with each of the other two worlds. The first world and the third world cannot interact, save through the intervention of the second world, the world of subjective or personal experiences" (155). That is, one knows the physical world only in a subjective, individual conceptual sense (in signs); groups cannot "know," and there are no universal essences of physical entities. Knowledge is based in the senses of the individual, but this knowledge is only via the intelligible, the crafted themes, the conceptual habits (World 3) of a group. The "third world is a natural product of the human animal, comparable to a spider's web" (112).[2] This third world is autonomous, "even though we constantly act upon it and are acted upon by it" (112); it cannot merge with any of the other worlds, and "it is through this interaction between ourselves and the third world that objective knowledge grows, and that there is a close analogy between the growth of knowledge and biological growth; that is, the evolution of plants and animals" (112).

Vico's social reality is also based on the communitas, a developed history of human ideas that forms the basis of the "metaphysics of the human mind" (1948, 347)[3]. Like Peirce and his analysis of the dangers of the "fixation of belief" by authority and his insistence on the necessity of our beliefs being reflexive and accountable by their pragmatic contextuality,[4] Vico points out that a metanarrative that is not accessible to human criticism, in which "men were for a long period incapable of truth and of reason" (350), would be governed by the "cervitude of authority," that is, only by a superficial "outer justice" (350). The metanarrative of Vico is public; it is reflexive, for "truth is sifted from falsehood in everything that has been preserved for us through long centuries." It exists as a mental but not actual language, a "mental dictionary" that is part of the community but is, however, capable of recrafted diversity in its expression. Importantly, this mental dictionary is not singular and original. There is no original first identity of its existence as there is in the unilevel architecture with its requirement of an original purity of form, and "this same axiom does away with all the ideas hitherto held concerning the natural law of nations, which has been thought to have originated in one nation and been passed onto others" (146).

The metanarrative that we are here describing is not external to the organism and operative as a tyrant, for "though but one person suffices for the purpose of organization, what he has organized will not last long if it continues to rest on the shoulders of one man" (Machiavelli 1983, I,9, 132). Northrop Frye said that "society, like the individual, becomes senile in proportion as it loses its continuous memory." This "habit" is reflexive, by which I also mean ethical, in that it is dialogically interactive with the non-recursive or random variations present in reality. Therefore, "the possible *practical* consequences of a concept constitute the sum total of that concept" (Peirce: 5.27, emphasis added), and if "what we think is to be interpreted in terms of what we are prepared to do, then surely *logic*, or the doctrine of what we ought to think, must be an application of the doctrine of what we deliberately choose to do, which is Ethics" (5.35).

Vico writes that if the metanarrative (his terms are *verum factum*, mental dictionary, common sense, and natural law) had been a human creation, "it would have been a civil law communicated to other peoples by human provision, and not a law which divine providence ordained naturally in all nations along with human customs themselves" (1948, 146). The point here, and I think we must translate from his eighteenth-century vocabulary—is that the metanarrative is not the result of Cartesian rationalism; it is not something articulated within the dyadic mechanics of an individual action, something also critiqued by Popper under the "subjectivist theory of knowledge" (1972), and by Aristotle under the theme of the particular "act of perception" (*Posterior Analytics* Bk. I)—which would make it simply a collection of formal, finite signs produced within thermodynamic codifications, of which "no science is possible." It is instead an active codification that produces a "spreaded sheet" of interlocked pulsating or interactional networks that is time-enduring (reversible), and repetitive, and that establishes a law of order that is hierarchical over thermodynamic codal forms. The metanarrative must remain a communal and local interaction to maintain both universal semiosis and the adaptive functionality of that particular codal regime. This means that it is a product of both "our minds" and our historic behavior, and that its reality is always accountable to both natural and historic reality. It cannot be abstracted from these two horizons; in that sense, our conceptual reality is interactive with our pragmatic, sensual reality. There are "two common human traits, on the one hand that rumor grows in its course (*fama crescit eundo*), on the other that rumor is deflated by the presence [of the thing itself] (*minuit praesentia famam*)" (Vico 1948, 121).

The metanarrative is not an accumulation of sensible, particular knowledge, such a perspective very aptly critiqued by Popper in his condemnation of the bucket theory of the mind, with its "emphasis on the perfect emptiness of the mind at birth." Popper's argument, like Peirce's critique of nominalism, "is that the bucket theory is utterly naive and completely mistaken in all its versions," which includes such illogicalities as "knowledge is conceived of as consisting of things, or thing-like entities in our bucket.... Knowledge is ... *in* us ... there is *immediate* or *direct* knowledge (1972, 60–67). The bucket or formalist theory of knowledge is obviously a unileveled frame. The metanarrative cannot be reduced to its nominalistic parts; it is not something "consisting of things, or thing-like entities in our bucket (such as ideas, impressions, sensa, sense data, elements, atomic experiences, or—perhaps slightly better—molecular experiences or *'Gestalten'*)" (62). The poetic knowledge of Vico is "composed of divine and heroic characters, later expressed in vulgar speech, and finally written in vulgar characters" (Vico 1948, 456). As Peirce notes, our signs cannot fully mimic the world. The metanarrative is a law of potentiality, divine in its stability and its indifferent permissiveness of the variations of human expression, "which the Latins called *ious* and the ancient Greeks *diaion* ... derived from *Dios* and meaning celestial" (473). The metanarrative is developed via poetic logic, which is to say, by sensual contacts with reality, which are then molded within the existent or historical logic into an ever more complex grammar, a communal logic of being, over time.

Popper divides theorists into two camps; those who accept and those who reject the idea of a third world, of a metanarrative.[5] On a first point, he is critiquing the nominalists who deny this conceptually created objective reality—those who, "like Locke or Mill or Dilthey or Collingwood, point out that *language,* and what it 'expresses' and 'communicates' is *man-made,* and who, for this reason see everything linguistic as a part of the first and second worlds, rejecting any suggestion that there exists a third world" (158). This is the unilevel world of the nominalists who move their stability into structuralism, in this case, using language as the formal system. Popper is considering this third world as "autonomous," which I feel is an error of term, but not of concept. To make it autonomous will indeed accord with those who "like Plato, accept an autonomous third world and look upon it as superhuman and as divine and eternal" (158). However, Popper deviates from the Platonic idea of this third world as divinely created, and instead suggests that it "originates as a product of human activity." "One can even admit that the third world is man-made and, in a very clear sense, superhuman at the same time. It transcends its makers" (159). In a footnote, he says that "although man-made, the third world . . . is superhuman in that its contents are virtual rather than actual objects of thought, and in the sense that only a finite number of the infinity of virtual objects can ever become actual objects of thought" (159). He differentiates himself from the Platonic Forms, for "Plato's third world was divine; it was unchanging and, of course, true. Thus there is a big gap between his and my third world: my third world is man-made and changing. It contains not only true theories but also false ones, and especially open problems, conjectures, and refutations" (122). That is, it is a socially created Peircean habit of thought, "that which is what it is by virtue of imparting a quality to reactions in the future" (1.343). It is not the thoughts themselves but the network of order, and "not only will meaning always, more or less, in the long run, mould reactions to itself, but it is only in doing so that its own being consists" (1.343). And so Teiresias warns Cadmus:

> Do not trifle with divinity.
> No, we are the heirs of customs and traditions
> hallowed by age and handed down to us
> by our fathers. No quibbling logic can topple *them,*
> whatever subtleties this clever age invents
> (Euripides, *The Bacchae,* lines 200–204).

This third world, this social construct, should be understood as the codal order for the conceptual themes of a whole social body; it is "*the unplanned product of human actions*" (Popper 1972, 160; italics in original). Popper sees it as autonomous because it does not merge with the other two worlds; it is not a direct product of either of the other two worlds, and, as he says, "we can act upon it, and add to it or help its growth, even though there is no man who can master even a small corner of this world" (161). The unileveled understanding is "the dogma that the objects of our understanding belong mainly to the second world, or that they are at any rate to be explained in psychological terms" (162). However, the activity of understanding consists essentially in operating with the concepts of the third world. Further, arguments, understood as dialogical reflexions between the second and first worlds via the third, are "among the most important inmates of the third world" (123).

> A man, though wise, should never be ashamed
> of learning more, and must unbend his mind
> The ship that will not slacken sail,
> the sheet drawn tight, unyielding, overturns,
> She ends the voyage with her keel on top (Sophocles, *Antigone*, lines 710–716).

Society is an order of law, developed over time, within a community: it is a communal text. The metanarrative, constructed within a people's ongoing experience over time, is the means by which we are human; "heroic education began to bring forth in a certain way the form of the human soul which had been completely submerged in the vast bodies of the giants" (Vico 1948, 520). The polis, which is to say, a particular codal regime, is based on a *public* articulation of its codifications. *Apo-deixis* means a "public-presentation"; the polis is governed by its laws, which must be presented to its people by *sema*, (signs). These signs are accountable; they represent the interaction of the heroic codalities with the codifications of other regimes, both natural and social. *Deixis* refers to "descriptions," that which clarifies; *apo* is "public" (Nagy 1990b, 217). The metanarrative cannot be privately owned and kept hidden, though many, over many years, have so tried. Codification can only live within semiotic dialogue, otherwise, as a fruit, it withers and "the cracked waste of African Ammon dries up, dies, never knowing dew, robbed of the beautiful rain that drops from Zeus" (Euripides, *Electra*, lines 733–736). We can consider other terms with this same prefix of *apo* or public: *apoikia* (settlement); *apoina* (compensation); *apokoruphoo* (sum up). These terms show us that the individual and the metanarrative are accountable to each other; they are in constant dialogic interaction. In a dialogic society, there will be a sense of a constant aesthetic interaction, such that "there were songs, hymeneals and nuptials"; in a monologic society "there were no such things to be seen" (Vico 1948, 683).

Certainly, it is a mistake to make this activity into a formal structure, as did the modernists and structuralists, for this will submerge our minds in that mountain's caves and not only prevent the development of complex and expansive dynamic codification but also prevent interactions with the random "strangeness" of thermodynamic codification. Postmodernists reject any aspect of dynamic codification. In their quite valid rejection of the subjectivist mediatory structures of modernism, they also deny any sense of a communitas network, any hierarchical and interlocked network of codal orders. Effectively, postmodernism isolates each sign into the random, haphazard, brief flickering appearances of thermodynamic codal forms, all ignorant of each other, all blindly engaged in a dissolute, shiftless dance. Postmodernism moves vagueness—which is to say potentiality—from its correct nodal sites of Firstness and Thirdness and shifts it to Secondness, the site of the particular and irreversible sign, removing the indexical specificity of this sign[6] and instead investing it only with spuriousness. This is an astonishing action that destroys all possibility of stability in human thought; all possibility of accountability of action (the basis of ethics); and, furthermore, all possibility of evolution and development. Indeed, postmodernism is the "devil"; it began as a healthy action of "deconstruction" of the static codifications of nominalism, but its continuity beyond the destruction of the modernist architecture will result in the complete dissipation of energy to its "energy death." On this subjectivist path, as energy tries to prevent its own death, we will almost certainly move back, not merely into the cave, but thence into the hands of the tribe, with their insistence on homogeneity of belief and behavior; and thence into the fundamentalism of authoritarianism. Instead of the final node, Secondness, being a result of the dialogic interaction of *active* hierarchical interlocked networks of dynamic and thermodynamic codes, the postmodern sign becomes merely an Erigenist "trace" of mystic essentialism—and ultimately, of complete silence.

Perceval kept himself in a dyadic bond of "fact," the singularity of each sign, never asking how they related each to each. *Sema* also means "tomb" and this monadic state of being, with no mediative interaction, meant that Perceval, who did not question the signs he saw, who accepted them each by each, as sealed monads, was the cause of the desolation of the people and the land.

> Et sez tu qu'il en avenra
> Do roi qui terre ne tanra
> Ne n'iert de sa plai gariz? (Chretien de Troyes 1990, lines 4605–7)
>
> ... Tuit cil [mal] av[en]ront par toi!" (line 4613)[7]

Why have mediation, a metanarrative, as well as the direct experience? The human reality operates on two levels; the human being's "body" is finite but the knowledge base within which this body operates must exist as a continuity before and after this finiteness. Within Homo sapiens, this knowledge is primarily a communal and acquired, rather than innate, realm. Therefore, the material body must become the social body; the only way that it can do so is within the development of a pragmatic communal knowledge base, the metanarrative.

THE SIGN

The particularity, the knowability, the individuality of the human conception, is akin to Peircean Secondness, in its specificity. "We become aware of ourself in becoming aware of the not-self. The waking state is a consciousness of reaction . . . the idea of other, of *not*, becomes a very pivot of thought. To this element I give the name of Secondness" (1.324). The sign-unit is the actual particle in its immediacy as substance, a spatiotemporal entity rather than the potentiality of the wave.[8] It is "position" sealed to momentum. The sign exists, in its brief life as "itself"—whether as a quark, a fly, a human being, a word in "the now" of time—which is in itself a limiting factor (Aristotle *Physics* Bk. IV: Chs.12, 13, 14). This haecceity, "thisness," is Aristotle's definition of the present-state, which is "something that is an extremity of the past (no part of the future being on this side of it) and also of the future (no part of the past being on the other side of it): it is, as we have said, a limit of both" (*Physics* Bk.VI:Ch.3, 234a).

The sign, as substance, or encoded matter, is basically divisible and must be finite, closed within the protection of its opposition to Otherness to prevent, for its life-span, entropic loss of energy. "The membrane of a cell, a bilipid structure, forms spherical closed surfaces because that is its lowest energy state" (Kauffman 1993, xvii). This closure is the reason for Peirce's concept of "the element of struggle" within the Sign, for "a thing without oppositions *ipso facto* does not exist" (1.457). We have already stated that *sema* "sign" also means "tomb," and specifically, the tomb of a hero, which is to say, a force that can mediate between the two basic forces of life—potentiality and actuality. The sign "encloses" the power of "being heroic" (mediation as transformation of codifications) within matter/energy, and thus traps, confines, entombs it into the finite fragility of substance. A true hero, a force of constant recodification, cannot remain entombed. Semiosis must therefore constantly confront its own closures, its own heroic rage "against the dying of the light." A sign, once entombed as a "substantial being," begins to disintegrate and escape from that tomb, much as the gods will move into and depart from all and every disguise they so choose. The sign as substance is finite, and "everything that changes must be divisible. . . . Every change is from something to something. . . . Part of that which is changing must be at the starting point and part at the goal" (*Physics* Bk.VI;Ch 4.234b10–15).

Popper posits the second world as "the mediator between the first and the third" (1972, 155), whereas Peirce is suggesting Thirdness as the mediation between Firstness and Secondness. Despite this phrasing, I consider their statements compatible, for Peirce considers that the sign, which only exists within a state of Secondness, acts as that mediative force of Thirdness. Popper is suggesting that the *second* world is the articulation, the "making-material-thisness" of the "interaction" between the first world (physical sense) and the third world (conceptual themes). Peirce's Secondness, the sign, functions in exactly the same way, and "substance is the starting-point of everything. It is from 'what a thing is' that syllogisms start" (Aristotle *Metaphysics* Bk.VII:Ch.9. 1034a30). Secondness is the site of our substantiality, our existential reality. Popper continues, "one of the main functions of the second world [is] to grasp the objects of the third world" (1972, 156). That is, our spatiotemporal existentiality, operative as sign-actions, permits us to live within the reflexive generalities of the communitas. "Achilles is the great hero of *bie,* force; Odysseus, who is not lacking in *bie,* also has the complementary quality of *metis,* craft" (Nagy, 1979, viii), and can thus create, and not merely react to, signs.

LANGUAGE AS A
METANARRATIVE CODAL FORMAT

Insofar as language actually says or states, or describes anything, or conveys any meaning or any significant message that may entail another, or agree or clash with another, it belongs to the immediacy, the finiteness, the haecceity of the second world; insofar as it has the capacity to codify any of the above, it belongs to the third world, the *metis*-narrative, the *crafted* narrative of mediation. For the human species, language is one of the most important means of codification, because the semiotic operations of our species are so overwhelmingly a conceptual rather than genetic action. However, we must not consider language itself as the formalized articulation of a metanarrative, or as the only means of conceptual codification. This would make it a *metalanguage*—a theistic and authoritarian monologue. As Aristotle notes, this makes the potential, actual, and this is a basic fallacy of logic. "If they are universal, they will not be substances; for everything that is common indicates not a 'this' but a 'such', but substance is a 'this'" (*Metaphysics* Bk.III.Ch.6 1003a5). This "materialisation" of the metanarrative into the particular sets up the third man syndrome, which nullifies its generalizing capacities and inserts linear, regressive authorial precedence.[9]

I am in total agreement with Peirce's oft-stated dictum that "all thought is in signs" (5.253), but these signs are not necessarily words. The metanarrative is a logical order; multiple codal systems, in varying degrees of stasis and flexibility, operate within this logic. Penrose argues against "the thesis, so often still expressed, that verbalization is necessary for thought" (1990, 548) and quotes Einstein that "the words or the language, as they are written or spoken, do not seem to play any role in my mechanism of thought. The psychical entities which seem to serve as elements of thought are certain signs and more or less clear images which can be 'voluntarily' reproduced and combined.... The above mentioned elements are, in my case, of visual and some muscular type. Conventional words or other signs have to be sought for laboriously only in a second stage." And there is Galton, who wrote, "It is a serious drawback to me in writing, and still more in explaining myself, that I do not think as easily in words as otherwise," and Hadamard, who wrote: "I insist that words are totally absent from my mind when I really think." Penrose says of himself that "almost all my mathematical thinking is done visually and in terms of non-verbal concepts" (1990, 548–549). No one is suggesting direct intuition, no one is suggesting that we do *not* think in signs; rather, the suggestion is that, despite its importance, language is not the only codal system available to the human mind. We can examine their *formalized* versions as semantic descriptions of a current semiotic version of a metanarrative, but we must never confuse these descriptions of a code with the real metanarrative. To do that is to "cut off a part of being and investigate the attribute of this part," to investigate the particular as a universal (Aristotle *Metaphysics* Bk.IV.Ch. 11003a25).

Breal comments that "we must not demand much clarity or logic from the followers of this doctrine. Some believed in a single language taught directly by God, of which all modern languages are the degenerate descendents.... Others asserted that privileged peoples ... had been endowed with a special form of intuition" (1991, 202). Following this nominalist theme, "it was appealing to attribute perfection to the original state of things [and] the same views were developed by Savigny in the history of law, Creuzer in the history of religion, and Stahl in political law as were developed by Grimm and Humboldt in linguistic history. At the bottom of these speculations lurked a fundamental disdain for reason. A certain caste pride was mixed in: the notion of privileged races, including of course one's own, was not to be shunned" (202). Rather, "language resides in the intellect; it cannot seriously be conceived to be elsewhere. It existed before us and will outlive us because it resides in the intellects of our neighbours just as in our own. It existed for our parents, and we in turn shall hand it on to our children. It is made of the consent of many intellects, the concurrence of many wills, some present and active, others long gone" (203).

He denies "that there is a necessary link between words and ideas which it is still possible to recover" (123). Words "sleep in us as long as we do not need them. When called, they seem to awake and line up at command. They are like actors waiting in the wings or dressing rooms for the moment of entrance on to the stage, ready to disappear as soon as they have played their part" (145). He continues, "we are gifted with a unique faculty. During the moment we are using them we forget every other meaning they can have, and are aware only of the usage which accords with our thinking. Yet the other meanings of the word are perfectly well known to us. How is it that those meanings do not also appear? " (146). What Breal is referring to here is the codal network of the dynamic architectonics of language, which is quite similar to the codal nets of a biological genome (species). It is most certainly *not* made up of iconic signs (words) waiting in the wings; but is rather the regulatory networks, the functional self-regulating systems (Jacobs, 1973; Monod, 1971; Prigogine, 1984; Brooks and Wiley, 1988; Kauffman, 1993) that together form "ensemble constraints" (Kauffman, 1993) in the production of words of that particular language. These constraints act as a *forcing structure* that defines the nature of the sign-units that may develop and "blocks the propagation of *varying* gene products from genetic loci that are not parts of the forcing structure" (Brooks & Wiley, 133). A codal grammar sets up a network that permits a finite, if multileveled and pluralistic, semiosis. In a particular semiosic action, the architectonic bonds produce "that" particular sign and not another; in a different situation, they would establish different dyadic interactions—and produce a different sign.

Breal states quite clearly that language has no specific beginning: "I do not believe language had a beginning; rather, language emerged from its first verbal gropings after lengthy evolution, the transitions of which are almost indiscernible" (1991,135). It is a complex codal form that is made up of hierarchies of interlocked levels. He denies that "language is an organism with a life of its own and that it develops apart from man" (135). Breal unfortunately considers that the natural sciences are locked into a unileveled consideration of only dynamic codification, and therefore places the study of language firmly among the "historical" rather than "natural" sciences, somehow ignoring that the humanities can be as trapped in monologic structures as the sciences. However, he states that there is no ideal first language, no pure parent form, no first language that was "transparent" and directly reflective of the external world.

Dynamic codal networks do have a history; they retain the memory of past networks: However, a past network is only "sealed" into an authoritative metalogue[10] within a unileveled architecture. In the bilevel architecture, such networks become merely "tried paths" that may be used again and again, generalizing systems that act to increase the complexity of the codal procedures. A past usage establishes possibilities for future networking. The function of a metanarrative is to establish possibilities of metaphoric or transformative codification.[11] Kauffman refers to Jacob's concept that "adaptation typically progresses through small changes involving a *local* search in the space of possibilities" (1993,33). These possibilities "optimize" semiosis, or the transformation of various forms of energy into new signs. We can compare this with a biologic codification, for

> the genomic regulatory system of 25,000 to 250,000 components can be thought of as a kind of chemical computer. Each component is a node in the computer and receives inputs from those other components which directly regulate its activity. Whenever I refer to the "architecture" of this genomic regulatory system, Monod's "cybernetic system," I simply mean the "wiring diagram" showing which component affects which component. Of course, the wires are not physical connections; . . . thus the wires are better thought of as directed arrows pointing from the regulating to the regulated component. This is no mere abstract image. Although we do not yet know the architecture of the genomic system, it surely has one (Kauffman, 1993, 418).

The idea of wires as "directed arrows" rather than actual linear "roads" is an excellent image, following the understanding of *sema* (sign) as an "indicator." Breal continues, "if we return to our initial question and ask whether words are arranged in our minds in historical order, we are obliged to answer in the negative" (1991, 149). The metanarrative, then, is not an essentialist monologic force, but an architectural construction of *active* interlocking networks. These complex systems remain "poised in the complex regime on the boundary between order and chaos" (Kauffman 1993, 30).

We learn the "diagrams" of codification, we learn that the "arrangement of the interior vocabulary differs among people according to their personal experience, their education, their habits, their ways of thinking and feeling" (Breal 1991, 150). But "to be precise, we should speak neither of ideas nor of words, for there are no such things: there are only states, the habits of our brain and the movements of our vocal apparatus" (151). Breal argues that a society's "constantly growing weight of knowledge, invention and ideas" of previous ages is "condensed in language" (151). I would compare this with the biological development of the "genomic regulatory system." As a society or other organism becomes more complex, its interlocking networks become integrated with one another, and its ability to encode more energy will increase. "[A] language is not merely a bundle of words, but also consists of preassembled groups with joints in place, so to speak" (164). A dynamic codal network "is something acquired through time, through the common effort of an entire people, which becomes consolidated through usage, and which ends up so ingrained in our mind that we usually are not conscious of it, and have some difficulty abstracting from it on the spur of the moment" (171). Breal is referring here to language, but I consider it an excellent description of the metanarrative.

The metanarrative is a formula for codification; it is not operative on the unileveled frame of nominalism and therefore, cannot be commodified into the specific or formal entities of a metalanguage or metastructure. It does not operate with any linear authoritarianism. The metanarrative, in this case expressed within language, works in a dialogic and transformative fashion. "The acquisition of a new word . . . is relatively rare. Much more frequent is the application of a new idea of a word already in use. Here lies the real secret of the renewal and growth of languages. I should add that the emergence of a new meaning in no way undermines the old one. . . . The more advanced the culture of a nation, the more the words it uses acquire varied usages" (156)."Who could have known that Phaeton, the god of the sun, would become the name of an automobile, and that *plateforme* (platform) would enter the current vocabulary of politics? In order to predict such leaps of meaning, which we have no trouble following once they have occurred, but which are impossible to gauge in advance, we would have to anticipate the large and small, necessary and contingent events which transform human society, the revolutions and chance occurrences to which our physical, social and intellectual universe is exposed" (154). The metanarrative, as a network of codification, permits its synaptic bonds to multiply and/or change. As a society increases its population or develops its means of interaction with its environment, its organization becomes more complex, and, therefore its various forms of codification (not necessarily or only language) increase their complexity to permit this semiosis. "The word *operation* uttered by a surgeon conjures up a patient, a wound, and surgical instruments; by a military man, an army on the march; by a banker, the movement of capital; by a math teacher, addition and subtraction. Each science, art and profession, in creating a terminology, puts its stamp on the words of the common language" (156). So, the architecture of the metanarrative develops. As it develops, it "self-organizes," develops its own order, and develops "grammar models of functional integration" (Kauffman 1993, 644) that do "not produce either obscurity or confusion" because "the word comes prepared by what has preceded it and what surrounds it, has been put in context by time and place, and has been defined by the actors on the scene" (Breal 1991, 157).

This insistence on the dialogic interaction—on an understanding of language not as a structure of communication of essentialist "bits" but as an active means of constructing knowledge, which means that both its "luggage" of past meanings, *as changed and reformulated* within current contexts is part of the meaning—is an aspect of Voloshinov/Bakhtin's critique of Saussure. Saussure is criticized for focusing only on the unilevel existence of the sign "with its individuality and randomness," which operates not "as a process, but as a stable system of linguistic norms" (1973, 63). This abstract objectivism sets up Saussure's "langue" as operating within a modernist purity by inserting a regressive "third man" standing as an a priori authority behind the current usage of the signifiers. Saussure's differentiation of the two forces of synchrony and diachrony (somewhat comparable with dynamics and thermodynamics) is correct, but his rejection of their interaction trapped him. Working within the idea of language as a key codifying system, Voloshinov offered the "utterance" as a means of interaction between these two forces. He notes "language exists not in and of itself but only in conjunction with the individual structure of a concrete utterance. It is solely through the utterance that language makes contact with communication, is imbued with its vital power, and becomes a reality"(1973, 123). However, the mere fact of the utterance is not enough; if the interaction is not between different codes (dynamic and thermodynamic), then the utterance is not a transformation of energies but merely a reiteration of what has already been said.

Another analysis that can be used to clarify the complexities of the metanarrative is that of Popper's four functions of language, which explain hierarchies of codification.[12] The first is that of "self-expression" which I would compare with Peircean Firstness in that it is a nonreflexive burst of energy from a source. It is not yet a sign; it has not met up with the limitations to its expansion via the intrusive walls of otherness; it has not been "received" and therefore is not a *sema,* sealed within the spatiotemporal limits that permit it to exist as an indicator. The second function of language refers to the state in which that burst of energy has been sealed into itself by the insertion of limits, via the interaction of the receiver, such that the expression has been heard and accepted as a sign. This is, so far, a unileveled and mechanical action. These first two aspects of communication, expression and signal, are the basis of most communication theories—the sender's expression of the sound-bit and the carrying of that bit to a receiver. However, there are two "higher" functions of language, described by Popper as descriptive and argumentative functions, in which, with "the descriptive function of human language, the regulative idea of *truth* emerges, that is, of a description which fits the facts" (1972, 120). A description is true or false based on its "fit" with whatever it is describing. However, the "argumentative function of human language presupposes the descriptive function: arguments are, fundamentally, about descriptions: they criticize descriptions from the point of view of the regulative ideas of truth; content; and verisimilitude" (120). The argumentative function does not only involve the true/false description, but inserts the values or regulative ideals of the communitas towards that described reality. This argumentative function is akin to the *apodeixis* "public presentation" of various themes; it not only presents an enumeration, but requires a judgment of data. The descriptive function is accountable only to the specific realities of individual entities, whether sensual or conceptual. This is a unileveled process of nominalism. The argumentative/prescriptive function brings in the ethics, the crafted values, of that community, and, therefore, brings in the metanarrative. It operates, therefore, on a bileveled codal network; it is dialogic and reactive to the realities of the situation. Popper's comments of "the futility of all theories of human language that focus on *expression and communication*" (121) can be used to express the futility of a unileveled architecture. Without *dike* (judgment), one moves directly to hubris (outrage), from a first sensual contact to a more complex sensual effect—neither of which have any validity beyond the flush of their experience.

What we see in a bilevel architecture is the development of a semiotic network permitting the dialogic interaction of these two codal formats, the dynamic and the thermodynamic. Within a social frame, this is the ordering of social organization that functions as "complex systems poised in the complex regime on the boundary between order and chaos . . . an entire ensemble coursing back and forth along a high-dimensional boundary between order and disorder" (Kauffman 1993, 30). This does not mean a borderline or fragile existence; it means a society that functions within both forces—the stasis of dynamic reiteration and the spurious variety of thermodynamic randomness.

PART III

Interaction

5

CODAL REGIMES

We cannot long endure the sterile iconicity of dynamic codification. "So long as the mind keeps silent in the motionless world of its hopes, everything is reflected and arranged in the unity of its nostalgia" (Camus 1955, 22). Equally, we cannot exist solely within the chaotic randomness of thermodynamic codification, for "with its first move this world cracks and tumbles" (22) and "an infinite number of shimmering fragments is offered to the understanding" (22). But we are part of those structures and therefore if they are harmed, we too are harmed, and "I am poured out like water. And all my bones are out of joint" (Ps. 22). I have taken a position in this book of an analysis of semiosis as operative within a bilevel architecture, which establishes a metanarrative, or a force of generalization, a force that mediates particulars to explore the commonality rather than the isolating specifics of their existence.

Energy, the basis of life, can exist only if it is codified, in which state it can be considered *information*. This means that it must assume a *form*, a coherent spatiotemporal entity-event, which is physical and/or conceptual in nature. I will substitute "energy" for Nietzsche's "god," and read: "God as the supreme artist, amoral, recklessly creating and destroying, realizing himself indifferently in whatever he does or undoes, ridding himself by his acts of the embarrassment of his riches and the strain of his internal contradictions. Thus, the world was made to appear, at every instant, as a successful *solution* of God's own tensions, as an ever new vision projected by that grand sufferer for whom illusion is the only possible mode of redemption" (Nietzsche 1956, 9–10). Such is the nature of energy. There is no essentialist teleological goal; there is only the desire of energy to exist.

Variable, contrary, and hierarchical codes; interlocking and isolate codal networks—they all operate for the semiosis of energy, for its transformation into those brief breaths of life, signs, or events-of-information. Dynamic codification establishes a web of habitual interactional bonds that permits continuity of semiosis; thermodynamic codification establishes heterogeneous variation. Any regime of knowledge that uses only one of these two major formats *cannot maintain* its ability to be semiosic and thus exist as energy/information. Both forms of codification must be engaged in a dialogic interaction via the mediative actions of the metanarrative. This requirement for interaction is a stress-inducer and may emerge only at various sites (synaptic nodes) or times (birth, mating, feeding, death).[1] In the normative phase of semiosic existence, the dynamic or iterative codification will be dominant. However, human beings, alone of all species, have attempted to completely reject the indeterminacies of dialogue for the securities of a unileveled architecture. How can they be blamed? The separation, in Homo sapiens, of the sensual from the conceptual semiosic action has provided humans with the ability to conceive of the image separate from the actuality. The resultant capacity for reflexive action has enabled the human species to be immensely inventive, capable of a dazzling rapidity of technological change and therefore able to encode seemingly infinite amounts of energy. We, in our blind egocentrism, have considered that these powers have all been for our sake, to develop us as supreme masters of the earth; we have drawn many maps and diagrams that show this linear evolution. Of course, we are wrong; it has nothing to do with us. Behind every action, are the gods, the *daimos* "forces" of energy. Semiosis has nothing to say with any clarity; it does not dictate the nature of form; it merely permits its existence. Semiosis is all for the sake of energy. It is completely indifferent, totally uncommitted, to the actual forms of its existence. "The Lord whose oracle is in Delphi neither says nor conceals: he indicates (=verb *semaino*)" (Heraclitus; in Nagy 1990b, 234). Energy is only interested in those networks that ensure semiosis, the on-going production of *sema*, signs. "The *sema* is not just the "sign" of death; it is also the potential 'sign' of life after death" (219). The human species is its very special *xenos*—"someone who is bound by the ties of reciprocity between guest and host" (147, n.7). The cost of being this special *xenos* of energy, of being the supreme medium of energy, has been that humans are cognizant of their fate as transient semiosic events:

> Because I know I shall not know . . .
> Because I know that time is always time
> And place is always and only place
> And what is actual is actual only for one time
> And only for one place . . .

I pray that I may forget
These matters that with myself I too much discuss (Eliot, *Ash-Wednesday*, 1930, 93).

Regimes of knowledge that continuously operate within both codifications, the dialogic interactions of the continuous and the spurious codes are defined by Kauffman as "complex networks"; they exist within a "state which optimizes the complexity of tasks the systems can perform and simultaneously optimizes evolvability" (1993, 174). These regimes have a strong capacity to develop profitable strategic adaptations. Systems that have less ability to adapt are less dialogic, they privilege either the dynamic or thermodynamic codification, and Kauffman terms them "ordered" and "chaotic" networks. "In the *ordered* regime, many elements in the system freeze in fixed states of activity. . . . In the *chaotic* regime, there is no frozen component. Instead, a connected cluster of unfrozen elements, free to fluctuate in activities, percolates across the system, leaving behind isolated frozen islands" (174). The ordered regime, whose "elements fall to fixed active or inactive states" (234) has little capacity to evolve; "alterations in other parameters lead to only minor modifications of dynamical behavior. . . . [It is] insensitive to small alterations in the system" (209). The chaotic system, on the other hand, is highly sensitive to any changes (initial conditions) but these are "too disordered to be useful. Small changes at any point propagate damage to most other elements in the system" (219). We can easily see the modernist and postmodern eras in these two regimes of the ordered and the chaotic.

The complex networking of the two oppositional codes that are operative within the bilevel architecture forms "the transition regime, on the edge between order and chaos" (174). Kauffman defines them as: "complex systems poised in the complex regime on the boundary between order and chaos . . . an entire ensemble coursing back and forth along a high-dimensional boundary between order and disorder" (30). Complex systems make use of both networks, order and chaos; it is a state of "parallel-processing networks—located in the ordered regime but near the edge of chaos—which may simultaneously optimize the complexity of tasks such a network can perform and also optimize the capacity of the network to evolve. . . . Parallel-processing systems lying in this interface region between order and chaos may be the best able to adapt and evolve" (218). The complex regime has the highest capacity to maintain a web of interactive circuitry that permits both a continuity of codification *and* the functional use of spurious random codification. "The ability of an optimal parallel-processing network to perform some task or computation is governed *by the task*. If the task is very simple, a simple system will suffice. If the task is more complex, a more complex network will be required" (221) The parallel-processing system, the bilevel architecture, can carry out these different tasks. Complex systems, those systems that establish interactional networks with *both* dynamic and thermodynamic codifications, may have "fitness landscapes whose ruggedness optimizes the capacity of the networks to evolve by accumulating useful variations" (174). Again, "evolvability is high in networks near the order-chaos boundary because here many mutations cause minor changes and some mutations cause major changes. In a changing environment, this range of responses provides adaptive buffering: If the abiotic or coevolutionary world changes dramatically, large useful changes due to single mutations can be found rapidly; if the world changes only slightly, minor useful changes in behavior lie to hand. In contrast, systems deep in either the ordered regime or in the chaotic regime are probably neither capable of complex behavior nor highly evolvable" (232).

The most functional agent of adaptive change is the human species, precisely because of its conceptual capacities, which have enabled its members to rapidly and drastically, without any other codal adjustment (the biological, chemical, or physical composition of the species Homo sapiens) change their technology or means of interaction with the environment. The price to pay for these powers is consciousness of that borderline life, of a sense of a precarious life lived within the two oppositional forces of semiosis. Is it any wonder that humans have fled to the isolate certainties of either the frozen stability of dynamic codification or the irresolute indifference of thermodynamic codification? "A man defines himself by his make-believe as well as by his sincere impulses" (Camus 1955, 17).

We define the a priori beliefs of dynamic codification as pure and completely dedicated to our beneficence. By doing this, we have calmed our souls. *Credo ut intelligam* (I believe in order to understand). This is Anselm's and Augustine's credo, in which one begins and ends with the certainty of faith. However, the very instant that we commit ourselves to any monologue, we become trapped within the blindness of its hubris, the arrogance of its certainty. Energy cannot permit such entropic isolation and that is why it will always destroy our monolithic systems, it will always tear us away from both the mountains that we have built and the freedoms in which we bathe. As Caesar said in 63 BC, " take care . . . how your present decrees may affect posterity. All bad precedents spring from good beginnings." Abelard insisted on the question, the opening up of our beliefs to the cracks of questions, "such as may excite tender readers to the supreme endeavour of inquiring for truth and may render them sharper by their inquiry. For this is the definition of the first key of knowledge, namely assiduous or frequent questioning. . . . By calling into question [*dubitando*] we come to inquiry; by inquiring we reach the truth" (Abelard, *Sic et Non*, 103; in Haren 1992, 108).

THE CODAL JOURNEY: PRISMS AND NETWORKS

The gods shook with "uncontrollable laughter" when they saw what the lame, slow-footed, and yet immensely pragmatic Hephaestus had done upon discovering his wife, Aphrodite (she, a lover of laughter), in bed with Ares. He had bound them, tied them, wrapped them up fast to the bed. Zeus, still laughing, asked Hermes, "Tell me, would you, caught tight in these strong fastenings, be willing to sleep in bed by the side of Aphrodite the golden?" And Hermes answered, setting the gods into even more laughter, "I wish it could only be, and there could be thrice this number of endless fastenings, and all you gods could be looking on and all the goddesses, and still I would sleep by the side of Aphrodite the golden" (Homer 1965, Bk. VIII, lines 335–342).

That which is meaningful, that which "says something" is a sign—a result of intricate bonds with other signs. Signs are always moving along networks, always attracting other signs, always interacting with each other; that is the nature of semiosis. Hephaestus, the craftsman, was skilled in setting up such semiosic nets. To avenge himself on his mother, Hera, for her rejection of his lameness, he made her a throne that held her fast when she sat on it. That was a *sema;* it "indicated" his anger in a sign, a "tomb" of heavily silent meaning. Dionysus had to get him drunk to release the nets.

I repeat my basic axiom that energy cannot exist except when codified. Jacob points out that "the reactions in living organisms always proceed in the same direction, towards a decrease of free energy" (1973, 301), and therefore, towards meaning. There is no such thing as pure uncodified energy, no untransformed or uncodified sign; there is no meaning separate from its actualization within the codal network(s). "The word does not exist in a neutral and impersonal language (it is not, after all, out of a dictionary that the speaker gets his words!), but rather it exists in other people's mouths" (Bakhtin 1981, 294). Therefore, to suggest that the various "mediums" of language, image, and gesture and the various organizational formulas of metaphor, metonomy, irony, and synecdoche; and other additional "twists" such as paradigm and syntagm are structures separate from meaning ignores this basic fact that the codal actions are agential constructs of meaning.

All signs exist within the spatiotemporal confinement provided within organizational codes and networks. The sign is a closed event-unit; it exists within that restraint of Peircean Secondness. "Constraint is a Secondness" (1.325); "the second is therefore the absolute last" (1.358)—which points out its state of isolation; "the genuine second suffers and yet resists" (1.358); "this notion, of being such as other things make us, is such a prominent part of our life that we conceive other things also be exist by virtue of their reactions against each other" (1.324). The sign in a state of Secondness is a closed result of a semiosic codification; this closure can last for one millisecond or one hundred years; it can be a quark, a cell, a word, a gesture, a bird, a statue, a statute of law. For that period, it is "frozen"; however, its energy/information quickly begins to decodify or dissipate, providing the intentionality for more semiosic interactions, which form yet new signs—whether they be similar quarks, mimetic or mutant cells, written words, drawings of that statue, or versions of that statute.

As noted, the particle-as-meaning, once encoded, will begin to dissipate, and "even when localized as a position state, a particle begins to spread out at the next moment" (Penrose 1990, 326). Energy needs to develop the means of stabilizing its semiosic existentiality. It does this via the development of a "skeletal frame" of *interactive codal networks* that establish interconnected links with other codal regimes, and permit contact with and usage of diverse and polyphonic codifications, and so maintain the adaptive strengths not only of stability but also of diversity. The development of these indexical networks within the expansion of the semiosic cytoskeleton is a second and vital phase of architectonics after the establishment of the unilevel or bilevel infrastructure of the regime.

We can postulate that there are three key types of regimes of knowledge or semiosic architectures, which will be further discussed in the next chapter. One type may privilege the dynamic code and permit an iterative replication of a stable semiosis. Another privileges the thermodynamic code; its key characteristics will be a plethora of accidental and polyphonic semiosic "events"—a state of chaos and information-ambiguity that cannot last for any period of time and should be considered a liminal regime. The third regime, the complex, permits a dialogic interaction of both codifications, and is both the most difficult to maintain and the most strategically adaptive regime. Kauffman's analysis of three types of Boolean systems is comparable to these three regimes. As previously noted, the "ordered regime" of dynamic codification is repetitive, with few deviations: "the system tends to return to the same cycle after perturbation and maintain phase" (1993, 479). The signs of the chaotic regime, in which thermodynamic codification attracts loose energy, are "unfrozen," and "alterations in the activities of one or a few genes unleash cascades of change, or damage. . . . [C]haotic networks exhibit sensitivity to initial conditions . . . [their] cell types, rather than exhibiting homeostasis, show massive sensitivity to initial conditions" (471). The chaotic regime "picks up" any deviation, even from afar; its previous brief order collapses and a completely new sign appears in an "endless interpretation," as the deconstructionists have repeatedly informed us. The "complex regime," which Kauffman calls "parallel-processing," is comparable to the bileveled semiotic structure, and operates within the triadic semiosis of Peirce. It "occurs at the boundary between the ordered and the chaotic regime" (471) and permits a complex semiosis or transformation of energy. Therefore, "parallel-processing systems in the solid regime but near the boundary of chaos could perform the most complex controllable behaviors and also adapt optimally in a fixed or changing world" (471). The architectonic codal infrastructure of a bileveled system is capable of extreme complexity. It is made up of multiple interlocking networks of information-gatherers, information-reformulators, and information-distributors. These information strings and their interlocking networks can be compared with a prism. The definition of a prism is that it is a polyhedron, a closed figure made up of interacting segments. As such, it is a "refracting medium." A prism will deviate or disperse, and thereby either recode or encourage, the recoding of a beam of light with or without loss of energy content. Add other prisms within the boundaries of the one, and you get multiple networks, permitting a rich interconnectedness and expansive potentialities for transformations of energy within these nets. It is a reflexive action rather than a reflective medium.

We can think of not merely biological, but also social examples of these three types of regimes. The society or species that is isolated—that maintains a small, no-growth population within a stable and effective resource base—will privilege dynamic codification as the most efficient means of perpetuating self-continuity.[2] Tribal groups with simple economies are well able to maintain their identity and integrity for thousands of years; the dominance of the dynamic code in these societies maintains and assures a habitual and productive interaction with the environment. Such a regime ensures, for energy, a continuity of semiosis. We will usually see that in these societies, thermodynamic codification is either ignored as irrelevant, denigrated as irreverant, or temporally and spatially confined to certain times and certain peoples—the dangerous rituals of shamans, sacred days, special initiations. Any "non-normative" problems or needs will be specifically dealt with at these times. If an individual makes too much trouble at other times that person will be rejected from the band. This ordered regime of knowledge—which I would compare with Peirce's fixation of belief, with Plato's inductive certainty—permits a comfortable and low-energy maintenance continuity. Dynamic codification will therefore, as Peirce said, function in whatever its varieties, as a universal codal activity, whether operating alone, or more often, as the basic semiosic infrastructure of a more complex semiosis. I will repeat this: the privileging of dynamic codification and the marginalization of thermodynamic codification provide the basic semiosic stability for all life forms.

A semiosic regime whose codal operations are in increasing contact with Otherness, either because its population and resources are out of balance or because of active intrusion from external codal forces, cannot maintain the isolationist safety of a dominant dynamic codification; it becomes too expensive, energy-wise, to build stronger and higher walls against these other networks and semiosic attractors. We can observe that fundamentalist-governed societies become more violent as their self-sufficiency collapses or as their isolation is threatened. When a regime cannot maintain a codal isolation that is productive and regenerative, this imbalance will engender an entropic collapse into chaos, followed by a grab-all, spontaneous, new semiosic regime that may result in several new orders/societies. The disintegration into a chaotic regime permits a redistribution and reorganization of energy that will then be organized within one or more robust and adaptive semiotic regimes. Again, all three basic codal regimes—the dynamic, the chaotic and the complex—may be operative as separate systems, or cooperative within parallel levels in the more complex semiosic networks.

SEMIOSIS AS A DYADIC OR TRIADIC INTERACTION

Codal reorganization takes place at nodal points or synaptic sites; these sites function as attractors of similar and different encodements as well as catalytic agents for the recodification of this energy/information. At this site of prismatic intersections, energy is attracted, collected, dissipated, and reorganized. The codal organization of the resultant discrete sign is itself not totally new or completely introduced at that site; it is in large part carried within the current information-forms that have entered that nodal site. That is, recodification includes the codal logics of the old information. There is no need for a total deconstruction for semiosis to produce a new form. Rather, within semiosis, there are different levels of decodification, different levels of reformulation and transformation of codalities. This sets up a situation in which the energy of the transformation is in small or great part shared with those of the earlier forms, and the codification of the new sign is in small or great part shared with those of the earlier forms, and yet, because it is being organized in a different way, the new form or forms are Other to the previous forms. Otherness, then, is the dialogic interaction between and reorganization of both shared and not-shared energy and codalities, situated at sites that are spatiotemporally and organizationally different from each other. Semiosis can be understood as the indexical transformation of energy into metaphoric states of Otherness. Multiple, both plural and hierarchical, rather than single nodal sites permit a great flexibility of codification (and ultimately conservation) of energy. Multiple codal sites also permit energy to quickly adapt, to organize itself into a variety of forms, to change its abilities of interaction with Otherness, to grab or release more loosely encoded energy, and so to permit semiosic transformation.

The actual action of "making a sign," a unit/event of informed energy, is either dyadic or triadic. I am accepting both the Saussurian model of *semiology*, which is dyadic, and the Peircean model of *semiotics*, which is triadic. That is, both dyadically and triadically produced signs, have their operative functionality within semiotic architectures. The dyadic semiosis operates on a one-dimensional frame, using either the dynamic or the thermodynamic codification; it has, as unileveled, no means for their interactive dialogue, and, therefore, no capacity for a transformative semiosis. Therefore, it will produce either iterative, mimetic signs or transient, once-only signs, both of which are made up of a sensual expression bonded to a specific meaning (Firstness bonded to Secondness), with no opportunity for transformative expansion. The dynamic significations operate within a closed logistics, for "the signifier . . . is fixed, not free, with respect to the linguistic community that uses it" (Saussure 1964,71); its flexibility is "checked not only by the weight of the collectivity but also by time" (74). This type of semiosis presents us with signs that are nonreflexive and require behaviorist reactions; we stop at the stop sign. Semiology, using these same two nodal sites of expression and meaning, but unbonded rather than bonded, will produce arbitrary or "unmotivated" signification; both the signifier (sensual expression) and the signified (meaning) are, as separate from each other, ungrounded and random, and must be considered as accidents, since "nothing acts on, or is acted on by, any other thing at random" (*Physics* Bk.I:Ch.5.188a32). If the codal formula of this mutant sign is not accepted into a communal semiosis, its codal identity will vanish with the decay of its particular expression. Accidents, therefore, need not destabilize a semiotic population. Dyadic semiosis is simple, uncomplicated, and functional at the most general level of semiotic architectures, such as basic cellular organisms or normative rules of societies.

However, a more complex semiosis, providing for diverse codifications that permit cross-regime expansion, requires a triadic interaction, operating within the three nodal points of expression, mediative generalization, and specific articulation, (or Firstness, Thirdness and Secondness—in that order). The interaction both uses established networks and sets up new ones between these three nodal points, using the two processes of dynamic and thermodynamic codification. The semiosic interaction, the *act of codification*, in its triadic or fully dialogic state, relates these three major codal focal points within the bileveled frame, and permits a semiosis that seeks their commonalities—that actually generates commonalities, such that the various codal logics can interact and share logics and energies. Because the energy is not simply passed along (as on a conveyor belt) but is transformed at each node, the codal organization that takes place at the nodal points[3] is open to diversive expansion. This combination of both resistance to dissipation within a reiteration of type, as well as an acceptance and incorporation of diversity, is the adaptive strength of the triadic semiosic act of generalization.

The triadic semiosis action can be explained in Peirce's analysis of the interactive nature of the three categories of existentiality of Firstness, Secondness, and Thirdness. As with the Aristotelian refusal to separate the matter from the formula (*Metaphysics* Bk. VII), the three categories or processes cannot be separated, except analytically, from one another. Peirce explains this in his discussion of the three categories within a chemical body, with a first state of feeling based on the actual "complexity of the protoplasmic molecule"; a next force of reaction "emphasized in the nerve cells," which "is the property by which any state of high cohesiveness tends to spread through the albuminoid matter"; and a "synthesizing law," found "in the power of assimilation, incident to which is the habit-making faculty" (1.351). He warns against their separation into self-sufficient forces. The triad can be understood, as Spinks has pointed out, as a geometric triangle, with the emphasis being that the interaction of the codal energies of this triangle is not as a serial algorithm but as a geometric prism. This spatial reality—and Peirce was a realist—cannot be divided, cannot be reduced; it consists in a relationship of three axial areas within one another.

For, "A REPRESENTAMEN is a subject of a triadic relation TO a second, called its OBJECT, FOR a third, called its INTERPRETANT, this triadic relation being such that the REPRESENTAMEN determines its interpretant to stand in the same triadic relation to the same object for some interpretant" (1.541). This transformation is not linear. A metaphor does not translate directly into another metaphor, leaving the former behind as an empty shell. Semiosic formation is not equivalent to the chrysalis of a pupa to a butterfly; this is a serial, Hegelian movement of a primary intentionality, involving monologic, goal-directed changes in codal formation. Triadic semiosic codification has no original essentiality, no first intentionality hidden as its animistic essence. It is not cumulative, with each new metaphor layering itself on the back of the former. Rather, codification (and, therefore, signification) must be understood as the ongoing transformation of both old and new *relationships*. I am removing from my analysis the concept of the sign as an intact entity; I am considering instead, the concept of the sign itself as a nodal event, an action of *lines or strings of codal formulas* meeting with other lines and with the multiple codal formulas encrusted on these strings. A sign, a conceptual entity, is a spatiotemporally bound event of strings of codal formulas that coalesce at nodal points and transform their energies/codes into new signs or events-of-information.

INTENTIONALITIES

A sign-entity operates as strings or lines of codal intentionalities, acting within a codal or knowledge regime. These organized strings of codal energy exist, as wave/particle, in a state of both potentiality and actuality,[4] permitting a constant phase of intentionality to interact, as well as a constant phase of results of interaction; Firstness and Secondness are coexistent. As soon as these strings of intentionalities, these forces of potentiality, meet with other strings of energy, they instantly jump into a particle form (Secondness), a resting stage from the intentionality stage. This particlestage permits them to retain their energy/information from potential loss within the "crash," and the stage is also a means for them to grab hold of the new energy/information available in the interaction and bond it, hold onto it by reorganizing it within their holding patterns.[5] Then, replenished, they move again into the string or attractor state of intentionality and seek other interactions. What is the source of these lines of interaction? First, a sign, as a formation of spatiotemporal energy, is always emitting energy, in both an iterative and an entropic sense; this is its "will to power," its attractor state of potentiality. Energy moves in codal strings (waves); these are single or group packets of strings of different amounts of differentially organized energy. Kauffman uses the same image of strings as do the physicists—"Polymers can be regarded as strings of symbols" (1993, 369)[6]—and says that "most strings are legal both as program and as input" (372); that is, the codal pattern or logic is existential within the potentiality of the wave (program) and the actuality of the particle (input). "The catalytic and other chemical rules governing the ways enzymes catalyze ligation and cleavage among proteins can be thought of as a kind of *grammar*. In this grammar, strings of symbols act on strings of symbols to yield strings of symbols" (369). He continues, "each such grammar is a kind of hypothetical set of chemical laws. Each will yield a world of symbol strings and their joint transformations. Such symbol strings can be thought of as polymers in a prebiotic soup, molecules in an organism, goods and services in an economy, and perhaps even conceptual elements in a cognitive web or mythic elements in a cultural systems" (369). The point is, these codal strings network with one another, in both a determined and spurious manner, and "become models of functional integration, transformation and coevolution" (369).

Semiosis, then, operates in interactive networks of codal grammars within which organized "strings" of potential interactions—strings of codified intentionality—"reach out" to other energy formations, meet them, and are transformed into events of information, or signs. This "attractor intentionality" of dialogic and expansive transformative contacts is not the same as an ego-centered intentionality with its authoritative intention of making copies of an essentialist, abstracted original.

> A wealth of molecular signals pass between a bacterium and its environment. The signals entering the bacterium are harnessed to its metabolism and internal transformations such that, typically, the cell maintains itself, replicates, and passes its organized processes forward into history. . . . The niches occupied by each organism jointly add up to a meshwork in which all fundamental requirements for joint persistence are met. Similar features are found in an economic system. The set of goods and services making up an economy form a linked meshwork of transformations. The economic niches occupied by each set allow the producers of that set to earn a living and jointly add up to a web in which all mutually defined requirements are jointly met. Both biological and technological evolution consist in the invention of slightly or profoundly novel organisms, goods, or services which integrate into the ecological or economic mesh and thereby transform it. Yet at almost all stages, the web retains a functional coherence. Furthermore,

the very structure and connections among the entities set the stage for web transformation. In an ecosystem or economic system, the very interactions and couplings among the organisms or among the goods and services, create the conditions and niches into which new organisms, goods, or services can integrate. The web governs its own possibilities of transformation (Kauffman 1993, 370).

I have quoted at length because this so clearly outlines the semiosic transformations of dialogic networking.

"Language is not an abstract system of normative forms but a concrete heteroglot conception of the world. All words have the 'taste' of a profession, a genre, a tendency, a party, a particular work, a particular person, a generation, an age group, the day, the hour. Every word tastes of the context and contexts in which it has lived its socially charged life; all words and all forms are populated by intentions. Contextual overtones (generic, tendentious, individualistic) are inevitable in the word" (Bakhtin 1981, 293). When one energy packet of strings meets with another at the nodal sites, they both become "excited" and open to interaction and the exchange of energy/information. Any meeting of energies causes a "jump," a sudden coalescence from the "reaching-out" strings into a sign-unit, a particle, a tightly bound form of energy/information. At this interaction, the string-form of the entity can reject new energy/information, not absorbing it into its codal actions and resultant sign(s). If no new energy is accepted, then the resultant sign (any meeting of strings produces a sign) will be a much weaker, even though near-mimetic copy of the previous sign(s). By near-mimetic, I mean that any contact with energy, whether accepted or not, is going to change the energy content and organization of both strings. Signs can be considered a defensive state for energy; they bond (entomb) energy to prevent its potential loss within the interactions of strings. As a sign, the boundaries of the unit/event become thicker, the nodal points or points of energy contact for both acceptance and loss of energy become less accessible. As soon as signs are produced, they become entropic, dependent on the codal form; this dissolution can be immediate or can take many years. The energy moves back into string-like interactional states and moves off, seeking new contacts. However, if the energy exchange reaches a critical threshold of excitation, then the codifying organizations—both near and far—may collapse in whole or in part. The energy, at this critical state, can be explosively "lost" (the big bang); or the codal logics can equally, suddenly, self-organize into one, two, or many new forms. From one regime, suddenly, many more will exist. There is no deterministic agent, no path of evolution, no predetermination for the emergence of these codal formations. Certainly, the whole point of dynamic codification, common to all organisms, is to inhibit the potentiality for change to prevent far-reaching deviations from current codification possibilities, and thus to prevent a possible loss of energy to semiosis. But codal logics and signs cannot be completely predicted by the previous semiosic actions.

The sign, therefore, is a particle event of information, a result of the interaction amongst multiple lines of encoded energy or lines of intentionality. As Eco has said, "the classical notion of 'sign' *dissolves* itself into a highly complex network of changing relationships. Semiotics suggests a sort of molecular landscape in which what we are accustomed to recognize as everyday forms turns out to be the result of transitory chemical aggregations and so-called 'things' are only the surface appearance assumed by an underlying network of more elementary units" (1976, 49). I would disagree with the "layering" image; the sign is not simply a macroscopic collection of simpler entities, but is a complex transformation of polyphonous forces. Eco's concept of the code states that "it is not true that a code organizes signs; it is more correct to say that codes provide the rules which *generate* signs as concrete occurrences in communicative intercourse" (49). Regimes of knowledge operate within those three key types of logics, which will be further discussed in the next chapter under the theme of rituals and which we can summarize here as a priori or historic, laterally transmitted or co-interactional, and spontaneously generated. Codes have only one role—the conservation of energy—and semiosic regimes have developed multiple strategies for this purpose.

Ego-centered intentionality operates within a dyadic semiosis. It is based around the psychological or mechanical framework of (1) a separation, a distinction between; and (2) a direct, dyadic bond between potentiality and actuality, between sender and receiver; an understanding that the "medium" and the "message" can be separated, that the medium is a transparent conveyor, and that the meaning can be "authoritatively" put through, intact, into the hapless and helpless receiver bucket. Barthes notes, "semiology is a science of forms, since it studies significations apart from their context" (1972, 111). This belief forms the basis for the "conceptual wars" of deconstructionism, which attempt to destroy the bonds of these dyadic forms and so permit the receiver to resist the power of this monologic purity; the result is a chaotic plurality of non-signs—self-referential units twisted, fetally, each into themselves and totally incapable of any semiosis whatsoever. The relationship between the dichotomic pairs of langue and parole, signifiant and signifie, diachrony and synchrony—and the syntagmatic and paradigmatic axes of language (Saussure 1964)—are a topic of frequent, tortured semiological and semiotic discussion.[7] The first deconstructionist was God, who threw Adam and Eve out of Eden (purity) when they became aware that the bond between the "thing" and its "image" was conceptual and triadic rather than innate and dyadic, that there were two levels to reality instead of one, that behind the "thing" was always the whisper of others. Such knowledge was meant to be confined to the gods; it was not meant for the human mind. "A man, a man, and nothing more,/yet he presumed to wage a war with god" (Euripides. *The Bacchae,* lines 636–637).

Ego-centered intentionality, which does exist and has its uses, is limited in its productivity, confined to the signification of only one image. It is not evolutionary and cannot adapt. Such authoritarianism is quite useful and necessary in preventing dissipative use of energy. A red light means stop; a green light means go. There are no options. A codal format for a particular hormone should not produce a different hormone. This iconic rigidity, this desire to pass on the sign in its exact form from one site to another, is not wrong; there should be no sense, as there frequently is, of any conspiracy against freedom of the right to be individual.[8] Conspiracy theories, operating within this assumption of the isolate integrity of the sign and the uniqueness of its production, consider any action that produces a mimetic sign to be dysfunctional; the cause of this dysfunctionality is equally operative within an ego direction: that of the evil Other, who is somehow understood as promoting collective behavior. Barthes wrote that "the signifieds of historical discourse can occupy at least two different levels. There is, first of all, a level immanent to the material stated; this level retains all the meanings the historian deliberately gives to the facts he reports.... If the 'lesson' is continuous, we reach a second level, that of a signified transcending the entire historical discourse'.... In this historical discourse of our civilization, the process of signification always aims at 'filling' the meaning of History" (1986, 137). Barthes rejects the possibility of a "pure" knowledge of "facts," but only because he feels that language is creative rather than reflective. However, he still provides us with the idea of an ego's "deliberate" codification, a conspiracy to corrupt certain purities, particularly the individual's ability to contact an external, Platonic purity. The frequent correlation of Saussurian semiology with psychoanalysis and with the structuralist theories of hegemonic domination shows how easily this framework operates within an ego-centered intentionality. Ego-centered intentionality is a factor of communication theory rather than semiosis.

COMMUNICATION THEORIES

The nominalist/structuralist understanding of codes is that they are *mediums* (rather than mediative); they are transparent mechanisms and must, if they are any good, convey an intact meaning originating from a first cause. Thus, there is, as Derrida claims, a potential conflict between "the force of accentuation and the force of articulation" (1981, 228).[9] I use the image of a prism to move our conceptualization of semiosis away from the older, serial, linear images of the triangle (Ogden and Richards, 1936),[10] the Saussurian dyad (1964), and the linear path of communication diagrams (Shannon and Weaver, 1964). The mistake has been to use these diagrams as images of semiosis. They are not: they are describing the mechanics of *communication,* the movement of a static sign-unit from one spatial site to another. This has nothing to do with cognition, but considers only and strictly the *mechanical* process of moving a sealed package of energy from one site to another. Communication theories must be distinguished from semiotic theories.

Communication is interested in the sign in its spatiotemporal "frozen" state of Peircean Secondness. Communication theory is not interested in the ongoing transformation of codification. It considers only the current entity, the sign, as existent in a "fullness of meaning," its Form.[11] The concern of communication theories is how to move this purity from site A to site B. Any deviations in form or content of the package at subsequent sites are considered a loss or damage, by inserting ambiguity within that basic meaning. One can put a better face on any changes that might take place in this journey and consider them tropic additions of the intellect (metaphor, parody)—but this does not change the conceptual infrastructure that is based around a concern with an original purity of meaning, as carried within a potentially denigrating medium.[12] "The movement of the wand is rich with all possible discourses but no discourse can reproduce it without impoverishing and deforming it. . . . The gesture, that of passion rather than need, considered in its purity of origin, guards us against an already alienating speech, a speech already carrying in itself death and absence. That is why, when it does not precede the spoken word, it supplements it, corrects its fault and fills its lack" (Derrida 1981, 234–235).

Communication theory understands the sign in the binary Saussurian sense, as made up of a meaning (signified) and a carrying codal medium (signifier). This Platonic perspective sees meaning as existential without a code: the code is no longer the organizing format of energy, it simply carries the intact energy/meaning on its journey. Dissipation of the code may harm the meaning; or the actual code, intentionally or not, may hide or obstruct the meaning. Communication theory is concerned with the meaning of *one* sign, in *one* particular state of Secondness, one particular frozen phase of spatiotemporality. This is a valid concern, but has absolutely nothing to do with the development of cognition or meaning. We might here consider Eco's famous statement of "every time there is a possibility of lying, there is a sign-function" (1976, 58).[13] As he says, the function "is to signify (and then to communicate) something to which no real state of things corresponds" (59). This suggests at first glance that there is an original purity of meaning, and any changes are a "lie," a deviation.[14] This is a unileveled analysis, considering only that there is a truth, and that codification enables one to deviate from that original state. This would confine semiotic actions to deviational codes, to thermodynamics. However, Eco continues, semiotics exists on the threshold "between *conditions of signification* and *conditions of truth*" (59), between thermodynamic and dynamic codification. This threshold state is that complex regime of Kauffman, and what I am defining as the bilevel architecture. It is in this state that the triadic interaction of semiosic codification occurs.

There is nothing wrong with communication actions: they are quite necessary—indeed vital—in the development of strong dynamic networks, whether these are biological links, laser tools, or telecommunication lines. But they must not be confused with semiosis, which is about *codification* or *cognition*—not about the mechanical movement of an encoded particle from one site to another. Theories that mistake the two force us to pay a heavy conceptual and emotional price. Freudian analysis considers that much of this original fullness of meaning may be "repressed" or hidden; its repression may be unconscious but the supposition is that this "part of the whole" is hidden due to one's own actions of rejection, one's selectivity; and thus, one's inability to accept a full reality. Analysis attempts to uncover these omissions and so to restructure the past "fullness" or original purity and potentiality of that particular person, as well as a current emotional structure that seemingly permits an acceptance of this "fullness of being," of this original Firstness. This perspective rejects the concept that life is a semiosic (transformative and evolving) experience, and that there is no purity of being either in the beginning or the end.

The separation of our codification nodes into sensual and conceptual means that such a direct linear bond between the two nodes is not part of our cognitive framework. We are born with the ability to formulate multiple and therefore, different codifications; this ability has enabled the human species to develop into the most complex and adaptive of all forms of life. The price we pay for this adaptive nature is the loss of purity; the rejection by the gods; or, rather, the ultimate indifference of each to the other. Cognition theories based around the conceptual viability of the single node, bonded node, or direct link between nodes are all fallacious. They are based around a false belief that cognition is a serial, algorithmic development. One begins with a set of bags and contents, and carries this same bag, simply adding (but not changing) contents as one walks along the cognitive path; signs are frozen commodities, external to us, that we pick up as products in the supermarket; they are never our own dialogic creations. This is also the mind-set of "false memory syndrome" patients, whose purification baths operate within this same concept of a "pure original" of which parts have been forgotten; the therapeutic bath will slough off the thickened skin and so "reveal" these basic lost memories. As I have said, purity is always about power. One must always consider who is empowered and who is destroyed in these psychological traumas.

This confusion of semiosis with communication is also found in literary criticism that focuses on language as a social construct and that therefore illogically concludes that the task is to "deconstruct" it and release the pure meaning beyond the language; this is that opposition between the primary text and the secondary discourse. We find here the many studies of the figurative aspects of language, the many ways of codifying and seemingly obscuring "purity." Kenneth Burke "mentions *deflection* (which he compares structurally to Freudian displacement), defined as "any slight bias or even unintended error," as the rhetorical basis of language, and deflection is then conceived as a dialectical subversion of the consistent link between sign and meaning that operates within grammatical patterns; hence Burke's well-known insistence on the distinction between grammar and rhetoric" (in De Man 1979, 8). This is that distinction between the meaning and the code. As Wlad Godzich has described "it opposes the immediately apprehensible darkness of the sensible to the eventuality of the great clarity of the intelligible, yet makes the first the condition and means of access to the second. . . . The immediately perceptible materiality of the poem—its verbal component—is a means of access, yet a barrier, to the central core of meaning of the poem" (Introduction, De Man 1983, xix). Communication theories deal with closed entities in a state of Secondness; they have nothing to do with the creation of sign-units, with the triadic transformation of energy.[15]

Communication has no need for gods, or even, for human beings. It is in that state of Thirdness, the metanarrative of semiosis, where the gods, who are infinite potentiality, and human beings, who are conceptual reality, meet, discuss, argue, and set up semiosic regimes, the codal narratives by which all life exists.

CODIFICATION AND HIERARCHIES

Words are like boulders torn from mountains and carried along by rivers at the beginning of their course: their rough edges having been already smoothed halfway along, they finally end up as those little round pebbles continually washed and worn down by the surf.

—M. Breal (1991, 105).

Codes are the basis of semiosis. Their inhibitory laws prevent energy from ultimate dissipation. Their normative intentions reject many spurious strings and prevent energy from being wasted by the exhaustive need to develop new networks. Their openness to new networks permits evolutionary development and the ongoing preservation of energy. A code is a "habit of action," and "the identity of a habit depends on how it might lead us to act, not merely under such circumstances as are likely to arise, but under such as might possibly occur, no matter how improbably they may be" (Peirce 5.400). We have many codes; language is only one of them—even though it is the most important within human cognition. Codes are not isolated in practice; they interlock with each other. This networking increases their capacities to organize energy.

In his introduction to Breal, concerning the relationship between language and the world, between the symbolic and the objective reality, Wolf notes that "from the beginning Breal urged against the form of the problem as it has tended to be addressed since Saussure's *Cours* and Wittgenstein's *Tractatus*. Instead, Breal stressed that language is not a mirror of the world, or the mind, as general grammarians in the lineage of Aristotle and Port-Royal held, but is more like a lens through which the world is refracted according to the light in our perspective" (1991,16). As Breal writes, "a word's body and soul (its form and meaning) do not exactly fit together" (81). Further, "I should like to show that it is in the nature of language to express our ideas in an incomplete way, and that language would be unable to represent even the simplest, most elementary thought, if our own intelligence did not constantly come to the aid of speech and with its own lights did not compensate for the insufficiency of the medium" (81). He continues, "it is because language leaves an enormous amount to the imagination that it is able to lend itself to the progress of human thought. A language which represented absolutely everything which existed in our minds at a given moment, and which supplied an expression for every movement of the intellect, would hardly be of use. It would instead be a hindrance, since either the language would have to change with each new notion, or our mental operations would always have to remain the same in order not to disturb the linguistic mechanism" (81–82). We have here the "fuzziness" that is the openness of semiosis (in contrast to the closure of communication). As Peirce wrote, "all the evolution we know of proceeds from the vague to the definite . . . the undifferentiated differentiates itself. . . . The homogenous puts on heterogeneity" (6.191). And even, "we cannot suppose the process of derivation, a process which extends from before time and from before logic, we cannot suppose that it began elsewhere than in the utter vagueness of completely undetermined and dimensionless potentiality" (6.193).

Language is, therefore, not a medium but a codal network of interactions, and the "subject and the object are at least as much logical notions as they are grammatical ones"(Breal 1991, 51). The modernist unileveled frame analyzes codes as carriers, its focus on words as discrete entities separates matter and form: If you use this frame, you will inevitably search for the ultimate purity of that matter as unsullied by its form. "We can see how rash is the confidence of those who claim to discern in roots like those of Indo-European an echo of the impression which the external world made on the ancestors of the race. To find onomatopoeia or natural cries in these syllables, which have already been worn down by the friction of centuries, is to begin the *Cratylus* all over again" (105). Modernist linguists "imagine origins as simple" or "have thought that the oldest form was the most complex" (107). However, we cannot observe "the first"; "our very percepts are the results of cognitive elaboration" (Peirce 5.416), and "either the basic premisses will be demonstrable and will depend on prior premisses and the regress will be endless; or the primary truths will be indemonstrable definitions" (Aristotle *Posterior Analytics* Bk II: Ch. 3. 90b25). We live within an ongoing semiosis; the origin and the finality of semiosic realities has no validity.

The "fundamental view of comparative philology is that languages have a continuous development which must be traced back in order for us to understand the facts encountered at a given stage of their history. The error of the old grammatical method lay in the view it presupposed: that a language is a whole, complete in itself, and can be explained by reference only to itself" (Breal 1991, 38). This is an important concept: we see here a unileveled versus a bileveled architecture. Modernism seeks the original, essentialist purity of origin. But languages "are full of forgotten metaphors, faded images, often incomprehensible allusions to dead beliefs and abandoned usage: they are the legacy of the past. . . . [T]hat legacy, instead of serving us, would have hindered us if it had not in the passage of time conformed to new needs and to different habits of thought" (56) and "It is therefore not just at the origin of races that the creation of languages is to be placed: we create them at every moment; for every change which affects them is of our own doing. . . . Words "exist only when we think them and understand them" (61).

If the unheard, unspoken
Word is unspoken, unheard (Eliot *Ash-Wednesday.*1954, lines 150–151).

We must assume that languages continuously develop; language change is natural, not within an inherent or intentional agenda, but within a pragmatic functionality, and "language forms change in conjunction with speakers' perceptions of those forms, perceptions which in turn are determined by speakers' communicational purposes in time" (Breal 1991, 5). Essentially, there is no such thing as a non-metaphoric cognition. Our reality consists of interlocked and hierarchical metaphoric complexities.

Vico examines the hierarchical structure of language or codification. Within his three ages of gods, heroes, and men, we find three languages, or what I will term "phases of semiosis."[16] He states that the "first language had been hieroglyphic, sacred or divine; the second, symbolic, by signs or by heroic devices; the third, epistolary, for men at a distance to communicate to each other the current needs of their lives" (1948, 432). This first aspect of the hierarchy—by which I do not mean increasing in power but increasing in complexity of organization—is that pure force of sensuality and emotion, "clothed in the greatest passions and therefore, full of sublimity and arousing wonder" (34). The first phase of semiosis is Vico's first speech, the mute divine, with muteness understood as the fullness of its Peircean Firstness: it is "full" in that it is, in its string nature, open to many network links; it is sensual, powerful, and mute; it is not yet a particular sign and is therefore not accessible to human reason. This first phase of codification is the "reaching out" of string potentialities: it is the activation of the network; that is why it is "divine"—in that it is considered closest to basic energy in its uncoded potentiality. Energy that is in the boundary stage, the synaptic stage—between one codal form and another—is mute.

It has, as potentiality, an enormous power to mean many things. Codification narrows potentiality into the specifics of an actual sign. The word "logic" comes from logos, whose first and proper meaning was *fabula* (fable), carried over into Italian as *favella*, (speech). In Greek, the fable was also called *mythos* (myth), whence comes the Latin *mutus* (mute). Vico criticizes Plato for attempting to clone this mute potentiality with codified meaning—the Form directly linked with the image.[17] Instead, what must happen is an increasing complexity of organization of this energy within a variety of codes; this gradually narrows the conceptual parameters, leading to a specification of meaning within that particular context. However, the potentiality that was there within the mute phase of Firstness provided for a diversity of possible meanings. Thus, the fact that energy must be encoded, and that this codification is not inherent in the expression, permits life to exist in diverse and highly adaptive forms. Vico adds, "as these vast imaginations shrank and the power of abstraction grew, the same objects were apprehended by diminuitive signs" (402). "Jove becomes so small and light that he is flown about by an eagle. Neptune rides the waves in a fragile chariot. And Cybele rides seated on a lion" (402). Uncoded energy cannot exist; energy that has only a few codes available to it will produce life-forms that are necessarily simple, stable and unable to adapt on their own. Complexity is a factor of strategic adaptation.

Vico continues, "we must here uproot the false opinion held by some of the Egyptians that the hieroglyphics were invented by philosophers to conceal in them their mysteries of lofty esoteric wisdom" (435). This conspiracy theory can only operate in a unilevel architecture, based on an assumption of an original purity as "owned" by one agent/class versus another agent/class. The "second kind of speech, corresponding to the age of the heroes" (438) is the establishment of the syncretic continuities of symbolic bonds. "In consequence, they must have been metaphors, images, similtudes or comparisons, which, having passed into articulate speech, supplied all the resources of poetic expression" (438). Codal networks develop within these heroic statues, mythic forms bond people into a communitas of shared knowledge. There is, finally, the vernacular, the "epistolary or vulgar language." This vulgar language was "introduced by the vulgar" (443) or common people; its meaning was related to the individual's real interactions with the external world. This is the particular sign, specific in its individual pragmatism, but produced within the codification processes of the community. As a semiotic process, all three forms of language or codification are in a prismatic, dialogic (not serial, algorithmic) relationship; "we must establish this principle: that as gods, heroes, and men began at the same time (for they were, after all, men who imagined the gods and believed their own heroic nature to be a mixture of the divine and human natures), so these three languages began at the same time, each having its letters, which developed along with it" (446).

Nietzsche's reactive procedures consider two systems—the unconscious and the conscious, which I would compare with dynamic and thermodynamic codes. The "reactive unconscious is defined by mnemonic traces, by lasting imprints. it is a digestive, vegetative and ruminative system, which expresses 'the purely passive impossibility of escaping from the impression once it is received'" (Deleuze 1983, 112). But "adaptation would never be possible if the reactive apparatus did not have another system of forces at its disposal . . . a system in which reaction is not a reaction of traces but becomes a reaction to the present excitation or to the direct image of the object. This second kind of reactive forces is inseparable from consciousness: that constantly renewed skin surrounding an ever fresh receptivity, a milieu 'where there is always rooms for new things'" (113). As with dynamic and thermodynamic codes, these two forces do not blend. "The two systems or the two kinds of reactive forces must still be separated. The traces must not invade consciousness" (113). Instead, the separation is maintained by consciously forgetting the traces, by releasing the momentary semiotic bond between the two levels. Oblivion, or forgetting, is the action of releasing the semiotic bond. "Oblivion is not merely a *vis inertiae*, as is often claimed, but an active screening device, responsible for the fact that what we experience and digest psychologically does not, in the stage of digestion, emerge into consciousness any more than what we ingest physically does" (Nietzsche 1956, 189). Codal networks interlock the forces of the two levels, the unconscious with the conscious, the mnemonic trace with the present, the dynamic with the thermodynamic. The sign is, as a prism, made up of multiple correlates within each plane. Each plane is its own prism: Putting them together increases the multiplicity of refractive potentiality. Each touch of the prismatic view (a single view, made up of its own multiplicity of prismatic lines) brings more encoded energy, more networked strings into play. Cognition is a myriad of potentialities.

Codification is any figurative form that encodes energy. An hour's observation anywhere can provide confirmation of the enormity and complexity of their chemical, biological, and cognitive variety. Research has attempted to systematize codal correlates into bundles of co-ordinated semiotic behavior. We are already familiar with the triadic interactions of Aristotle, Peirce, Popper, Vico, and Plato.[18] These can be understood as attempts to analyze the actions taking place within the *single action* of semiosis, the semiosic action. But there are other analyses that try to categorize the increasingly complex development of semiotic behavior into hierarchical phases or stages of an increasing complexity of cognition.

For example, Guibert of Nogent (circa 1084) had four such bundles of signification: historic, allegoric, moral and aesthetic, with each bundle bringing in other correlates of meaning. The historic would bring in traces of the past; the allegoric brings in metaphoric versions of the present and past; the moral brings in a comparative and restrictive reflexion; the aesthetic brings in the sublime. We can compare these four with Vico's tropes of metaphor, metonomy, synecdoche, and irony, which also create meaning within interlocked conceptual networks. I would also remind the reader of Popper's four "bundles" of language functionality: the symptomatic, the signalling, the descriptive, and the argumentative. The first two establish an entity as a discreet existence: The first is an agent's expression of a state of being, somewhat similar to Firstness; the second is the reception of this unit such that it signifies "something." The next two Popper considers definitive of the human cognition. Third is the ability to describe something, in its truth or falseness of being. This description requires a trace, a memory of identity for this comparison. And then there is the fourth, the vital action of decoding and recoding the coded forms in a reflexive, comparative manner. These four functions represent different levels of the complexity of codification. There are many other such systemic analyses, and they share a sense of a hierarchical development of complexity. There are Aristotle's four faculties of the soul, beginning with Nutrition, having to do only with the expression of existence; and the Sensate, referring to the reception of sensations. The two higher faculties are the Volitional, referring to a sense of self-direction; and the Rational, referring to analysis and the use of symbols. The comparison to Popper's four categories is obvious. Plato's four categories of knowledge are similar. One begins with the helpless observation of the images in the cave; one can only accept these at face value. The next stage is the awareness of the visible or possible actuality of whatever causes these images; these are dealt with by induction. The next two higher stages deal with the awareness of relationships between entities, particularly within a study of mathematics; this is a deductive knowledge. The final stage is the intuitive awareness of the pure reality, the Forms.

We may even consider another set of four forces of organization of energy—that within physics. There is gravity, a long-range force, operating within a "field" or limit of extensional range around a particle. Then there is electromagnetism, which is not universal (as is gravity) but appears within a specific interaction. And finally, there are the strong and weak nuclear forces: The former binds the protons and neutrons together in the nucleus, the latter brings about the transmutation of particles. There are even more interactive forces of organization. There are three types of exchange forces that act between particles: each corresponds to the sharing or exchange of different properties. The Heisenberg force is an exchange of charge; the Bartlett force is an exchange of spin direction; the Majorana force is an exchange of position due to exchange of charge and spin. Codification, or the organization of energy, is the most important force for the formation of life; the more complex and interactive these codes—the greater the preservation of energy.

The social text is organized within multiple interlocked codal networks that organize and transform energy. All spatiotemporal reality exists within such networks, which permit repetition of form and also the generation of variation; together, these two actions prevent entropic loss of energy. Each form of energy, organized and therefore differentiated from others, is in itself part of other organizations of energy. The same codal form of life is also part of an energy content as organized within a larger group, and that is part of another code system or group, and so on—which is what we should really understand within Peirce's continuity of semiosis, rather than the endless interpretation of the deconstructionist. As Aristotle noted, "To rely on mere thinking is absurd, for then the excess of defect is not in the thing but in the thought.... The thought is an accident" (*Physics* Bk.III:Ch.8.208a15).

However, this very fact of the constant *motion*, the endless "semiosic churning" of signification, as operative within the multidimensional and polyphonic state of interconnecting codes and interlocked hierarchies of the bileveled architecture, results in a state of existence—Kauffman's "borderline" wherein one is subject to a constant loss of clarification of meaning, an open debate on the integrity of being, leading, one might fear, to a final state of entropic decay and anomic dissolution. Certainly, Plato feared this dissolution of meaning in his polis; the medieval church argued against dialogue, with Augustine, for example, arguing against the "vice of curiousity," a "certain vain and curious longing, cloaked under the name of knowledge and learning ... the lust of the eyes ... this malady of curiosity" (*Confessions*. Bk X, Ch.35, 174). How does one deal with these two seemingly oppositional requirements of energy for stasis and heterogeneity? The variety of codification, the complexities offered by hierarchies, provide a means for these oppositional forces to interact rather than obliterate each other. Let us now consider such interactions within their formalization in rituals.

6

RITUALS AND REGIMES OF KNOWLEDGE

RITUALS

Rituals deal with stability, with the invariance of time; they support the preservation of energy and therefore are heavily operative within dynamic codification. They are, in this sense, "planular" or spatial: they operate as smooth planes of order, with a "plane" understood as the spatial extension of a code exclusive of temporal incidents: Indeed, rituals attempt to deny temporality; they ignore time as an irrelevant and irritating intruder. In this sense, they at first glance seem to be anti-dialogic; they preserve the *sema* against the intrusion of the question. Whenever one is in a synaptic site at which different codalities and different energies meet, and different Selves and different Others come together, one must be cautious. Such a mingling can drown one's identity, and the inclusion of time—that sharp arrow-head of reality into this confluence—will suddenly set that new identity, freeze it into a sign—fresh indeed in its sudden passion, but a tomb from which one may not easily escape. So was Aeneas warned of the results of his passion for Dido. "This vision stunned Aeneas, struck him dumb. . . . What can he do? With what words dare he face the frenzied queen? What openings can he employ? His wits are split, they shift here, there; they race to different pieces, turning to everything" (Virgil 1990, lines 373–381). It is in this state that one must affirm one's commitment to the restrictions of one's own codality; one must remember the rights of semiosic iteration. "Are you forgetful of what is your own kingdom, your own fate?" (lines 356–7). "For evolution is the result of a struggle between what was and what is to be, between the conservative and the revolutionary, between the sameness of reproduction and the newness of variation" (Jacob 1973, 310). Rituals are mediators of this struggle for meaning.

As noted, the nodal sites of semiosis are synaptic phases for the interaction of multiple and diverse string-like intentionalities of contact between the Self and Otherness. These phases sit—or, more accurately, act on—an "edge," a synaptic cleft, a borderline of contacts. The cleft phase moves energy to the peripheries of existent codal controls, it exposes it to the intrusive codifications of Otherness, and thus moves energy from a closed codification to a state of openness; a state of Firstness; an intense fullness of desire-for, without a conception of that which is desired.[1] In this ambivalent state, these interacting energies will suddenly coalesce into a sign—but the actual sign thus emergent cannot be completely controlled or predicted and is—must be—open to chance. As such, this phase is highly dangerous to the stasis of both the Self and the Others, as well as to the viability of continuity of semiosic codification. Interactions at these sites are therefore stabilized by the development of various forms of ritualistic behavior, reified codes that serve to defuse the deconstructive potentialities of this phase of semiosis. It is here, at these nodal phases, that we will find formalized patterns of behavior within societies and, indeed, all organisms. In many societies, the last day of the month, the day between the old and the new, is a crisis point. "This is the day that people spend by sorting out what is truth and what is not" (Hesiod, *Works and Days,* lines 766–768; in Nagy 1990b, 62). Odysseus, in preparing for action, sacrificed "the barren heifer, the best I had . . . a ram, wholly black, the goodliest of my flocks . . . and milk and honey, sweet wine and barley meal" (Homer, 1965, Bk. XI, lines 24–54). These are the ritual signs that one offers to Otherness: a ram, a bull, and a boar that mates with sows—and the first few words of greeting the multitudinous forces would be carefully and cautiously selected. We see here the rigid codal etiquettes in human interaction, both on the individual and group level; the highly ritualized forms of interaction between animals, birds, and insects; and biological and chemical immune interactions. We can include here all "meeting sites" of different codifications: for example, the most dangerous time for an airplane is when it makes a transition from a codified reality that is airborne, to a codified reality on land; it is at this synaptic phase that the strictest forms of operational behavior will be required. I will consider three forms of ritualistic codification of behavior under the Peircean terms of iconic, indexical, and symbolic—which I will define, to differ them from these sign-units, as iterative, evolutionary, and lyric rituals.

Rituals encode interactive behavior in a repetitive, homogenizing, and therefore group-bound or communal form of behavior. Ritual behavior and beliefs inhibit thermodynamic spuriousness by their social authority: they provide stability for the individuals in the group—one *knows* how to behave. There are many levels of ritual, from the simplest daily interactions to complex sacred interactions laden with multiple meanings and confined to only a few practitioners. They are all a means of providing normative standards and therefore syncretic continuity to a regime of knowledge. Traditional analyses of ritual have provided us with two major paradigms. Both see ritual behavior as not necessarily simple but certainly irrational; both acknowledge the reality of biological and conceptual diversity, as well as the possibility of iterative and stable behavior as a means to diminish the dangerous effects of this instability. Both consider rituals functional to certain goals and, following simple oppositional binarism, can see possibilities of those same functions' being achieved without rituals. In these analyses, human beings are faulted for a view that seemingly locates the authoritative control of stability outside individual rationality and within some theistic, irrational force that must be dealt with by ritual. These paradigms understand rituals as indicative of a primitive understanding of the forces of stability, and, therefore, these analyses understand rituals as symptoms of intellectual incompetence. The functionality of the ritual as the conceptual articulation of the acceptance of dynamic codification and its limitations is ignored. I am suggesting, however, that rituals are absolutely vital not only for their articulation of dynamic codification but also as a mediative and structuring action between the oppositional dynamic and thermodynamic forces of codification.

The iterative ritual, following Peirce, will produce codal forms whose behavior resembles an original or desired form. The evolutionary ritual will produce codal forms that "dynamically connect" an agent to the ideal or next stage. The lyric ritual is associated with an outcome by virtue of "the idea of the symbol-using mind" (2:299); it is more "general" and open to variation than the specifics of the iconic or indexical form of ritual. Some societies or groups will define interactive behavior around one or even the first two types of ritual; the fully textual or bileveled society will have all three ritual forms.

ITERATIVE RITUALS

The first type of ritual, the iterative, focuses on the codal definitions of an existent central authority, located within the past of the knowledge regime, which provides an assurance of iconic stability. The goal of this ritual is mirrorlike replication of developed, long-term, normative standards of what-ought-to-be within current reality. The second type, the linear ritual, focuses on the means of ensuring the evolutionary movement of current reality—viewed as developmental—to a final, fixed goal. This perspective understands energy as coded within a number of distinct and sequential phases; the rituals move it from one phase to another. In a very real sense, these two analytic frames are similar, in that both operate within a conceptual frame of the authoritative power of an instructional, goal-directed process; both are focused on the dynamic code of a clear definition of "what-ought-to-be" behavior. The complete definition of this behavior lies within the authority of the group, not the individual; and perhaps that is why modernism and postmodernism, with their privileging of the individual, have condemned rituals. In both these rituals, the choice of codification is severely restricted by a conscious attempt to marginalize the effects of any aberrant codes that may affect semiosis in the nodal phases of transition. Both forms of ritual function as a means of preventing deviation from the authoritative interpretation. Any specious interaction between "the possible" and "the actual" is defused by these rituals.

Douglas defines ritualism as a "heightened appreciation of symbolic action" in both primitive and modern cultures, and "a concern that efficacious symbols be correctly manipulated and that the right words be pronounced in the right order" (1973, 26, 28). This is a definition of dynamic codification; therefore, we must assume that for Douglas, all codification is dynamic or operating within a repetitive and centralist control. Her analysis of such codification is based within an oppositional polarism; there are two extremes of this code: irrational and rational, understood as group-bound and closed-minded on the one hand, and self-sufficient and individual on the other. This might seem to set up a bileveled frame, but in reality it is unileveled. The deeper level of semiosic generalization has moved up to the surface level and become particularized as one of the polar nodes. There is only one type of code, the specific, and it exists in two forms that are both within the control of the individual. We may understand these two forms as similar to the sensual and rational nodes of the surface level of the bileveled architecture. Taking an analysis of language use from Bernstein (1971), Douglas defines these two codal types as "restricted" versus "elaborated." The former defines knowledge that is "firmly embedded in a stable social structure" (1973, 49), primarily because knowledge is accessed via the sensual or "natural" node and is based around a system of unarticulated, a priori and "abstract principles," which are stabilized by group authoritarianism. Therefore, "when the social group grips its members tight in communal bonds, the religion is ritualist; when this grip is relaxed, ritualism declines" (32). Sensually accessed knowledge is defined as "ritualistic"; rationally accessed knowledge is seen as emancipated from such social controls, and it establishes the individual as a free and self-sufficient agent. The sensual is considered polluted and weakened by the passions of the body, and must be supported by the strictures of group structures or rituals; the rational is considered capable not only of a direct access to knowledge but also of its examination and justification (49–51)—without the mediative interactions of a metanarrative.

This suggests that society is a collection of Hobbesian/Lockean social-contract or self-organized individuals, devoted to unilevel themes of rhetoric, psychology and epistemology, rather than the bilevel ones of logic.[2] I maintain that no individual, of any species whatsoever, can develop to a decision-making capacity without being a member of a grounded, reflexive and group-based metanarrative—whether that metanarrative be solely biological or, as in the human species, also conceptual. Second, it suggests that some forms of knowledge are asymbolic, intuitive rather than semiosic. To repeat the words of Peirce, "we have no power of Introspection, but all knowledge of the internal world is derived by hypothetical reasoning from our knowledge of external facts. . . . We have no power of Intuition, but every cognition is determined logically by previous cognitions" (5.265). Again, without a metanarrative, adaptive knowledge—which is a syllogistic action of reflexive mediation against a background of symbolic continuity—is impossible; a regime operative within a unileveled frame is mimetic by procedures of authoritarian reproduction. Such an architecture may seem viable for simple organisms and basic infrastructures, but adaptive strategies are inaccessible on this level. Therefore, in this understanding of ritual, we end up with an iterative and unmediated codification—whether it is sensual and unarticulated (and thus seemingly ritualistic), or rational and articulated (and thus seemingly non-ritualistic). In both cases, it is non-reflexive—and that is the syncretic power of the iterative ritual—that its codal actions can slide through spatial territories and ignore temporal randomness. As Kauffman describes structurally stable systems, "their dynamics typically changes only slightly as parameters change" (1993, 181), or for "systems deep in the ordered regime . . . virtually all mutations cause only minor changes in behavior. While landscapes are smooth, achieving large alterations in behavior is cumbersome" (232). We may understand a "smooth landscape" as one with few nodal or semiosic transformations. This is the iterative regime.

Douglas assumes that rituals are factors of restrictive societies: rituals are understood as iconic images of the societal psychic core; its symbolic expressions are seen as subversive and hegemonically destructive of individual desires. We have here a unilevel architecture that pits the group against the individual. "The most important determinant of ritualism is the experience of closed social groups" (Douglas 1973, 33). This assumes that there is such a thing as uncodified or unritualistic behavior, and she therefore observes that "pygmies move freely in an uncharted, unsystematized, unbounded social world" (34)[3]. Within this unilevel architecture, the human is understood as someone who "ought to" operate only within the rational node of "elaborated" thinking and is hampered by the strictures of the irrational group. Douglas examines "three phases in the move away from ritualism": "the contempt of external ritual forms; . . . the private internalizing of religious experience; . . . [and] the move to humanist philanthropy" (25). We see here the increased power of individual, random behavior over the supposedly irrational discourse of the group heritage. It is not that Douglas asserts, as does postmodernism, that a society can exist without symbols, within a denunciation "of ritualism as such; exaltation of the inner experience and denigration of its standardized expressions; preference for intuitive and instant forms of knowledge; rejection of mediating institutions, rejection of any tendency to allow habit to provide the basis of a new symbolic system" (40). Rather, in "its extreme forms anti-ritualism is an attempt to abolish communication by means of complex symbolic systems" (40). She sees ritualism as codification within "natural"(or sensual), subjective, and restrictive codes; and warns against the "destructive lure of the natural system of symbols, equally when it devastates category boundaries as when it wrongfully closes them" (200).[4] However, despite her promotion of the rational node, "the power of our own unconscious mental activity" (199), and the "analytic power of an elaborated code" (200), her insistence that it is an action released from group codification sets up an isolated, self-referential, noninteractional articulation—and thus actually establishes a regime whose members are semiotically incapable of debate or analysis. The choice she is asking of us refers to the type of ritual that can offer an "open" or "elaborated" semiosis rather than a "closed" or "restricted" semiosis. However, the semiosic actions of a regime that operates either aloof from or without the communal reflexions of a metanarrative—whether based within a sensual or a rational symbolism—will become "frozen" into theistic signs; alienated from further semiosis; and, therefore, only able to repeat their iconic images.

A clearer assessment of regimes that privilege ritual or dynamic codification is that which was previously discussed within Kauffman's "orderly regimes," which privilege dynamic codification and therefore exhibit "smooth" or stable behavior with relatively few mutations. The orderly regime permits long-term continuity of type: "energy flux in an initially homogenous system sets up a spatially ordered pattern" (1993, 180). The orderly type of regime sets up a codal system whose codes are "functionally isolated islands of elements" (205), by which I understand that the codal format of each nodal site is "frozen into a fixed value" and the action of semiosis does not dissolve or semiotically transform these values/codes but uses them in a repetitive semiosis. Energy moves from nodal site to nodal site in a homogenous and undisturbed manner. This pattern is a specific evolutionary adaptation with a particular functionality and can be the correct choice for a particular type of semiosic regime—that of a relatively stable and self-sufficient biological or social regime, or an equally stable, larger organism/society with fixed hierarchical levels/classes. The whole point of iterative ritualistic behavior is the provision of a continuity of type: This is actually a highly effective adaptation. The established rituals require little expenditure of either conceptual or physical energy, and reap great benefits in their provision of stable and efficient interactions within a particular environment. Iterative rituals will form the substratum of every long-term semiosic regime—indeed, of every stable species: The difference will be only in the proportional percentage of their operations.

EVOLUTIONARY RITUALS

Moving away from this iterative ritual—from what Turner has defined as "the implicitly theological position of trying to explain, or explain away, religious phenomena as the product of psychological or sociological causes" (1969, 4)—an evolutionary view of ritual can be found in the anthropological analyses of "rites of passage," which view ritual not simply as an iteration of the dominant psyche, but more specifically as mediatory agents for the evolution of a particular expression of a genre or knowledge regime. Rituals are understood as the "process accompanying the movement of people from one social status to another" (Davies; in Holm and Bowker, 1994, 1). Arnold van Gennep's 1908 study of rites of passage saw them as "organized ritualistic events" that deconstructed individuals from one social state of being, or codal form, and reconstructed them into another social state of being. There were three parts to the rite: the "first separated people from their original status, the second involved a period apart from the normal status, and the third conferred a new status upon the individual.... He spoke of the three phases as (i) pre-liminal, (ii) liminal, and (iii) post-liminal" (Davies 1994, 3). This is a Hegelian serial algorithm of gradually increasing complexity of codal form (to a teleological final goal) and, therefore, increasing complexity of knowledge and strategic interactions with the environment.

Victor Turner's work (1969) on rituals and rites of passage followed van Gennep's theories of the three stages: first was the separation of the individual from a previous identity; second, the "limen," or threshold, phase; and third, the reaggregation of the individual into a new status. Liminality, the second stage, is a condition of not being fully organized into a particular definitional and holding pattern of energy and, therefore, as in the synaptic cleft phase, subject to entropic loss of energy or even worse, the intrusion of alien energies and codal formats into the individual's spatiotemporal frame. Obviously, this "gap"—this phase of being between two stable holding patterns—is extremely dangerous, and yet is the only means of changing from one form of existentiality to another, from one "species" to another.

The unilevel frame rejects the analysis of the transformation of energy from one form to another as operating within a state of unpredictability and, therefore, potential disaster. Instead, as with Darwinian gradualism, it sees energy as moving: the slippery signified of deconstructionism, simply and easily, from external cause to internal sign, moving within the focus of a predetermined goal, as if it were a cloak easily cast aside—as if it were to be done with the ease of a god moving from hiding place to hiding place. However, the codal form is not a cover for infinite essentiality; is not a cloak but a part of the existential nature of the energy in its spatiotemporal existence as a sign. It is not merely "bonded to" (Saussurian) or "slipped into" (deconstructionist) by the essence of meaning. Neither is energy existent "in itself," as Aristotle, Peirce, Duns Scotus, Aquinas, and others so clearly explained; it does not exist per se, simply covering its nakedness with a code form. Energy that is released from a coded form—that loses any bond with other forms of energy—rapidly disperses. It becomes available to other forms—in possibly beneficial but more probably harmful ways. The coded format—the sign-unit that supposedly cloaked this energy—ceases to exist. Therefore, changing a codal form from one organized state to a different one is a traumatic event, and the basis of tragedy. That is why Priam had to bury Hector with all the proper rituals: to prevent the dangerous dissipation of his soul, to preserve the energy of his identity within the communal codality of his society.

Turner notes that "at certain life-crises, such as adolescence, the attainment of elderhood, and death . . . the passage from one structural status to another may be accompanied by a strong sentiment of 'humankindness', a sense of the generic social bond between all members of society" (1969, 116). The nodal phase is a decodified and therefore non-individual (non-sign) phase and must necessarily rest its existentiality on a common, and quite possibly universal, human experience.[5] Turner focuses his attention on this "communitas" state of participants during liminality, in which all are rendered equal members of the same bonded group. Members in this liminal or nodal phase are, as isolates, necessarily bonded into a communitas: this new brief and emotive bond prevents complete dissipation of energy. This may, at first glance, have some comparison with the dissolution of hierarchies and subsequent equal relations during the Bakhtinian carnival, in which current realities are suspended and "people [are], so to speak, reborn for *new, purely human relations*" (Bakhtin 1984b, 10; my emphasis), along with a phase of "change and renewal, with a sense of the gay relativity of prevailing truths and authorities" (11). Although both the carnival and the liminal are partly[6] decontextualized states of existence, Turner's liminal state exists within a serial network: it is bonded to a specific future, while the future of Bakhtin's carnival is open. I would explain Turner's three-stage ritual as an analysis that focuses on the movement of selected sets of already-existent group codifications into the operational knowledge codes of individuals. Tribal members in the liminal state are kept securely within the group; they are never permitted to "regain" a sense of individual identity, which might leave them open to an awareness of their current decodification and, thus, subject to individual pathological disintegration or a recodification into a codal format that is alien or unacceptable to group norms. Members in this state are, as noted, open to dissipation of form and consciousness; the society prevents such entropic loss of energy (and potential madness and/or loss of that member to social functionality) by having these individuals, via strict rituals in which all participate, temporally formed into a tightly bound group.[7] The liminal stage and its instructionist rituals are abandoned when the individuals are reformulated into the new, socially ratified codal forms. It is perhaps incorrect to consider these people as "individuals" for they are rather parts of the collective: there is no escape; everything is "done to achieve something else, and always in obedience to orders from above" (Calasso 1993, 335).

Turner, following van Gennep, separates the nodal actions into separate and sequential linear phases, suggesting a future-oriented bond with the way things "ought to be." That is why he comes up with instructionist rather than selectionist actions at these sites. This evolutionary development of knowledge permits a more complex semiosic regime than that of the iterative, which is limited to iconic mimesis; the evolutionary ritual has the ability to incorporate change within the regime. The sign can begin within a simple semiosic codification, and it can develop its codal properties to a particular threshold of complexity; it will then shed some of the holding patterns of this simple semiosic state and, incorporating some of the codal factors gained so far, reorganize itself into a more complex semiosic state. This is a remarkable accomplishment, permitting an increase in the sign's ability to attract, hold, and store energy; however, the greatest danger to the success of this sign-growth is during the nodal phases of the transformation of its codal organization. Rituals or highly organized and limited behavior during these nodal phases prevent loss of energy and codes: We can observe such strict orders not merely within the finely-tuned states of biological species but also and above all, within human interactions.

LYRIC RITUALS

The nodal phase can also function as an open site for conflictive confrontation of a polyphonic cluster of codal forms that meet, disintegrate, and formulate new codal forms. The selection is made during this phase and deals with the factor of choice of a contextually based "what will be" rather than with the authoritative and aloof "what ought to be." Like the natural world, human semiosis, via the openness of these nodal points, permits deviations that can be incorporated into the knowledge regime and so permits "more complex structures, new organs, and new species.... The actual living world, as we see it today, is just one among many possible ones" (Jacob 1994, 15). The lyric ritual is quite different from the iterative and evolutionary ritual in that it does not function within the monologic instructionalism of "what ought to be." The lyric ritual can be explained within Bakhtin's comments on both the lyric and the serio-comical genres.

A genre of any type, as a stable codal regime, provides intrinsic boundary conditions to the experience of reality. It does this because, as a regime—which is to say, a communal network—it links an individual to a wider knowledge base. A code system is, by its very nature, communal and meant to broaden the existentiality of the individual to membership within a group, for "always preserved in a genre are undying elements of the archaic" (Bakhtin 1984a, 108). Within biological analysis, genres or knowledge-regimes can be compared with Sheldrake's morphogenetic fields, which provide a "resonance from previous similar systems [such that] . . . the most specific morphic resonance acting upon (an animal) will be that from its own past" (1981,170). The morphogenetic field or codal regime is a situation in which "the form of a system, including its characteristic internal structure and vibrational frequencies, becomes present to a subsequent system with a similar form; the spatio-temporal pattern of the former superimposes itself on the latter" (96).

Genres or codal regimes can be of different types and can thereby inform the individual experience in multiple ways. Literary genres, such as the epic, tragedy, history, and classical rhetoric forms, are monological and privilege dynamic codification; the serio-comical genre of the novel is dialogical and operates within Kauffman's "borderline regime." The dialogics of the serio-comical genre provide it with an openness to novelty and a capacity to provide "an indeterminacy, a certain semantic open-endedness, a living contact with unfinished, still-evolving, contemporary relativity (the open-ended present)" (Bakhtin 1981, 7). As such, this genre has a "joyful relativity" and possesses "a mighty life-creating and transforming power, an indestructible vitality" (1984a, 107). This genre exists "in the living present, often even the very day"; rather than relying on legend, it relies on "experience" and on "free invention," and is deliberately "multi-styled and heterovoiced" (108). We have in the serio-comical genre a means of polyphonic expression and transformative change. As such, this genre supplies the stability of instability, the ability to adapt.

The traditional lyric *genre* form is quite the opposite of the serio-comic genre: The lyric interaction between the author and the Other, with the latter understood as the hero, gives the author immense monologic powers over the hero-Other. The lyric, in opposition to the dialogic, specifically does not "localize" and, therefore, is not individualist and "provides no clear-cut impression of a human being's finiteness in the world" (Bakhtin 1990, 168). In this sense, the lyric genre is uninterested in the polyphonic nature of the individual and is primarily interested in the iterative stability of the universal. It is, therefore, an important aspect for those codal systems that insist on and provide for stability and continuity, because it is essentially uninterested in the arguments of reason, in any proof of the rationality of its forms of behavior. What is, is what works, and the collective asks for no other explanation. However, the lyric *ritual* to which I refer is a combination of these two generic types, the lyric and the serio-comical, and is particular to the bilevel architecture. Following my use of Peirce's definition of the symbol, the lyric ritual permits growth and variation. As Peirce said of the symbol: "symbols grow. They come into being by development out of other signs, particularly from icons, or from mixed signs partaking of the nature of icons and symbols. . . . So it is only out of symbols that a new symbol can grow. . . . A symbol, once in being, spreads out among the peoples. In use and in experience, its meaning grows" (2.302). To be meaningful, a symbol or metaphor requires the factor of mediation: that is, it requires the interventive offering of a choice of codal paths that will be acceptable/possible codifications to the majority—though not all—of the energy intentionalities at that site. The power of the lyric ritual is that it provides for such choices.

The lyric ritual seemingly combines two contrary textual genres: the dialogue and the monologue, the novel and the lyric, the individual and the universal. This nodal phase is a center for the interaction of both existentialities—not individual with individual—but individual with collective, and individual with universal. Their meeting must have the particular qualities of both forms—the specific with the general, the *explicatio* with the *implicatio*,[8] the existential with the potential, the "what-is" with the "what-ought-to-be," the instability with the stability—and yet, it must respect their differences and never, ever—as Aristotle warned, merge them. In the lyric ritual, the two genres are associated with each other, much as every type of particle has an associated anti-particle, "in which all distinguishing qualities except mass are reversed" (Davies 1988, 21). Indeed, this mixture of the lyric with the serio-comical genre, would be understood in the *contaminatio* terms by the sixteenth century, within a society that separated life into grid systems of purity, and moral and intellectual pollution.

The lyric ritual, as operative within a bilevel architecture, is more adaptive than the iterative or evolutionary ritual, with its monologic instructionist intentionalities. The lyric ritual, in differentiation from Douglas's understanding of ritual, is both emotional and rational and is, therefore, fully capable of accepting and encoding the explicable—and yet maintaining within the society an acceptance of the potentially inexplicable. The normative and the deviant, the rational and the irrational, the Self and the Other—all of these forces intersect at these nodal sites. It is the ability of the lyric ritual to accept and consider polyphonous forces that gives it its strength. For "in all cases where the hero begins to free himself from possession by the other—the author . . . where he suddenly finds himself to be in the event of being, in the light of to-be-attained meaning" (Bakhtin 1990, 172)—that is, where the seemingly inviolate boundaries of the individual's codal format are shredding, opening up to multiple Others; where the actual semiosic act is beginning to come into being—the lyric ritual must attempt to recover this dissipating energy. Within the potentialities of the universal nature of being human, and combined as it is with the serio-comical codal nets, it has the power to reformulate that influx of new energy into a new codal format that becomes, not marginal to, but centrally part of, that particular text. "It is precisely those endlessly and meaninglessly shifting colors that lie at the heart of the divine" (Calasso 1993, 331). It is here, via the lyric ritual, that the "what-is" becomes part of the "what-ought-to-be; "that a choice is made, and specific codal forms are selected and accepted by that regime as part of its normative framework.

> He came down from the craggy mountain. . . . He harnessed under his chariot his bronze-shod horses, flying-footed, with long manes streaming of gold; and he put on clothing of gold about his own body, and took up the golden lash . . . and climbed up into his chariot and drove it across the waves. And about him the sea beasts came up from their deep places and played in his path . . . and the sea stood apart before him, rejoicing. (Homer 1951, Bk. XIII, lines 17–29).

Choices, once made, clarify; they empower.

The bileveled ritual as a lyric is both a chorus, and a singular voice. The two are interactive, for we must, as semiosic agents, provide support for the individual as a separate and unique voice; we must understand that the individual "can sing only in a warm atmosphere, only in the atmosphere of possible choral support, where solitariness of sound is in principle excluded" (Bakhtin 1990, 170). It is this emphasis on the emotional bonds with human potentiality rather than the closed separatism of the already-socialized collective that is the strength of the lyric genre. Bakhtin points out that "lyrical self-objectification is a seeing and hearing of myself from within with the emotional eyes of the other and in the emotional voice of the other: I hear myself in the other, with others, and for others" (170). The lyric network permits the human being a contact with the potentiality of the uncoded; "we enter the mythical when we enter the realm of risk, and myth is the enchantment we generate in ourselves at such moments" (Calasso 1993, 279). Myth refers to *muo,* which means "to have my mouth closed" in everyday situations, but also to "say in a special way." Myth means "special speech" derived from "special seeing" (Nagy 1990b, 31–32), and it is this vision that is the basis of lyrical or poetic semiosis.

> Make bright the air, and give sight back to our eyes; in shining light destroy us, if to destroy us be now your pleasure (Homer 1951, Bk.XVII, lines 645–47).

All three forms of ritual may be found within a bilevel architecture. The iterative replicates the synechestic continuity of both the group and the individual as codal forms. Any group will have iterative rituals of self-identity, whether it be a political party, a business organization, a professional society, or a kin group. It will also have stable and acknowledged rituals for meeting with other groups. Iterative ritual is "redundancy reduced to its essence. . . . It is a faith in redundancy as the way in which the cosmos makes itself manifest" (Calasso 1993, 331). As authoritative forces, iterative rituals are domineering in a way that provides continuity of type. They are the backbone of any organism, and Peirce was quite right to assert that "the method of authority will always govern the mass of mankind" (5.386).

Evolutionary rituals are equally important because they permit development of the codal form. They are more active than iterative rituals, even if their nature is serial and monologic rather than diverse and dialogic. Serial codification is an efficient, energy-saving method of increasing the complexity of a species. One begins with a small amount of energy, operative within a basic codal format: The fetus develops from within the most basic chemical and biological codes. Energy support is provided by external forms that are already operative in a stable, complex form. Gradually, the chemical and biological codes increase in complexity, and gradually the cognitive codes emerge. These latter increase in complexity of behavior and adaptive powers as the child grows to adult form. The group will closely monitor these transformations: the final product must be a member of the collective. Group rituals will be primarily iterative, because the group is focused around stable continuity. The rituals of development of the parts of the group (individuals, social systems) will be both iterative and evolutionary.

The lyric ritual is more complex than the iterative or evolutionary ritual. It permits multiple forms of energy to be woven into codal networks, such as those found in art, music, literature, and film. It is here, in these deliberately fragile networks, that different codal realities meet: the individual and the group, the biological and the social, the finite and the infinite. The lyric ritual encodes the interactions of these energies. At this site, the individual-entity is deconstructed; the energy is left as open potential for a now-choice to be made, a choice invested as much in the present as in the past. It is at the lyric nodal site that the universal potentiality and the individual immediacy are presented to already-stable codal networks, in which new codal forms have the possibility of existence. The lyric nodal phase permits, not final forms—never admitting even the possibility of such a travesty—but rather codification that acknowledges the multiple potentialities of semiosis. The lyric ritual, with its ties to both the universal and the specific, is more flexible, more amenable to the acceptance and therefore codification of deviation and innovation. It is, therefore, of primary importance in a bilevel architecture, with its capacity for both stability and strategic adaptation.

As a nonevolutionary action, in contrast to Turner's rites of passage, the lyric ritual does not conclusively define the nature of the codal form, for "the lyrical work does not seek to proclude a finished character for the hero, does not draw a clear cut boundary around the entire whole of the hero's souls and all of his inner life (it deals only with a constituent of that whole, with an episode from his inner life)" (Bakhtin 1990, 168). The lyric ritual is, by its very nature, a chorus of voices—interactive, separate, competing, conflicting, harmonizing, parallel. The results of this ritual interaction are not bonded to any one reality, but float with many realities. The lyric ritual's accessiblity to multiple codal forms, and its offering of these codal forms to the many energies existent there at the nodal site, permits the dialogic reformulation of what we call human existence. It is, therefore, the essence of a semiosic society.

As pointed out, the nodal phase is a site of potential destruction because of the conflictual nature of the polyphonic voices at that site, and because of the possibility of degeneration of the codal regime by interaction with these other energies. Energy may be lost, new energy may intrude; the old codal forms collapse. Rituals prevent the destructive aspect of this fission and fusion by strictly defining its format and thereby the amount of energy that may be codified and used; this prevents explosive dispersion of energy at contact points and, equally, potentially explosive inclusion of energy beyond that which can be normatively codified by the code systems of the individual and the society. Popper speaks in favor of indeterminism and unpredictability: "I personally believe that the doctrine of indeterminism is true, and that determinism is completely baseless" (1950, 41). This does not mean that he rejects determinism completely: "we can still obtain predictions, *for any given* instant of time, of the state of the mass-point, provided we measure its initial direction with a degree of precision. . . . What we *cannot* predict is the behavior of the system *for all* instants of time" (40). The dynamic level is predictable, simply because there is no difference between the past and the future. The thermodynamic level is completely unpredictable. In the adaptively functional semiosis, both levels are linked together by multiple codal networks. It is this necessary interaction, and the awareness of the enormous potentialities of this meeting site, that brings in the concept of ethics, or the idea of a conscious awareness of the two opposite codal forces. That is, both predictability and unpredictability are necessary; the conscious bonding of the two is the subject of ethics, as pointed out by

Monod: "This prohibition, this 'first commandment' which ensures the foundation of objective knowledge, is not itself objective. It cannot be objective; it is an ethical guideline, a rule for conduct" (1971, 176). By "objective knowledge" I understand him to mean the permission to reject teleology and permit both chance and transformation; it is a choice made by the human subject to reject the desires of the Self for the security of either dynamic predictability or thermodynamic freedom, and to permit their dialogue.

INTERACTION

Saussure, with monumental, mechanical indifference, made cognition a mechanism, defining the sign as a commodity made up of an essentialist value (content/signified) and marketed within a package (signifier). Language and other codes became marketing tools. He ignored the codal network, that network that develops within interaction; indeed, his concentration on the sign isolated it from interaction and set up semiology (as differentiated from semiosis) within a structuralist, modernist framework that was based around a mechanical examination of the linguistic code. His error was to consider the sign an artifact, an end in itself; in reality, the sign is only a momentarily sealed instant of the codification networking. For Saussure, the codal network of *logos* became instead *langue,* a dictionary, rather than a mediative action. The word became an artifact, an arbitrary bond of original purity glued to material form. People, such as Barthes and Saussure, did not take the concept of codification far enough: they considered the code only a means of signifying or carrying meaning. This makes both meaning and the code existential particles—signs. Semiology, therefore, consists of two particles: that of the essence, or meaning, and that of the code.[9] When you bonded the two together, you came up with a sign. This is an error. An entity, in its string or intentional state, is *already operating within a code.* As previously noted, Kauffman states that "by construction, most strings are legal both as program and as input" (1993, 372). That is, a string affects another string not merely by "input" of energy but also via the codal program of that energy. Barthes commented that "semiotically, the 'concrete detail' is constituted by the *direct* collusion of a referent and a signifier; the signified is expelled from the sign, and with it, of course, the possibility of developing a *form of the signified,* i.e., narrative structure itself" (1986, 147). I understand this to mean that a referent (object) meets with a code-form (signifier); this makes a sign, which permits meaning (signified). Notice that each entity in this semiological analysis is understood as discrete: referent, signifier, sign, signified. Or, in my terms: object or energy, code, entity, or meaning. Such self-sufficient entities cannot exist within the network analysis of semiosis.

We cannot have direct contact with the object or with energy; certainly, we must have contact, but we do so via the codal systems of our biological and social metanarratives. These codal systems cannot exist "in themselves": they exist as logical patterns of order *within* the coded sign; they are the wave to its particle, and both are complementary to each other. For Barthes and for other structuralists, the pattern or the code is that "form of the signified"; a narrative structure. Barthes states that "the goal today is to empty the sign and infinitely to postpone its object so as to challenge, in a radical fashion, the age-old aesthetic of 'representation'" (1986, 148). This is similar to Popper's "bucket-theory": the sign is a bucket; empty it and you will lose contact with the object of which that sign is a copy; you may thus find purity rather than false representation. This concept of "emptying" the sign functions within a unileveled perspective that sees the purity of meaning (understood as the sight of pure uncoded energy, the object) as denigrated by the various code systems. Again, no object can exist unless it is coded; no code can exist except with the encoded. It is impossible to "empty" the sign, to return to purity—unless, of course, what is meant is a return to a zero-point energy, a state of absolute zero in which energy cannot exist in particle form and, therefore, where semiosis, the state of signs—cannot exist.

> This mountain is such
> That the first part of the ascent is always hard
> And the higher a man goes, the less hard it is (Dante 1993 *Purgatorio* IV, lines 88–90).

Bakhtin's utterance, Peirce's semiosic act, and Benveniste's "enonciation" all leave their traces (shared energy) in the utterance (enonce); these varied metaphors of the semiosic prism, these correlates that each reach out to and from each other—that, as long as they interact, spin their interwoven networks—this is the basis of the sign. The sign is made up of conceptual "lines" that never blend or merge but instead—acting in the manner of quantum strings of different energy forces—bond briefly into semiotic units, and then move away, carrying some of their past with them. "Thought is a thread of melody running through the succession of our sensations" (5.395), for, within the principle of continuity, "all is fluid and every point directly partakes the being of every other" (5.402,ff 2). Codification of energy is based around increasing specification; prisms will interlock with other prisms. As Peirce notes, "The actual world cannot be distinguished from a world of imagination by any description. Hence the need of pronouns and indices, and the more complicated the subject the greater the need of them" (M 5.296). This increasing deixis, or specification, is the increased complexity of organization of semiosic networks. Philosophical reasoning "should not form a chain which is no stronger than its weakest link, but a cable whose fibers may be ever so slender, provided they are sufficiently numerous and intimately connected" (5.265).

PART IV

Evolution

7

EVOLUTION OF THE METANARRATIVE

I will sing of that second kingdom
In which the human spirit cures itself
And becomes fit to leap up into heaven.

—*Dante (Purgatorio I, lines 4–6)*

I am taking a position in this book that the human agent is existential within two types of codification, the dynamic and the thermodynamic, that of the regime and that of the specific experience. What I most emphatically do not mean by this is the quite dull and tired adage that "humans are social animals"—which suggests merely that we live in communities out of individual functional necessity, that we like to gossip and need to exchange goods and services with each other. I mean instead that our individual mortal nature is a combination of two quite opposite codifications of energy: dynamic codification operates within a constantly generalizing commonality of codal form that is stable, iterative, and continuous; thermodynamic codification is spurious, random, irreversible, and most definitely not shared with the group. These two codal patterns are located within the biological and cognitive frame of the single individual; this is valid for all species. There is no such thing as an "individual" in the sense of a codal entity separate from the codification powers of the communal forces of the species or regime of knowledge. The modern and the postmodern glorification of the self-sufficient sign is completely invalid: such entities are physically, chemically, biologically, and cognitively impossible. The individual exists within a perpetual conflict of two oppositional codifications: the *dunamic* force of potentiality that belongs to the regime, and the *energeia/entelechia* force of random and individual specification. This is the crux of the superlative adaptive powers of Homo sapiens as a species, and our tragic existentialities as individuals.

Modernism made the mistake of denying transformative mediation, of insisting on an immediate bond with an a priori truth; postmodernism repeated this error and compounded it by denying any access to truthful situations and focusing on the solipsism of thermodynamic codification.[1] What was it all about? Power. A unilevel architecture, even if it seems to operate as an attempt to escape power, will always trap itself within its bonds. Each interaction supposedly creates a new sign; and its author, whether an essential god or an existential individual, is readily understood as its source of life. This is superficially valid, but—and this is the factor ignored by the isolationism of these two theisms—energy cannot exist within such isolation.

The synaptic "gap," the site of the semiosic interaction, is the site for the actions of the transformation of, and bonding of, multiple forms of energy. As soon as an entity becomes existential—which is to say, as soon as energy is measured within an interaction and so becomes bonded within a codal form as a sign-action, becoming a "once-occurrent event of Being" (Bakhtin), or existing in a state of Secondness (Peirce)—then the stability of meaning that comes within that interactional action of measurement slides and glides away from the tropic codal forms. This disintegration of the codal form is based around both the actions of natural entropy, which set in once the measurement (interaction) stops, and also around the "Self-and-Other awareness" of a bonded form within a state of Secondness, the self-awareness of its borders and the realities of Others, resulting from the differentiation of the Self and the Other.

This constant awareness of the Self as "what is" and the Other as "what is not" is also and always an action of desire. Desire for the "not" is basic to the existence of the "is." As Lacan notes, "desire begins to take shape in the margin . . . the margin being that which is opened up by demand, the appeal of which can be unconditional only in regard to the Other" (1977, 311). Semiosis, or the transformation of differently coded energies into a sign-entity, can take place only within a state of desire for connectedness. When semiosis encodes energy into a sign, that sign exists within a sense of itself as both not-Other and Self. Its awareness of its own connectedness, and therefore its identity, involves an awareness of that integrity being Other to other signs, and their being Other to its own self. This intense "state of attraction," this non-isolation, this awareness of other codifications of energy, is expressed as a movement toward the Other, a state of desire for that Otherness. This sets up an entropic dissolution of the codal integrity of that sign—toward an interaction with the codal networks of the Other. Desire, existing within dissolution, is the basic action of semiosic transformation. The only way for energy, as desire, to exist is via the development of guarantees of codification. Peirce described this energy as "a chaos of unpersonalized feeling, which being without connection or regularity would properly be without existence" (6.33). These guarantees are achieved by the development of hierarchical levels of codification of both simple and complex—interlocking, delocking, relocking, new locking—networks of codification via which energy moves in a continuous production of signs. Networks of relationships, pragmatic and reflexive (which means an ability to be meaningful) are the infrastructure of semiosis.

DESIRE AND THE METANARRATIVE

Di Quoi li Graus sert?
Et Percevaus redit tot el . . .
Tant que il do Graal savra
Cui l'en an sert, et qu'il avra
La Lance qui saigne trovee
Tant que la verite provee
Li soit dite por qu'ele saigne.

—*Chretien de Troyes (lines 4656–4670)*[2]

Semiosis, the transformation of energy into spatiotemporal reality, is an action operating within the desire of energy for codification. This desire is expressed—is empowered in its search for codification—within the action of the question. The question opens the current state of codification, the current semiosis, to its potential transformation into a new semiosis. Life exists within the doubt of the question, and never within the fullness of the answer. "Love is not specially the cause of existence; for in collecting things into the One it destroys all other things" (Aristotle *Metaphysics* Bk. III: Ch.4. 1000b12).

The basis of semiosis is the desire of energy to be encoded. An immediate assumption by my use of the word "desire" is that I am denying what Monod defines as "the basic premise of the scientific method, to wit, that nature is *objective* and not *projective*" (1971, 3); I am completely in agreement with this statement—however, Monod continues that "the positing of the principle of objectivity as the condition of true knowledge *constitutes an ethical choice and not a judgment arrived at from knowledge, since, according to the postulate's own terms, there canot have been any 'true' knowledge prior to this arbitral choice*" (1971, 176; italics in original). I am therefore insisting on an original "teleonomy" or intentionality of desire, both within the origin of the mediative codal actions (to be discussed as agapastic desire) and within its ongoing operation (to be discussed as tychastic and anancastic desire). This first premise, which is and must be a conscious and therefore ethical choice, is that this semiosic desire—which is to say, the infinite action of questioning—can only exist within the reflexive capacities of a bileveled semiosis.

The codal operations that emerge within the semiosic states of desire develop in evolutionary processes. What is evolution? Evolution operates within the desire for the articulation or codification of energy and exists within the realities of entropy.[3] Codes emerge spontaneously within this state of desire. "The evolution of forms begins or, at any rate, has for an early stage of it, a vague potentiality; and that either is or is followed by a continuum of forms having a multitude of dimensions too great for the individual dimensions to be distinct. It must be by a contraction of the vagueness of that potentiality of everything in general, but of nothing in particular, that the world of forms comes about" (Peirce 6.196). This original intentionality includes no instruction, no agenda, no particular grammar for the metanarrative or the signs of semiosis. Semiosic intentionality must be understood as operative within "the realm of perennial metamorphosis . . . of every beginning, when the word has not yet detached itself from the thing, nor the mind from the matter" (Calasso 1993, 137). It is "a process which extends from before time and from before logic, we cannot suppose that it began elsewhere than in the utter vagueness of completely undetermined and dimensionless potentiality" (Peirce 6.193). Emergence of the basic code within a knowledge-regime is not simply and only tychastic and chance-driven; that is, isolate and unaffected by Otherness; but is also operative within the desires, the codal attractions imposed by adjacent codal networks.[4] And, therefore, "part of that which is changing must be at the starting-point and part at the goal" (Aristotle *Physics* Bk. VI: Ch. 4. 234b15); and "the unfailing continuity of coming-to-be cannot be attributed to the infinity of the material. . . . [Rather] the passing-away of *this* is a coming-to-be of *something else,* and the coming-to-be of this a passing-away of something else" (*De Gen.* Bk. I; Ch. 3.318a 20–25). Maturation, or the evolutionary development of these "selected" codes, will be anancastic—mechanically implemented, incremental networkings and "robust" or functional couplings with other codal networks. Therefore, within a state of desire for codification, actual codes emerge within the limited choices imposed by the current realities of codal Otherness, and this choice is made within the unpredictabilities of chance and accident; the "selected" or chosen codes, if successful within the limitations of the existent codalities of the Self and Other(s), quickly transform themselves into grammatical laws of regulatory order and, thus, increase the semiosic complexities and capacities of that particular regime of knowledge.

The codal grammars of the human species are expressed not merely within the physical, chemical, and biologic but also the conceptual codifications. This is the real reason why we define Homo sapiens as "social"—because the metanarrative is developed and functions within metaphors developed by the imagination, and the imagination is a communal and interactive force. "Experience is knowledge of individuals, art of universals . . . yet we think that *knowledge* and *understanding* belong to art rather than experience . . . [and] these things, the most universal, are on the whole the hardest for men to know; for they are farthest from the senses" (Aristotle *Metaphysics* Bk.I.Ch.1, 2). The perpetuation of life requires the development of a metanarrative that operates within the generalities of interconnected habits of being. This generality is not that of any differential specification but "looking upon the course of logic as a whole we see that it proceeds from the question to the answer—from the vague to the definite. The indeterminate future becomes the irrevocable past. In Spencer's phrase the undifferentiated differentiates itself. The homogenous puts on heterogeneity. However it may be in special cases, then, we must suppose that as a rule the continuum has been derived from a more general continuum, a continuum of higher generality" (Peirce 6.191).

Each society will develop a metanarrative grammar and its attendant networks over long periods of time—in a pragmatic, which means reflexive—sense.[5] These metanarratives are not rational architectures, concise blueprints of instructional goals, but are dialogic adaptations over time to particular stable and changing realities, beginning with a simple and moving into a complex semiotic architecture. "The activity of an organism in any living system must favour both the environment and the organism itself" (Harries-Jones 1995, 76). I am repeating Peirce's dictum "there are Real things, whose characters are entirely independent of our opinions about them" (5.384). I am quite capable of describing an alligator as a metaphoric clone of any ill-favored politician, but I am no more capable of creating that alligator than it can create me. My relationships with the Real must acknowledge the force of its potential impact on me; as such, these relationships develop within the basis of communal generalities developed over time. Vico points out two common human traits: that "rumor grows in its course . . . [and that] rumor is deflated by the presence of the thing itself" (1948, 121). Peirce again: "philosophy ought to imitate the successful sciences in its methods, so far as to proceed only from tangible premises which can be subjected to careful scrutiny, and to trust rather to the multitude and variety of its arguments than to the conclusiveness of any one. Its reasoning should not form a chain which is no stronger than its weakest link, but a cable whose fibers may be ever so slender, provided they are sufficiently numerous and intimately connected" (5.265).

The metanarrative of a society is an ongoing mediation, an ongoing development of habits of belief and behavior, within a pragmatic expectation of their validity in enabling us to deal with reality. "At any moment we are in possession of certain information, that is, of cognitions which have been logically derived by induction and hypothesis from previous cognitions which are less general, less distinct, and of which we have a less lively consciousness" (Peirce 5.311), for "that is called universal which is such as to belong to more than one thing" (Aristotle *Metaphysics* BkVII.Ch.13.1038b10). Again, Peirce: "the third category—the category of thought, representation, triadic relation, mediation, genuine thirdness, thirdness as such—is an essential ingredient of reality, yet does not by itself constitute reality" (5.436). Understanding moves from "sensible things" via this generality, "for learning proceeds . . . through that which is less knowable by nature to that which is more knowable" (*Metaphysics* Bk.VII: Ch. 3.1029b5). The modernist location of reality in a universal, a priori truth, whether conceptual or material, is theistic; the postmodern location of reality in individual actions within their "text" is comparable to the eidetic cave illusions of Plato's individuals trapped within the bonds of their self-isolation. Our knowledge is a social mediation of external reality but it cannot last long if it is a complete fabrication, a false image, of this reality. Knowledge is an adaptive bond with reality, a light but certain marriage; we can break it when we will but we know that while we are bonded, we must be true.

The whole point of the metanarrative as mediation, whether biological or social, is its adaptive flexibility in the evolution of codification. "The pragmaticist . . . makes it to consist in that process of evolution whereby the existent comes more and more to embody those generals . . . which is what we strive to express in calling them *reasonable*. In its higher stages, evolution takes place more and more largely through self-control, and this gives the pragmaticist a sort of justification for making the rational purport to be general" (Peirce 5.433). Bateson comments on this flexibility: "If mere survival, mere continuance, is of interest, then the harder sorts of rock, such as granite, have to be put near the top of the list as most successful among macroscopic entities. . . . The rock, we may say, *resists* change; it stays put, unchanging. The living thing escapes change either by correcting change or changing itself to meet the change or by incorporating continual change into its own being" (in *Mind* 1979, 103; quoted in Harries-Jones 1995, 77). Semiosis rests upon a basis of fuzziness, the ever-present Firstness, that fullness of the non-articulated desire to be articulated.[6] Fuzzy or simple desire, acting within the generalities of the metanarrative—those habits of behavior that are "hand-in-glove" with both Firstness and Secondness—is guided, handed over to the specifics of deictic and elenctic codal specifications that transform this desire within their multiple networkings—to a specific sign. Energy within semiosis becomes gradually more complex, more specific, less open. We may say that semiosis creates a charged particle desirous of existentiality; this desire becomes more specific within a particular electromagnetic field and, as it evolves, limits its own semiotic potentials. It sets itself up as a being that will be born and will, for the sake of that same semiosis, die. "I weep for Adonis; the gods of Love weep in answer. . . . Cypris was beautiful, when Adonis was alive, but her beauty died with Adonis. Alas for Cypris; all the mountains and the oaks cry 'Alas for Adonis.' And the rivers weep for Aphrodite's mourning, and the fountains on the hills weep for Adonis, and the flowers turn red with pain" (Bion, 120 BC; in Trypanis 1971, 343–344). It is a factor of a true semiosis that a limit to the codal capacities of these networks is reached; they will then dissolve in that action of *ricorso* into the freshness of Firstness, and we must ourselves, as the architects of these metanarratives of knowledge, begin a new semiosic regime. Societies must be capable, from time to time, of turning away from their texts, and living only within the fullness of poesis. Plato feared this regenerative semiosis: "we can admit no poetry into our city save only hymns to the gods and the praises of good men. For if you grant admission to the honeyed muse in lyric or epic, pleasure and pain will be lords of your city instead of law and that which shall from time to time have approved itself to the general reason as the best" (Plato 1935, 607a). Poetry is not to be taken "seriously as a serious thing that lays hold on truth, but that he who lends an ear to it must be on his guard fearing for the polity in his soul" (608a). Plato, committed to the stability of the polis, had to believe in the essentiality of a single, once-evolved, infallible a priori truth; everything else was an imitation "of images of excellence and of the other things that they 'create' and do not lay hold on truth" (600e). The poet is someone who just "roams about rhapsodizing," ignoring "public service."

What is it all about? Peirce points out that "fallibilism is the doctrine that our knowledge is never absolute but always swims, as it were, in a continuum of uncertainty, and of indeterminacy. Now the doctrine of continuity is that *all things* so swim in continuua" (1.171).[7] Further, "fallibilism cannot be appreciated in anything like its true significancy until evolution has been considered" (Peirce 1.173). "Evolution means nothing but *growth* in the widest sense of the word. Reproduction, of course, is merely one of the incidents of growth. And what is growth? Not mere increase" (1.174). Growth is "the passage from the homogenous to the heterogeneous . . . diversification" (1.174). Evolution is the increasing development of knowledge, which is to say an ongoing development of the complexity of both the possibilities and actualities of interactional codification. Complexity should be understood within this sense of a development of codification capacities; this can only be done within a fallibilistic or pragmaticist metanarrative that sets up a continuum of codal networks that permit both habitual and random codifications that function in a reflexive or "testing" situation. Jacob discusses complexity, seemingly against the terms:

> the words complication or complexity are hardly better. There are gratuitous complications, and others that, because of over-specialization, prohibit any possibility of further evolution. What is perhaps most characteristic of evolution is the tendency to flexibility in the execution of the genetic programme; it is an "openness" that allows the organism constantly to extend its relations with its environment and thus to extend its range of action. . . ."Success" in evolution leads to increases in both the ability to perceive and the ability to react. . . . At the macroscopic level, therefore, evolution depends on setting up new systems of communication, just as much within the organism as between the organism and its surroundings (1973, 307–308).

Again, evolution may be understood as "the tendency to increase interactions between the organism and its environment" (312).

My understanding of the evolution of a successful semiosis is of an increased complexity of interaction that proceeds via "punctuated equilibrium" (Eldredge and Gould 1972, 1985) or phases of stasis and phases of chaos. There will be long periods of stasis of dynamic codification during which increasingly complex interactive networks will be developed; these codes will reach a "carrying capacity" or critical threshold, at which point the anancastic specifications begin to prevent adaptive codification and the system will begin to entropically decay; this will be followed by short catastrophic phases during which the old, grammatical, dynamic codes are destroyed, either (more commonly) in part or (less commonly) in total. New codes and networks will then develop. Evolution, therefore, exists within long periods of stasis during which the regime develops its interactional networks and semiosic capacities; it will change these codal networks in "jumps," with sudden catastrophic eras of disintegration of codal networks and even of whole metanarratives, the equally sudden self-organization of new networks or metanarratives and the gradual development of the flexibility/complexity of these new grammars until they have again reached a pinnacle point, when a new phase will be again be required. This dissolution of the old grammar and the sudden emergence of a new grammar with simple rather than developed networks can be considered a reversal to an original simplicity of Firstness, to a "mute era" of the fullness of the gods. "The absurd is born of this confrontation between the human need and the unreasonable silence of the world" (Camus 1955, 29). It is an awareness that "definite potentiality can emerge from the indefinite potentiality only by its own vital Firstness and spontaneity" (6.198). The new metanarrative must be gradually articulated over time by the heroes and heroic events of a society. "The heroes were the first to look at the earth before them as an object" (Calasso 1993,358). It is our heroes who create our stories for us; the stories that we tell, over and over; the stories that permit us to be semiotic and so, to live. And just as we have many metanarratives, so we will always have heroes.

Therefore, we must ask: Is evolution a linear or cyclic process? It can only be cyclic; otherwise the idea of an infinite yet fallibilistic complexity, with all its variation and diversity, all its future-oriented potentiality, dies with an essentialistic infallibilism. Certainly, the idea of cyclic transformations of energy, moving from the simple to the complex to the simple, is a common theme: Vico is only one of many believers, with his "three ages: the age of the gods, the age of the heroes, the age of men—which ages not only interact, but also repeat, in phases, the dominance of one of those three ages" (Book V). There is Nietzsche's famed "eternal recurrence" as a result of the basic desire of life, of *amor fati*. Machiavelli speaks of a "return to original principles" for "those are the best constituted bodies, and have the longest existence, which possess the intrinsic means of frequently renewing themselves, or such as obtain this renovation in consequence of some extrinsic accidents. . . . [W]ithout such renovation, these bodies cannot continue to exist; and the means of renewing them is to bring them back to their original principles" (1983, III,1, 385). Regimes of knowledge become trapped within their codal grammars: they lose their adaptive flexibility, and catastrophic entropic dissolution will be not merely inevitable but necessary. As Peirce notes, "the long continuance of a routine of habit makes us lethargic" (6.301). Therefore, "a continuum which is without singularities must, in the first place, return into itself" (6.210).[8] And "time itself, unless it be discontinuous, as we have every reason to suppose it is not, stretches on beyond those limits, infinite though they be, returns into itself, and begins again" (6.210). This is comparable, also, with Aristotle's "rotatory motion" which is itself responsible for its motion (*Physics* Bk. VIII: Ch.5, 6).

This cycle is not, however, a reversal to an *original* typology: we do not reach a certain point and then begin all over again within the same typologies of semiotic codes and signs. We begin with a *simplicity* of semiosis and increase its *complexity*. The new metanarrative orders are random selections and presumably, never repeat themselves. There are no duplicate ages: There are, instead, multiple metanarratives that begin in the silent essentiality of the gods; are articulated as our heroes develop the authority and complexity of our communal networks; and are used, by us humans, as our laws of belief and behavior.

These new metanarratives are our *ainos:* "an affirmation, a marked speech-act, made by and for a marked social group . . . the *ainos* is a code that carries the right message for those who are qualified and the wrong message or messages for those who are unqualified. . . . [It is] predicated on an ideal: an ideal audience listening to an ideal performance of an ideal composition" (Nagy 1990b, 148). But "at the same time it is also predicated on the reality of uncertainties in interaction between performer and audience in the context of the actual performance of a composition; . . . [It is] ambiguous, both difficult in its form and enigmatic in its content." The essence of the *ainos* is that it is a general codality, it "restricts and is restricted by its audience" (148). The *ainos* is the metanarrative of semiosis.

THE DESIRES OF ENERGY

In the end, after it all, what we do is always for desire, for the hope of its attainment. It is all "for sake of Helen tossing her beautiful hair."

Semiosis has "intentionality;" indeed, it has "necessity." These are dangerous words, suggesting a priori determinism, goal-orientation, authorial power—none of which I mean. I define intentionality within the concept of the desire of energy to exist. Desire has three phases or states of existence. It begins within a vague, inarticulate awareness of the actuality of Otherness; this awareness is experienced within a sensual fullness, which is actually an action of entropic decodification in that it ignores, is completely indifferent, to the codal restrictions of both the Self and Otherness, and can therefore set up interactional relations. This is not an intuitive but is rather a poetic bond with the basic or simple shared codal potentialities of the Self and the Other. This is followed by the phase of tychastic desire, which is the chance-driven formation of an actual codification, a codal order that permits the relationship (positive or negative) of both Self and Other(s), and that emerges within both the randomness of chance and the limitations of the restrictions put upon this "choice" by the presence of the codifications already existent in the broader semiosic field of the Self-Other. The last phase is the anancastic desire for the specific and iterative articulation of that particular codification, which is accomplished via the mechanical development of complex interactional networks to replicate, in mimetic or slightly variant form, the codifications of that regime.[9] Essentially, what we see in evolution is what we have seen in the triadic action of semiosis—an increasingly narrow and specialized complex organization of energy into an actualization, a spatiotemporal particularity, of energy. Again, the interaction, as a result of semiosic desire, is: (1) the establishment of an interactional acodal field (which must rest within an existent or immediately self-organized codal base or metanarrative); within which (2) primary codification; followed by (3) secondary network codification can take place.[10] These actions can also be understood as the establishment of multiple dyadic bonds of desire, (Self-Other; dynamic-thermodynamic; sign-not sign), within which triadic semiosis can take place. Evolution, whether biological or social, is not a factor of one but of three intertwined desires or intentionalities.

DEGENERATE: NECESSITY AND CHANCE

The mistake has been to consider that evolution operates within only one, or at most, two, of these three intentions. The most common analysis of evolution suggests an ego-centered or instructionist teleology that exists *before* any of the three intentional phases that I outlined above. This was the "tradition of Natural Theology, a tradition in which organisms were considered to have been constructed by the agency of God" (Kauffman 1993, 11). In this situation, the anancastic or mechanical intentionality is privileged: "every single fact in the universe is precisely determined by law" (Peirce 6.36). Peirce's caustically concludes that this was "a style of reasoning so usual in our day with men not unreflecting as to be more than excusable in the infancy of thought" (6.36). This form of reasoning suggests that signs (the results of semiosis) and codification (the means of semiosis) exist apart from the interaction, as visualized in the familiar semiotic triangle of separate and cumulative nodes. This separation of the realm of knowledge from the realm of experience is a unilevel and nominalist architecture, and necessarily leads one to the concept of a linear progression of "purity."

A comparable monologue has been developed within the theme of natural selection, for years the backbone of biology and "thus from the war of nature, from famine and death, the most exalted object which we are capable of conceiving, namely, the production of the higher animals, directly follows" (Darwin 1963, 470). Selection is the "principle of preservation" and it "leads to the improvement of each creature in relation to its organic and inorganic conditions of life; and consequently, in most cases, to what must be regarded as an advance in organization" (110). Natural selection is God, is the Judgment of what "ought to be" in the future. It "should never be forgotten [that it] can act solely through and for the advantage of each being" (127). "Each slight variation, if useful, is preserved" (49) by natural selection, and "Natural Selection . . . is a power incessantly ready for action, and is as immeasurably superior to man's feeble efforts, as the works of Nature are to those of Art" (49). "The preservation of favourable individual differences and variations, and the destruction of those which are injurious, I have called Natural Selection, or the Survival of the Fittest. . . . [S]ome have even imagined that natural selection induces variability, whereas it implies only the preservation of such variations as arise and are beneficial to the being" (64). Natural selection operates within a unilevel architectonics, with the definition of "the pure" understood as a force of origin, in that it judges those existences that may be allowed to continue. Indeed, as Kauffman points out, "Darwin's notion of natural selection can be enthroned in God's stead as the creative agency" (1993, 11).

We must be extremely careful not to turn the concept of desire, and particularly agapastic desire, into a theistic or instructionist intentionality—whether such is found within rationalism or sensualism. A unilevel frame will access truth by a direct sensual or rational contact. Such intuition is strongly rebutted by realists such as Peirce (5.225–249) who insists on "inference from external facts"; that is, the descriptive immediate data is, as Aristotle also emphasizes, the basis of knowledge but "perception must be of a particular, whereas scientific knowledge involves the recognition of the commensurate universal" (*Posterior. Analytics.* Bk. I: Ch. 31.87b38). Lyotard says that there are "ideas of which no presentation is possible," which, again, Peirce would refute, for "the highest concept which can be reached at all—is the concept of something of the nature of a cognition" (5.257). This does not deny that there is more to reality than we can conceptualize; it instead concedes that we can have no "idea" external to an image of that idea; we "think only in signs." Lyotard's outline of avant-garde art is that it recognizes the "sublime" by not representing it (a Judaic and Islamic tradition); however, rather than seeing these religious traditions as an acceptance of the infinite codal potentialities of energy and a rejection of semiosic commodification, his concept of the avant-garde seems to be a form of nominalism; it rejects the materialistic form that guarantees limited access to the truth; instead, it accepts truth as existent (the sublime) even though unrepresentable. This sense of a "force "which does not allow itself to be made present" (1984, 80), invites a theistic perspective in that it is understood as an essentialist, mystic, asocial force whose authority is not equally amorphous and potential but a priori and necessary. Therefore, to Lyotard, "modern aesthetics is an aesthetic of the sublime, though a nostalgic one" (81). Derrida rejects encoded signs as semiotic traps: "the idea of the book is the idea of a totality, finite or infinite, of the signifier. . . . The idea of the book, which always refers to a natural totality, is profoundly alien to the sense of writing. It is the encyclopaedic protection of theology and of logocentrism against the disruption of writing, against its aphoristic energy" (1981, 18). Instead of the commodities within the book, he offers "Writing," which is not, however, agapastic desire to be encoded in any manner, but is an essentialist purity whose later codification is a degenerate state of its essential nature. Energy cannot exist in such an aloof or a priori form; it can only exist within semiosis. An essentialist or unilevel architecture will always consider that the semiosic or experienced version of pure knowledge is degenerate. "There is therefore a good and a bad writing; the good and natural is the divine inscription in the heart and the soul; the perverse and artful is technique, exiled in the exteriority of the body" (1981, 17). This sounds very like the instructionalism of both Plato and Descartes who also considered that semiosis, the transformation of energy into material existence, was a degenerate step down from absolute purity. Postmodernism, with its deconstruction of both the commodified and the commodifier, moves one into an asemiotic sense of "powerlessness of the faculty of presentation" and (they hope) a "nostalgia for presence felt by the human subject, on the obscure and futile will which inhabits him in spite of everything" (Lyotard 1984, 79). It may seem stabilizing to consider that the energy of the sign, once deconstructed, would feel a nostalgic bond with this purity of original presence—and indeed, energy bonds to energy—but there is no such thing as an existent or original purity. Energy that is deconstructed is not pure knowledge, is not pure will, is not pure origin; indeed, it is non-existent. However, for the postmodernist, being semiosic, being encoded, is akin to a fall from grace.

Lyotard and Derrida's aesthetic assumes a direct contact with purity. Lyotard speaks of forces that "allude to something which does not allow itself to be made present" (1984, 80); he refers to any allusions to these forces as an "aesthetics of the sublime," whose forces are concerned with the "unpresentable." Derrida comments that "the concept of writing exceeds and comprehends that of language" (1981, 8); that is, it provides something that is beyond codification. So that "writing is at the same time more exterior to speech, not being its 'image' or its 'symbol,' and more interior to speech, which is already in itself a writing" (46). Derrida's essentialism is clear: "what we call production is necessarily a text, the system of writing and of a reading which we know is ordered around its own blind spot. We know this a priori, but only now and with a knowledge that is not a knowledge at all" (164). Pure, elusive, essential. And, speaking of encoding (done by language), "the south is the place of origin or the cradle of languages. Thus the southern languages are closer to childhood, nonlanguage, and nature. But at the same time, being closer to the origin, they are purer, more alive, more animated. On the other hand, the northern languages are distant from the origin, less pure, less alive, less warm" (218). This can seem very similar to what I have discussed under the theme of a simple and complex semiosis, with the south being a less evolved, less specific semiotic regime than the north. Purity is about power, and themes of purity will include hierarchies of power. Derrida's Writing is a priori esssentialism, and languages are valued according to their bond with this mystic presence.

I will repeat: Energy has one intentionality—to exist; it has no interest whatsoever in the nature of the codal form of its existence. It has no identity, no plans for any development of specific codal forms; all that energy requires is its articulation in signs. Energy is "a spirit who plays naively—that is, not deliberately but from overflowing power and abundance" (Nietzsche 1969, 299). This indifference to the results of codification is seen by some unilevel purists as a sign of its actual purity and by others as an aspect of a hidden conspiracy against accessing truth. That is, purity is understood to have intentionalities of being "known" in its true nature; both its intentions and our own intentions of accessing this knowledge are sabotaged by the evils of certain types of codification. This is the basis of adversarial rather than interactional dualisms. We see in these assumptions the concepts of the "domination of the fittest," the "struggle for survival."

The government may be understood as "evil" and hegemonically dominant over the people who, as natural, are somehow closer to purity than the regulated bureaucrats—but are prevented by these same bureaucrats from expressing that purity. Alternately, the Platonic rulers may be considered closer to truth than the errant peasants. These serial analyses see an actual finite code, rather than infinite actions of codification, as the prime goal of all actions. Naturally, if one selects the code as primary, then the stability and maintenance of this particular code becomes vital; any deviation from its codal construction is seen as an "attack" on its ability to survive. Again, I remind the reader that themes of purity are always themes of power. Power, with its insistence on stasis of a particular semiotic frame, is, in the long run, asemiosic, because it renders that frame non-adaptive; the code, beautiful as it is, will decay from its very core.

The other factor in a unilevel architectural analysis of evolution is tychastic chance, the random mutations that provide change. This provides the potentiality to deviate from the authoritarian instructions of either a basic code or its anancastic networks—which is why the church, based around an a priori necessitarianism, has always opposed Darwinism.[11] If one thinks about it, the rise of a belief in random chance, the Epicurean *clinamen* or swerve,[12] was inevitable; it was the only way to offset the nominalist "fist of God." The problem, in the unilevel frame, is that the analysis of evolution becomes dyadic; there are only two forces: random tychasm and/or anancastic necessity. They can become confrontational and isolate authoritative voices; necessity and randomness; modernism and postmodernism. "The two creative tendencies developed alongside one another, usually in fierce opposition, each by its taunts forcing the other to more energetic production, both perpetuating in a discordant concord that agony which the term *art* but feebly dominates: until at last, by the thaumaturgy of an Hellenic act of will, the pair accepted the yoke of marriage and, in this condition, begot Attic tragedy, which exhibits the salient features of both parents" (Nietzsche 1956, I, 19). What is lost in their mutual antagonism is the reality of evolution as the dialogic semiosis of energy. Evolution, as the permission to be potential, can only operate within three intentionalities; the median force that disentangles the two isolate forces is agapism, the irrepressible and ever-present desire for interactional bonding.

SEMIOTIC EVOLUTION AND THE THREE DESIRES

How does it begin? I am going to define three different types of semiotic desire or codification intentionalities—the agapastic, the tychastic, the anancastic; continuity, chance, and necessity; and self-organized codes that develop spontaneously within communal interactions, laterally transmitted codes that occur by the chance "swerve" of current and local rather than communal interaction, and the necessities of the already existent or inherited code. I am going to describe the evolution of a semiotic regime, a logical and hierarchical systemic network of codal interaction, within these three correlated phases of organization. Semiosis should not be analyzed within the theme of the single sign[13] but within the codal orders by which energy can be transformed into that single sign.

Does codification begin with nothing? Peirce's comment on beginning with doubt is that such a state is "as useless a preliminary as going to the North Pole would be in order to get to Constantinople by coming down regularly upon a meridian" (5.264). Aristotle's comment is that "all instruction given or received by way of argument proceeds from pre-existent knowledge" (*Posterior Analytics* Bk. I: Ch. 1.71a). We do not yet know how codification began; we only know that the big bang, which was an action of codification, began. This codality spread via "inflation" whereby a codal form expands its homogeneity in the space of an instant; a proton inflates to a galaxy in a millisecond. Inflation nullifies monopoles or competing codes, making the semiosic universe "flat." This is a description of basic dynamic codification. Is this all? Is this flat monologue the basis of our world, with all subsequent codification dependent on a single will? Such is the answer of an essentialist regime. As soon as a codal order "flicks" into existence, then it will inflate. Why doesn't this code become universal? It is because universal homogeneity will destroy energy. All codified forms are subject to entropy; if the codal system can only encode one particular sign or even a regime of networked signs, then much of this dissipating energy will be lost because the single code will be unable to pick up energy in its less complex forms. Therefore, not merely multiple, but different codifications, are required.[14] This requirement for diversity sets up limitations on specific codes—they encode signs within that regime and not within another regime. Codification can only take place within such horizons. These are both internal and external restrictions. Externally, the code will meet with Otherness, whose codal operations will be closed to its energy and its codification. Internally, there will be codal restraints; it will only be able to encode certain amounts of energy, in a certain manner; other codes may grab and encode energy in a different manner. Semiosis is about order, not disorder.

The only a priori is desire, the desire to be encoded into a sign. Whether desire existed before the big bang, I cannot say, but I suspect that it did not; it certainly exists after, and is the basis of all semiosis. Desire is activated by the sense of Otherness, which sets up a heightened awareness, a phase of excitation, which brings semiosis into a state of readiness-to-encode.

AGAPASTIC DESIRE

Lord, thou hast been our dwelling place in all generations; Before the mountains were brought forth.

—Psalm 90

The continuity of freshness, of openness to contacts, must be maintained: a state of being "where the clear-singing nightingale warbles her song in the green glens, clinging to the wine-dark ivy, and to the untrodden grove of the god, thick with leaves and berry clusters . . . day by day the narcissus blooms in lovely clusters, fed by the dew of the sky" (Sophocles *Oedipus Colonus;* in Trypanis 1971, 225–226).

Energy moves towards the establishment of a semiosic regime when it first experiences an awareness of Otherness; it does this by moving—by chance, by intent—into a site, or rather, phase of contact, a phase of attractions, of different energies. This is a synaptic field, known in biology as a synaptic cleft; it is a meeting place beyond, yet "in touch with" the boundaries of the existent signs, and is the site where different energies will suddenly become focused intently, suspiciously, with a desire that may shock themselves, each on the other. In these sites, *both* decodification and codification occur.[15] It is in this gap that the agapastic desire of energy to exist explodes in all its generative power; one can readily say that one is "possessed" by its force, the silent overwhelming urgency of the invisible desire to be. "Only the lover is *entheos.* . . . Only the lover is 'full of god'" (Calasso 1993, 86). This is a sudden deconstruction of the Self: "whenever I look at you, even for a moment, no voice comes to me. But my tongue is frozen, and at once a delicate fire flickers under my skin. I no longer see anything with my eyes, and my ears are full of strange sounds. Sweat pours down me, and trembling seizes me all over" (Sappho, 600 BC; in Trypanis 1971, 146). This is agapastic desire. Evolution cannot take place without this desire and its action of deconstruction. It cannot take place within a homogeneity of type, where Self simply meets a version of Self. Differentiation, the awareness of otherness, is a basic requirement of semiosis, of the transformation of energy into existentialities, for, as Aristotle points out, "only those things which either involve a 'contrariety' or are 'contraries' . . . are such as to suffer action and to act" (*De Gen.* Bk.I:Ch.7.324a).[16] This agapastic feeling, in the fullness of a deconstructed Firstness, is without knowledge[17] of either the Other or the Self; it is a sense of a relationship of energy to energy, an intense desire for this merging energy to be encoded, which desire arises within the "charged" atmosphere of this larger "semiosic field." It is similar to an electromagnetic field that is activated and "excited" by the presence and input of other fields. Agapastic desire points to a "relationship, where the god of inspiration *semainei* 'indicates' to the *theoros* the inner vision" (Nagy 1990b, 164). A *theoros* is "he who sees a vision." What is this inner vision? One and only one—the desire of energy to exist, to continue into the future. A chance encounter will open up a new semiosic contact; tychasm bluntly introduces a new and shared code relevant to the local codal existentialities, it bonds the two together, so to speak; specific anancastic codification moves in and cools their desire down, limits its expression, orders the paths it may take in future and so develops and ensures a stable semiotic regime.

Agapastic desire is formless; "it has all the features of the arbitrary, of what is born in the dark, from formlessness, the way our world was perhaps once born" (Calasso 1993, 133).

"The agapastic development of thought is the adoption of certain mental tendencies, not altogether heedlessly, as in tychasm, nor quite blindly by the mere force of circumstances or of logic as in anancasm, but by an immediate attraction for the idea itself, whose nature is divined before the mind possesses it, by the power of sympathy, that is, by virtue of the continuity of mind" (Peirce 6.307). I remind the reader, that this basic desire is for semiosis, for the codification of energy, and not for any particular code or the codification of any particular sign. This syncretic desire for the infinite continuity of semiosis is "something whose possibilities of determination no multitude of individuals can exhaust" (6.170).

Agapastic intentionality is a continual openness of energy to energy; as such, it exists within a ready awareness and amorphousness of boundaries, a power of deconstruction of current boundaries. It is a sense of two things: first, of the codal differentiation between the Self and the Other, and on a deeper level, of the essential continuity or sameness of energy between the Self and Other.[18] Agapastic desire is both an action of deconstruction of this current semiosis of energy that has created the codal isolation of both the Self and the Other, and a bonding and desire for recodification which shares the energy between these two seemingly separate entities. It is Bakhtin's "will to destroy," which is also a "will to create." "Death is the necessary link in the process of the people's growth and renewal. It is the 'other side' of birth" (Rabelais 1968, 407). It is all emotion—grief, rage and joy; it is all sensuality, in the dionysian essence of "freshness, life and freedom." It breaks up current codes in their senility, their irresolute nature. This is "the glorious transport which arises in man, even from the very depths of nature, at the shattering of the *principium individuationis*, then we are in a position to apprehend the essence of Dionysian rapture, whose closest analogy is furnished by physical intoxication" (Bakhtin 1984b, 22). Bakhtin's carnival, along with laughter, as a deconstructive action, has an "indissoluble and essential relation to freedom" (89), for "festive folk laughter presents an element of victory not only over supernatural awe, over the sacred, over death; it also means the defeat of power, of earthly kings, of the earthly upper classes, of all that oppresses and restricts" (92). It should be noted that "humanity ceased to laugh from the fourth century on; it did nothing but weep, and heavy chains fell on the mind" (Herzen 1954, 223; in Bakhtin 1984b, 92). Not only did the Platonic polis condemn real laughter, but so did early Christianity, for "only permanent seriousness, remorse and sorrow for his sins befit the Christian" (73). "And so in regard to the emotions of sex and anger, and all the appetites and pains and pleasures of the soul which we say accompany all our actions, the effect of poetic imitation is the same. For it waters and fosters these feelings when what we ought to do is to dry them up, and it establishes them as our rulers when they ought to be ruled, to the end that we may be better and happier men instead of worse and more miserable" (Plato 1937, 606d).

> Here is no water but only rock
> Rock and no water and the sandy road
> The road winding above the mountains
> Which are mountains of rock without water
> If there were water. (Eliot 1954, *The Waste Land*, lines 331–335).

This agapastic phase of open desire "frees human consciousness, thought, and imagination for new potentialities" (Bakhtin 1984b, 49). Agapastic desire does not seek the replacement of one sign with another, the hegemonic domination of the one over the other, but a deconstruction of all boundaries and the transformation of the freed energies into new signs.[19] "Freedom can only manifest itself in unlimited and uncontrolled variety and multiplicity" (Peirce: 1.302). This basic interaction rests on an awareness of a "relational generality" between one entity and another. This may be our universal humanity, it may be a social commonality, but the idea of a shared generality is a required factor.[20]

This commonality is of three types: "first, it may affect a whole people or community . . . second, it may affect a private person . . . so that he is only enabled to apprehend the idea, or to appreciate its attractiveness, by virtue of his sympathy with his neighbors . . . third, it may affect an individual . . . by virtue of an attraction it exercises upon his mind, even before he has comprehended it" (Peirce 6.307). As such, agapastic desire is not an a priori *form* but an a priori *intention;* it is the desire of energy to be encoded. This desire is a primary will, therefore, even when codal dissolution occurs; the agapastic intentionality of energy will remain to be instantly articulated within another code.

> The infinite diversity of the universe, which we call chance, may bring ideas into proximity which are not associated in one general idea. It may do this many times. But then the law of continuous spreading will produce a mental association; and this I suppose is an abridged statement of the way the universe has been evolved. But if I am asked whether a blind 'agapke' cannot bring ideas together, first I point out that it would not remain blind. There being a continuous connection between the ideas, they would infallibly become associated in a living feeling, and perceiving general idea. . . . [W]herever ideas come together they tend to weld into general ideas; and wherever they are generally connected, general ideas govern the connection; and these general ideas are living feelings spread out (Peirce 6.143).

Agapastic desire moves into an excited or active state within the synaptic phase, when two codal forms move into an area/phase of interaction. In this phase, their current semiosic boundaries and current codal order become focused on each other's energy-content and codal orders of articulation; their boundaries and orders become flexible and amorphous, and subject both to deconstruction and subsequent construction. Prometheus gave men not only codification but also the gift of fire, and it is this agapastic fire that breaks open the tomb walls of the *sema*. Every action of semiosis takes place within this inflamed synaptic phase and therefore is always an action beyond individual existentiality, an action of both deconstruction and construction, of both terror and joy, angst and delight. Therefore "when we know for sure that a person is the agent of some action, then that action is mediocre; as soon as there is a hint of greatness, of whatever kind, be it shameful or virtuous, it is no longer that person acting" (Calasso 1993, 94), which is to say that one has moved into an agapastic state of decodification and recodification, an action that involves both Self and Other. This semiosis exists on all scales. There are miniscule variations, which hardly shift the codal architectures of both signs; more intense changes, which transform the secondary phase of network codifications; and, finally, more rare events, which deconstruct both architectural levels and result in an entirely new metanarrative code.

I remind the reader that semiosis is complex; it can but does not, for its own sake, operate within only simple and un-networked codes. It operates within a basic codal grammar, which itself can be complex and many layered. Then, parallel to this unconscious level, is the interactional level of the network codal formations that serve to increase elenctic and deictic complexity. The force of agapastic desire, in its synaptic phase, will not necessarily destroy all these codal formations; it may only sever the most immediate and superficial codes that serve to keep the two forms of energy separate, and will then link them into yet more plastic and robust forms of semiosis. Agapastic desire can be compared with Lacan's Imagination, Vico's mythic sense of poesis, with Peirce's Firstness, all of which express a "fullness of being" beyond any confinement in words or other material form, a purity or potentiality of full existence of life, whether you called it Nature or God. Agapastic desire permits a first relationship in its immediacy and fullness, with its people "unable to make use of the understanding" (Vico, 402) and "entirely immersed in the senses" (Vico, 378). The definition of Firstness "is predominant in the ideas of freshness, life, freedom. The free is that which has not another behind it, determining its actions. . . . Freedom can only manifest itself in unlimited and uncontrolled variety and multiplicity; and thus the first becomes predominant in the ideas of measureless variety and multiplicity" (Peirce 1.302).

This is the human experience in its Eden, its Dreamtime, its innocence. The truths of this experience "lay claim to divine authorship; and it is true that men have no more *invented* them, than the birds have invented their wings" (ff 1, 5.380). This is that direct confrontation with the gods, in which "every sudden heightening of intensity brought you into a god's sphere of influence" (Calasso 1993, 95). *Ate* means "divine infatuation," that sudden intense coupling with a god. The Homeric heroes "knew that this invisible incursion often brought ruin . . . but they also knew, and it was Sophocles who said it, that 'mortal life can never have anything grandiose about it except throught *ate*'" (Calasso 1993, 94).

The intense, open potentialities of agapastic desire meet face to face with the restrictive conditions of codification. Semiosis, the means by which energy exists, operates as the codification of energy. Energy is necessarily organized into systemic combinations with specific—and therefore limited, confined, selective, codal—agendas. In other words, the agapastic desire to encode must result in a codal format that is potentially operative within existent codal interactions. "Much of the order we see in organisms may be the direct result not of natural selection but of the natural order selection was privileged to act upon" (Kauffman 1993, 173). The noblest heroes, as Prometheus knew, belong to the confined realities of codification, the restrictions of life, and not to the irresolute openness of the gods. Heracles, the noblest of them all, chose virtue, based as it is around restrictions, the obligations to "what ought to be" rather than "what one desires." The awareness of the restrictions of codification humbles "not only their bodies but their minds as well" (Vico 1948, 502) and thus "arose the eternal property that minds to make good use of the knowledge of God must humble themselves, just as on the other hand arrogance will lead them to atheism" (502). Whenever one is in the agapastic situation, one must at the same time confirm one's commitment to the restrictions that belong with life. "Why does your heart sorrow so much for me? No man is going to hurl me to Hades, unless it is fated, but as for fate, I think that no man yet has escaped it once it has taken its first form, neither brave man nor coward" (Homer 1951, Bk. VI, lines 487–489).

What we must "insert" back into the linear, Darwinian concept of evolution, is this first form of evolution, agapism. "I have given you wings on which you may rise and fly with ease over the endless sea and over the whole earth" (Theognis 520 BC; in Trypanis 1971, 162).

TYCHASTIC DESIRE

Agapastic desire for codification includes no instructional intentionality; all it does is develop a sense of commonality. Whatever codal form that new fellowship eventually takes is arbitrary, a factor of chance. "Coronis was washing her feet in Lake Boebeis. Apollo saw her and desired her. Desire came as a sudden shock, it caught him by surprise, and immediately he wanted to have done with it" (Calasso 1993, 56). This sudden decision, this immediate clarity of one's mind, is tychastic chance. However, when I speak of chance, I do not mean that the results of semiosis are completely undetermined and ad hoc; the new codal formula is limited by the codification networks already locally existent at that site, and we cannot assume, ever, that such networks do not exist. Tychastic desire operates within the restrictions of local codal formulas, and its chance-mutations are products of those formulas. If codification did not exist, even if only within the regime of the Other, there would be no such thing as energy. Tychastic codification is the organization of newly freed, still codified, local formulas of energy; it is the essence of thermodynamic codification, that random, irreversible coalescence of different forces, operative within current time and current space, into actualities. "The tychastic development of thought, then, will consist in slight departures from habitual ideas in different directions indifferently, quite purposeless and quite unconstrained whether by outward circumstances or by force of logic, these new departures being followed by unforeseen results which tend to fix some of them as habits more than others" (Peirce: 6.307). And again, "By thus admitting pure spontaneity or life as a character of the universe, acting always and everywhere *though restrained within narrow bounds by law* continually, and great ones with infinite infrequency, I account for all the variety and diversity of the universe, in the only sense in which the really *sui generis* and new can be said to be accounted for. . . . Variety can only spring from spontaneity" (6.59; my emphasis).

Tychastic codification takes that newly freed energy, that newly fused potentiality of the local semiosic regime, and quickly, effortlessly, transforms it into signs. Where do its codes come from? From interactions that I shall define as *dialogic-chance* formations. New codes do not constantly appear, in the sense of completely random and never-ending mutations, which are then "offered" for the judgment of selection. The actual code offered to selection is a chance-driven but otherness-restricted form that will most certainly be immediately functional and interactive within its codal environment; there will be no need for time and energy to be expended in multiple tests, no depletion of energy caused by multiple mutant failures. This is why tychastic evolution can be considered as developing its codes within lateral or parallel (existent) networks. Relativism attempts to deconstruct these parallel relationships, seeing them quite rightly as a power, and quite wrongly viewing codal restrictions as a conspiracy against individual inventiveness; that is, conspiracy theories operate within a unilevel theme of the agential power of the individual sign, rather than the power of semiosis. However, formulating a new, separate codal pattern for the semiosis of each and every sign-unit would be an enormous, indeed extravagant, use of energy. Most of the available energy would be used as fuel for the continuous establishment of new individualized codes; very little would be left for the material content of the sign-unit. Second, it would be a highly precarious semiosis resulting in a continuous loss of energy via an inability to rapidly come up with new codal formats that would encode that energy before it dissolved into a lower state. And finally, the production of signs by instant, once-only codes would negate any possibilities of networking; networking is an energy-efficient means of ensuring stable codification and a continuity of semiosis; if one network doesn't codify the energy, an interaction with another one will. It also permits the development of more complex semiosis, with an ability to encode more energy within patterns that may overlap and shadow each other. Energy could never survive within such unproductive procedures as are found within relativism. "The din makes a great mountain murmur overhead" (Virgil *Aeneid* Bk. I, lines 79–80).

Even within the codal restrictions of the existent networks of otherness, the new codifications are not ordered by any monologic necessitarian intentionality. There could be quite a number of codes that could operate within that regime of networks; the one that emerges, is a result of that chance dialogue, that sudden decision to take this road and not that road.

ANANCASTIC DESIRE

The final step is the gradual development of the anancastic mechanical codal networks, those interlinked codal bonds that develop as secondary stabilizing forces that permit the continuity and elaboration of a basic code. Bonded as they are to each other, they can be understood within the traditional definition of "intentionality" or inheritance; their behavior is completely linked to the necessary principles of the existent order. "The anancastic development of thought will consist of new ideas adopted without foreseeing whither they tend, but having a character determined by causes either external to the mind, such as changed circumstances of life, or internal to the mind as logical developments of ideas already accepted, such as generalizations" (Peirce 6.307). "The present is connected with the past by a series of real infinitesimal steps" (6.109). These rules of codification are the second step in the two-phase Darwinian process of evolution: mutant chance and natural selection. Anancastic codes develop within a gradual *selection process* that affirms the viability of the basic code (as offered within tychastic chance) by establishing complex interlocked codal networks that "prove" the success of that basic code and ensures continuous semiosis of that particular codal regime. The fact is, however, that neither the basic code nor its selective success would have existed without that first step of a synaptic, agapastic collation of energies.

Networks permit indexical semiosis, signs that are codally "related" to each other. "The index is physically connected with its object; they make an organic pair, but the interpreting mind has nothing to do with this connection, except remarking it, after it is established (2.299). Smoke is not merely a symbol of fire; it is also a chemical aspect of that fire. The point of the indexical relationship is that it operates within multiple codal networks; it is a physical, a chemical, a biologic as well as a symbolic codal relationship. Its forcefulness in moving itself into semiosis is thereby more necessary than a semiosis that can use only one codal network: i.e., chemical *or* symbolic. As Coletta says, "any language which is rich in metaindices is an ecologically and evolutionarily 'fit' language: when humans use metaindices in their poetry, they are stretching human metaphoric capacity towards a before unrecognized ecological iconicity" (1993, 224). Indexical semiotic relationships are more evolutionary fit codal bonds than symbolic ones because they are more pragmatically interactive with the environment. Following this, Coletta says that "biological evolution will be seen as a system of the generation of biogeochemical icons and indices, chemical con-figurations or re-figurings, which are solutions to the problem of survival;" and "biologically extinct species are like Peirce's 'symbols': configurations for which there are no longer any indexical (or motivated) ecological linkages" (224); while "ecologically fit species are like Peirce's icons and indices: configurations with linkages to a/an (ecological) field of reference, linkages of either resemblance or causality" (224). A semiosis that operates within indexically linked networks can be understood as a more robust and "fit" species.

The energy of a codal regime is predominantly organized in an indexical or pragmatic manner; it is a syncretic forging of organized interactions within a particular ecological and social environment. It will develop within an agapastic desire to interact with the existent networks of that environment; this desire is satisfied with tychastic, chance-driven local codified interactions that, if successful, move into habitual anancastic codes, which will, over time, via bonds of "sympathy" or Peircean agapism, develop more complex networks, more specific interactions, and so contribute to the articulation of energy. Eventually, they will become overly restrictive, and will have to be decodified so that new networks (and new codes and signs) will be able to emerge spontaneously. The cycle renews itself.

This giant web of relationships permits energy to exist; it ensures that the dreaded deathly state of zero-point is never reached. Once the metanarrative and those interlocked networks of habitual codal relationships become established, these codes function as an instructional guide for semiosic transformation. As I have said, this is an energy-efficient and productive aspect of semiosis; habitual codal networks ensure semiosis.

Therefore, I am not denying but am insisting on the importance of an instructionist or mechanical intentionality. However, I am saying that it comes into play *after* codification has set up the basic codal regime. "The repetition that abounds in history presupposes the whole history of repetition. . . . The rarer written traces become, the more imposing is the part repetition plays in them. It seems that signs are drawn chiefly to indicate how something must be repeated" (Calasso 1994, 186). Again, "for something to have meaning, it must be repeated—and if one thing is to be repeated, everything must be repeated" (Ibid).

SUMMARY

Semiotic evolution involves all three phases of intentionality. There are the two processes that we normally associate within evolution—that random offering of a new codal format and the subsequent use of this new code within the development of interactive networks. These are the two steps as understood within Darwinian gradualism. Darwin's identification of basic intentionality with theism led him to reject agapism, the ongoing desire of energy for codification, which in his era of late modernism, had been commodified into the instructionist intentionality of God. Darwin's gradual codal changes ignore any and all dialogic relationships; in Darwinian thinking, the bond with the rest of life is not the *simple-coded or open-coded* synchretic generalizations of agapastic desire but is rather a confrontational relationship with otherness, that life-struggle of a *complex-coded or closed-coded* system to maintain its particular existentiality. Darwinian desire becomes a bloodthirsty struggle of an individual code system against other code systems—a semiosis quite understandable within a unilevel architecture but totally meaningless within a bilevel system. Darwinian "evolution is thus seen as an opportunist, remolding hard-won successes for novel uses (Kauffman 1993, 13). Agapism or the desire of energy to live is transformed into a particular species' strength to live. This is desire in its degenerate transformation into a commodity: purity-as-power continuously confronted by other purities-as-power.

On the other hand, indexicality, the organized linkage not merely of nominalist signs, but of codal networks, is the framework within which the bileveled semiosic evolution operates. It is the key architectonic infrastructure of life. Agapastic desire can establish the potentiality of a codal grammar that will permit a horse, a zebra, a mule or some other form that we have never seen. Then, tychastic or locally chance-driven codification will narrow the agapastic potentialities to a specific code—let's say a zebra.

Anancastic interactions will then establish the interlocked networks with other species that make the reproduction of zebra-signs in that area an inevitability for multiple generations. All three intentionalities operate together; all are both chance-driven and restricted by each other and the codalities of their neighboring networks. Semiosis is an action of increasing order and decreasing potentiality. We cannot say that evolution begins with random mutation (tychasm), whose results are then "selected" by a theistic natural selection. Evolution begins with agapastic intentionality, a desire of the fullness of energy-in-interaction, to exist.

Energy has been given the name of Zeus and what better image for its generative immensity: "The sea grew calm as he entered it, and the sea-monsters gambolled before the feet of Zeus, and the dolphin from the deep tumbled joyfully over the waves. And the Nereids came up from the sea, all riding on the backs of sea-monsters, and ranged themselves in rows ... and around him the Tritons gathered, the gruff flute-players of the sea, playing a wedding song on their slender shells" (Moschus, 150BC; in Trypanis 1971, 342).

EVOLUTION: THE THREE REGIMES

There are two types of evolution. There is the ongoing development of a regime, an interactional adaptation of a metanarrative that has already been established and that is developing and strengthening its networks. And there is the actual establishment of a metanarrative. I would compare the operations of the former with what Kauffman defines as "natural selection" and the latter with his "self-organization," which Prigogine has defined as "far-from-equilibrium states" and which Per Bak has defined as "self-organized criticality." The difference between the two is not one of degree: in the former, semiosis is operative within a metanarrative; in the latter, energy has moved to a peripheral state beyond the codal restrictions of a metanarrative and requires a new metanarrative. The two are both important, but should not be confused with each other. The first is microevolution, the latter is macroevolution.

Energy moves from general potentiality to specific particularity. The particularity of the semiosic codal form occurs at first by "interactive" chance,[21] but this chance appearance of a code may produce permanent effects if this code sets up networks that establish a continuity of its codal formation: "continuity consists in a binding together of things that are different and remain different, so that they are in a measure different from one another and yet in a measure independent, yet this is only true of finite parts of the continuum.... [A]lthough the other instants of time are not independent of one another, independence does appear at the actual instant" (Peirce 6.86). In other words, both continuity and independence, commitment and freedom, are interlocked. As Prigogine notes, "initial conditions and dynamics are no longer independent" (1984, 280). This positive sympathy permits the development of the interlocked codal networks within which the simple code is existential. The will of energy is not, in the beginning, goal-directed; but once interactive networks are formed, the codes act as restrictive anancastic instructions and will limit the type of possible new codifications. Chance, even though a vital force, is itself limited by the codal bonds that have developed within the local anancastic networks. These necessitarian bonds limit the possibilities of mutant code forms even appearing. Therefore, mutant codifications will succeed if they take place in peripheral areas, in areas where the anancastic codal networks are weakest. Revolutions always begin among the disenchanted, the unstable, the forgotten.

The continuity of life is achieved by the *self-organized* development of general orders or grammars of codification, within which specific and increasingly complex semiosis takes place. Jacob wrote that

> the notion that evolution results exclusively from a succession of microevents, from mutations, each occurring at random, is denied both by time and by arithmetic. For the wheel of chance to come step by step, sub-unit after sub-unit, with each of the several ten thousand protein chains needed to compose the body of a mammal would require far more time than the span generally attributed to the solar system. Only in very simple organisms can variation occur entirely in small independent changes. Only in bacteria can speed of growth and size of populations allow the organisms to wait for the appearance of a mutation in order to adapt.... The limits of life cannot be left to chance. They are prescribed by the programme which, from the moment the ovule is fertilized, fixes the genetic destiny of the individual ... death is an integral part of the system selected in the animal world and its evolution (1973, 308).

There are different types of semiotic regimes in which the interactions between the two basic codifications of dynamic and thermodynamics can differ. Kauffman sets up three regimes: "ordered, complex, and chaotic." "In the *ordered* regime, many elements in the system freeze in fixed states of activity. These frozen elements form a large connected cluster, or *frozen component,* which spans, or *percolates,* across the system and leaves behind isolated islands of unfrozen elements whose activities fluctuate in complex ways" (1993, 174). Prigogine states that "At equilibrium, molecules behave as essentially independent entities; they ignore one another. We would like to call them 'hypnons,' 'sleepwalkers.' Though each of them may be as complex as we like, they ignore one another. However, nonequilibrium wakes them up and introduces a coherence quite foreign to equilibrium" (1984, 180–181). Kauffman continues: "In the *chaotic* regime, there is no frozen component. Instead, a connected cluster of unfrozen elements, free to fluctuate in activities, percolates across the system, leaving behind isolated frozen islands. In this chaotic regime, small changes in initial conditions unleash avalanches of changes ... in the chaotic regime, the dynamics are very sensitive to initial conditions. The transition from the ordered to the chaotic regime constitutes a phase transition, which occurs as a variety of parameters are changed. The transition region, on the edge between order and chaos, is the *complex* regime" (1993, 174). This transition should not be thought of in a serial or cumulative sense. An orderly regime privileges the dynamic code; a chaotic regime privileges the thermodynamic code—and the complex regime sits on the borderline, with both codes in dialogic interaction. Within these tropic regimes, order is organized from within and not from an external codal authority. There may be small changes that only affect the superficial level of codification or large reorganizations which develop entirely new orders; and "one would get many little avalanches and fewer big avalanches, but if one waited long enough, one would get rare massive avalanches crashing down"(Kauffman 1995, 236). Most changes fall within the adaptive fluctuations of microevolution but, rarely, a macroevolution will destroy current metanarratives and thereby permit the self-organization of new orders.

"Orderly dynamics is due to the percolation of a frozen phase containing functionally isolated islands. ... Deep in the frozen, orderly phase, each functionally isolated island can perform its own computations but is unable to communicate with other islands. Conversely, in the chaotic phase, orderly computation seems improbable since any slight perturbation will cause damage to spread exponentially" (1993:221). "In the chaotic regime, nearby states diverge from one another. In the ordered regime, nearby states converge" (223). Both regimes are ill-equipped to make complex adaptation; at their extremes, the orderly is frozen into non-interaction; the chaotic cannot establish any interactions or continuity of order. The "poised state," where the two codifications are able to interact, is the only one capable of a continuous adaptive change. In the orderly state, codal interactions cannot "break through" the frozen codes; in the chaotic state, new codes are constantly emerging, but cannot establish interlocked networks that stabilize codification and thus dissolve. The only regime in which steady adaptive microevolution can occur is one that permits the interaction of both types of codification, the complex or borderline regime.

Prigogine defines these regimes as "dissipative structures," the two words acknowledging the two actions within the one organism, "to emphasize the close association, at first paradoxical, in such situations between structure and order on the one side, and dissipation or waste on the other" (1984, 143). "Dissipative structures actually correspond to a form of supramolecular organization" (143) and he calls this "order through fluctuation" (178); that is, nonequilibrium is a source of order. Energy within a dissipative structural regime exists in a constant "state of desire" for semiosis. Such a regime is one in which "alterations in the species at one site in an ecosystem can often cause neighboring species to undergo coadaptive changes" (263). As Kauffman states, "a phase boundary separates networks that exhibit frozen, orderly dynamics from those that exhibit chaotic dynamics. The existence of this boundary leads us to a very general and potentially very important hypothesis. Parallel processing systems lying in this interface region between order and chaos may be those best able to adapt and evolve. Further, natural selection may be the force which pulls complex adaptive systems into this boundary region" (218). "At the boundary between the order and chaos, the frozen regime is melting and the functionally isolated unfrozen islands are in tenuous shift contact with one another. It seems plausible that the most complex, most integrated, and most evolvable behavior might occur in this boundary region" (219). Again, Kauffman: "organisms adapt under natural selection via a *metadynamics* where each organism myopoically alters the structure of its fitness landscape and the extent to which that landscape is deformed by the adaptive moves of other organisms, such that, as if by an invisible hand, the entire ecosystem coevolves to a poised state at the edge of chaos" (261). Therefore, regimes that are able to use both dynamic and thermodynamic codification, that are bileveled, and able to use "parallel processing" are best able to adapt. These systems "appear able to carry out the most complex computations and yet may harbor sufficiently ordered fitness landscapes that the systems are able to evolve well" (237). Complex regimes are those using all three intentionalities: agapastic, tychastic and anancastic.

Peirce says it best:

> Habits are general ways of behaviour which are associated with the removal of stimuli. But when the expected removal of the stimulus fails to occur, the

excitation continues and increases, and non-habitual reactions take place; and these tend to weaken the habit. If, then, we suppose that matter never does obey its ideal laws with absolute precision, but that there are almost insensible fortuitous departures from regularity, these will produce, in general, equally minute effects. But protoplasm is in an excessively unstable condition; and it is the characteristic of unstable equilibrium that near that point excessively minute causes may produce startlingly large effects. Here then, the usual departures from regularity will be followed by others that are very great; and the large fortuitous departures from law so produced will tend still further to break up the laws, supposing that these are of the nature of habits. Now, this breaking up of habit and renewed fortuitous spontaneity will, according to the law of mind, be accompanied by an intensification of feeling (6.264).

Theories that state that order rises out of a chaotic regime are mistaken; they assume that a primal order sits underneath the chaotic flux, simply waiting for its time to emerge. This is a priori purism and I hope that I have shown that such a condition does not exist. "At all levels, be it the level of macroscopic physics, the level of fluctuations, or the microscopic level, *nonequilibrium is the source of order. Nonequilibrium brings 'order out of chaos'*" (Prigogine and Stengers 1984, 287). Prigogine continues, "as we already mentioned, the concept of order (or disorder) is more complex than was thought" and concludes that "irreversibility is the mechanism that brings order out of chaos" (292). Order is basic to life; what nonequilibrium does is to permit *codal stress,* the stress derived from maintaining a code against its own entropy and the excitations derived from interactions with other sources of energy, to reach a limit, a "bifurcation point" at which the existent codal orders will collapse and permit the introduction of new energy, which will lead to the development of new codification and a more robust semiosis. The basis of life is order, in any codification whatsoever. We cannot say that chaos is the primal soup, the beginning. This is fine for a California deconstructionist party, but all it can do is dissipate. The statement should read that *nonequilibrium is the source of the evolution of order,* what Prigogine has defined as "order through fluctuations" (178). It achieves this by establishing semiosic regimes that are capable of moving into borderline states, those agapastic states of excitation that are most sensitive to interaction with other sources of energy and to both forms of codification.[22] Prigogine points out that "it is very important to emphasize that the behavior of such systems depends on their history" (161); that is, the tychastic changes developed at these bifurcation or nodal points are not fully open but are related to the restrictions of already existent anancastic networks. This does not mean prediction. We cannot predict, by rational or scientific methods, future semiosic codifications and therefore, the future growth of scientific knowledge or of human history. The belief in any kind of linear destiny is sheer superstition; however, the potentiality of a particular codification is restricted by the "history," the currently existing codal networks that have already been developed in both near and far semiotic regimes.

An adaptive society will use both codes: dynamic and thermodynamic, as expressed within orderly and chaotic semiosis; it is capable of the "borderline" or complex regime, in which both codes are dialogically interactive, sensitive to fluctuations from other sources of energy, and capable of codifying that energy within their own boundaries. Such a complex regime need not use both codes at the same time; it might be easier to use them in a serial format. Carnivals may take place only at certain times of the year; there may be six days of work and one of rest; a wild bachelor party followed by a strict marriage ceremony. The society may use them in parallel format: some aspects of life are rigid, others are completely flexible. "It might be the case that coevolving ecosystems tend toward a state of 'self-organized criticality' in which parts of the ecosystem are frozen for long periods, such that the species in the frozen component do not change, while other species continue to coevolve" (Kauffman 1993, 256). However, the microevolutionary or borderline state is not the only possible regime; there still exist the orderly and chaotic regimes. I am considering that all three regimes are normative semiotic states. An isolate tribal group may have developed a normative behavior that is so rarely exposed to excitations from otherness of any kind, environmental or human, that its regime may be stable for thousands of years. A chaotic regime is not, by definition, a regime but is rather a state of indeterminacy. As such, it is a necessary part of semiosis, a phase of deconstruction (which, in a society, may last for a generation)—but it must be understood as a phase and not a self-sustaining regime.

How can a species or society prevent change? By moving to a peripheral niche in which its codal activities may become less accessible to external excitation from other societies *and* by a rigid control of that codality. Any fundamentalist group, be it the Platonic polis or the ethnic and ideological enclaves of our modern world—any group that is committed to the purism of a particular code must use a centralist authoritarianism to prevent its dissolution and the intrusion of different codes. The problem is, codal dissipation is ongoing even in isolation from external intrusions, and the energy required to maintain this strict mimetic reproduction is high. It is easier to maintain iconic reproduction of a particular code when the group is relatively isolated but it is difficult in areas with high populations, diverse groups, and global communication. In such situations, iconic reproduction requires that emotions be kept at a "feverish pitch" to constantly decodify these intrusive codes. Blind acceptance of the "mother code" and hatred of other codes must be maintained. This maintenance of codal purity requires such a high-input of energy that very little energy will be directed towards other activities; these groups will have a fragile and poor economy, and will inevitably collapse because of that entropic withering. Semiosis is a harsh master; it is indifferent to the emotional bonds of any code, indifferent to the loyalties of any historic networks, its only interest is in the survival of energy—never, ever, the code.

FAR-FROM EQUILIBRIUM EVOLUTION

These mountains are swarming, my kingdom is no longer of this world, I need new mountains.

—Nietzsche *Thus Spoke Zarathustra*, LXIX

How is a metanarrative developed? There are two phases: the appearance of the basic code, and the development of the complexity of this code. The basic code emerges in a critical act of abduction, a sudden immediate contact with the gods of poesis; it is a self-organized wholeness, an invention, in the true sense of the word, from within that site of energy. The second phase is that gradual evolution with which we are familiar, that serial algorithm of extensional cumulation of behavioral norms as developed within local chance-choices, and the spread of these choices via the mechanisms of anancastic interactional network bonds with other semiotic regimes.

Megacodification, the development of an entirely new basic code, is rare and can happen only when both the basic code and the secondary network codification have moved out of a state of equilibrium of codal operations; their semiosic activities have degenerated to a critical disablement of codification. It is here, at this bifurcation point, that the codal regime becomes incapable of retaining energy. The dissolution of the vital supportive network codes may have been gradual over the years; this will reach a decisive state of non-participation with the basic grammar. The basic grammar itself may be unable to establish new networks. At this point, the collapse of the basic grammar will be almost instantaneous. This can only be defined as "catastrophic" in every sense of the word. Energy cannot exist outside of codification; therefore, if a basic codal order collapses, everything that is encoded by that code, in both primary and secondary networks, will also dissolve. Energy, as in a nuclear explosion, will be released in an enormous expansion of chaotic or unrestrained energy. This type of energy is "simple," it is "primitive" in the sense that it *is* encoded but in a very simple code that can move into a multitude of other coded regimes, rather than being rejected by them as too complex for inclusion. This event is all to the benefit of energy; if it has been existing within a regime that has become incapable of encoding energy, then, to preserve itself, energy *must* find a new means of semiosis; it must leave its old home and go elsewhere. As with the effects of a nuclear explosion, these "primitive" codes may disturb and eventually destroy both the secondary networks and the basic codal order of neighboring regimes. A comparable image is found within the famous "butterfly effect," in which the flap of wings in one site disturbs the equilibrium of another site. This "butterfly effect" should not be understood in as light-hearted a sense as that image implies; it is not simply that the wing-flap causes the leaves of a tree to shake; in both cases, we are speaking about codification, not breezes; and energy that has been deconstructed to a simpler code form can intrude into foreign codal regimes and destroy them.[23] However, megacodifications should be understood as rare, though natural. The released energy may be absorbed by neighboring networks but as this would require in most cases a massive recodification of these neighbor regimes, and, as noted, if stable, they are immune to these butterflies, then the most energy-efficient means of dealing with this released energy is by the self-organization of a new basic code in that same niche. Therefore, to prevent the ultimate global dissolution of codal order and the necessity of developing millions of new orders, (a very energy-expensive process), a new codal order must develop—instantly—in that same niche of semiosis.

This phase of massive disorder will therefore spontaneously organize a new basic order, a new metanarrative. This new order is self-organized; the order must emerge from within the semiosic realities of that particular site of energy and not from any a priori or external force. It is chance-driven and yet restrained by the codes of the coexistent regimes of otherness. As Prigogine notes, in the far-from-equilibrium state, matter is highly sensitive to Otherness and "external fields . . . may play an essential role in the selection mechanism of self-organization" (1984, 14). Therefore, the codal order that emerges in this primary bifurcation is not inhospitable but necessarily compatible with the coexistent codes of other regimes. Prigogine comments that "the sensitivity of far-from-equilibrium states to external fluctuations is another example of a system's spontaneous 'adaptive organization' to its environment" (165). The new basic code that emerges inflates instantly throughout the ecosystem, as far as it can, in a phase of closed, or semiosically viable, self-identification; this is the age of the hero, whose image as victor banishes all other contestants. Then, gradually, supportive networks begin to appear that ensure its stability. Prigogine, speaking of chemical and biological processes, says that a fluctuation "that leads from one regime to the other cannot possibly overrun the initial state in a single move. It must first establish itself in a limited region and then invade the whole space: there is a *nucleation* mechanism" (187). The secondary phase of networks is developed by the less flexible tychastic and anancastic intentionalities. These supportive codes emerge within a state that cannot be described as completely chance driven but should rather be understood as operating within a "permission of chance." It includes the element of chance but the flexibility and openness of the resultant codification is already limited by that first codification and will be further limited by the developing support networks. The gradual development of the anancastic networks becomes less chance-driven and more necessitarian as more and more interactions develop. We will see "jumps corresponding to radical reorganizations followed by periods of more 'pacific' quantitative growth" (171).

What happens in the far-from-equilibrium states is a collapse of all three actions of codification. How does this come about? I suggest that the macrodissolution of metanarratives comes about because the basic code is no longer functional within the regime. More and more energy is not being codified, is dissipating and not being picked up within either the basic code or the extended networks. First, let us think of a biologic species that cannot adapt to a prolonged drought, or even the destruction of its ecological environment; its members become weak and vulnerable to prey and disease, and remaining members expend more and more energy travelling to fresh food areas and produce both fewer young and such malnourished ones as cannot reproduce. Think of a society whose population has increased beyond its technological ability to support those numbers; this has led to massive unrest, famines, disease, and war. The changes, the first indifference to the strictures of the codal regime, will appear first, as with all revolutions, in the peripheral areas, in the anancastically linked areas that are farthest from the domination of the dynamic codes. Such areas always exist and are part of the ongoing adaptive strategies of a healthy semiosic regime. These peripheral areas function within the borderline or "close-to-equilibrium" regime, and are more flexible than the rest of the system. In these areas, small changes constantly appear, small tychastic changes that are themselves, not as random as the name suggests, but are coevolving units. These changes may be rejected as "noise" by the centralist authority of the basic dynamic code, or they may instead move through the larger regime, and be taken up within the whole. This is normative and non-revolutionary adaptive evolution. It may be a state of hibernation for the biologic species, a new alliance that can provide sustenance for a larger population. This is microevolution, the ability of a complex regime to adapt, which Prigogine defines as "in many situations fluctuations correspond only to small corrections" (178).

But if the basic codal format is not functioning well, if the regime as a whole is semiosically dysfunctional and incapable of encoding energy with a certain percentage of stasis, then the entire central code must change. In a biologic species, it could be the isolation of the basic code by the destruction of the ecological environment; therefore, more and more members will be born that cannot survive for very long in that new ecosystem. In a society, the socioeconomic infrastructure will be unable to support its population, and in larger and ever-larger numbers, people will ignore the laws; at first this will be in the peripheral areas but this will quickly spread into areas closer to the basic codal orders. The regime will move into a state of chaos, of thermodynamic codification of self-referential individuals who have little loyalty to a central or group code. Then, at a crisis stage, not merely the whole anancastic network that supports the basic code will disintegrate—for it has already done so over the years—but the basic central code will disintegrate. The species will become extinct; the society will collapse. "Whenever we reach a bifurcation point, deterministic description breaks down" (177). In this far-from-equilibriuim state the regime is no longer protected from full dialogic interaction with other forms of semiosis both near and far; indeed, in this phase, energy is highly aware of other forms of semiosis. The adaptive benefits of such awareness are obvious; the new codal order that spontaneously emerges is one that is immediately capable of a high degree of integration with other codes in its environment. The actual selection of the new codal order is spontaneous and chance driven in that the immediate best order emerges. Other codal organizations are quite possible; there is no inherent need for a bird-form or for democracy. The only requirement of energy is its own conservation; this is only possible within semiosis.

Therefore, whichever semiotic order happens to coalesce and inflate through the system is the "best" order. This is what Peirce would consider a pragmaticist answer, for "the pragmaticist does not make the *summum bonum* to consist in action, but makes it to consist in that process of evolution whereby the existent comes more and more to embody those generals which were just now said to be *destined*, which is what we strive to express in calling them *reasonable*. In its higher stages, evolution takes place more and more largely through self-control, and this gives the pragmaticist a sort of justification for making the rational purport to be general" (Peirce 5.433). Essentially, semiosis is a highly pragmatic action. The Greeks knew that when one was in this borderline phase, this "far-from-equilibrium," that one was walking hand-in-hand with a god; indeed, the god might even have taken over one's body for its own purpose and such a purpose might be quite indifferent to one's own current semiosic identity. The goal of evolution lies in the future, in the continuity of the codification of energy. The collapse of the Soviet Union is a recent example; we can think of other situations in history that followed this pattern, including the various Inca, Aztec, and Mayan civilizations; the Renaissance in Europe; and the French and American Revolutions.[24] Immediately, a radical reorganization, a "spontaneous self-organization" of a new basic code will emerge. This new code, with its tremendous bonding desires, will inflate and rapidly spread throughout a semiotic territory; it will establish itself and codify new anancastic networks. It should be understood that the new codal grammar may not include the entire territory of the last society. When the Roman Empire collapsed, it split up into smaller nations. The Nazi attempt to codify a large territory collapsed into smaller areas; the Communist attempt was similar.

In simple semiotic terms, a codal grammar will collapse, and a new order will self-organize, will spread and develop its codal regime over an ecological terrain. What happens after this introduction of a new basic code, the new metanarrative? If the regime is capable of maintaining a borderline or complex status, using both dynamic and thermodynamic codifications in a dialogic manner, it will be able to strategically adapt and so maintain a robust state of semiosis; it is ensured of a stable regime—whether it be a biologic species or a society. If the codification is flexible and adaptive enough to other networks, the basic code may even spread its codification activities beyond its original niche. This is the case with any number of biologic species; this was the case with the British Empire; this is the case with global industrialization. If the codal order of the new regime is operative within a more restrictive niche—an "orderly regime" operative in a static and centralist code—then it is not that adaptive; it cannot absorb or interact with the minority codes of Otherness, and must remain relatively isolate.[25] If either the complex or isolate codes are dysfunctional, they will collapse yet again; this is the judgment of natural selection on the viability of the new code. However, as I have pointed out, it is extremely energy-inefficient for new codes to haphazardly appear and "wait for" the judgment of natural selection. Energy does not like being tinkered with in the fashion of a bricoleur. The bifurcation phase of a far-from-equilibrium state is so highly sensitive to the codal orders of neighboring regimes that it will necessarily develop a functional rather than dysfunctional codal order, and "there are, fortunately, few mistakes. The jumps are performed in a reproducible fashion. We might speculate that the basic mechanism of evolution is based on the play between bifurcation as mechanisms of exploration and the selection of chemical interactions stabilizing a particular trajectory" (Prigogine and Stengers 1984, 172).

In a small and isolate society with simple and homogenous codes that interact relatively quickly, there will be little need for dramatic codal changes. It will be easy for the small amount of energy used to be rapidly codified and recodified in the normative codes; there is little opportunity or even need for peripheral regimes to become established. Any non-normative behavior is sloughed off as irrelevant noise, and the commonality of sustenance activities discourages deviant behavior. We can see this type of regime in small bands of hunting-and-gathering societies which maintain a stable code of behavior and represent the longest-enduring socioeconomic pattern on earth. In a larger and therefore more specialized population, such as that found among horticultural and pastoral nomadic societies, a tighter codal regime with increased ritualistic behavior will prevent peripheral codification and maintain group functionality. In a large society, whose peoples are spread out over different geographic terrains, whose economy functions by specialization of tasks, peripheral regimes that are far from the codification powers of the dynamic order easily become established. These function to maintain the adaptive viability of a heterogenous society. Certainly, "the more complex a system is, the more numerous are the types of fluctuations that threaten its stability" (188). These fluctuations may be considered a threat only if one insists on a static homogeneity of existence or if their heteroglossic actions unbalance the dialogue with homogeneity. We must remember that reality requires an active semiosis—and semiosis requires diversity.[26]

The old code is no longer functional, and a new ideology must be developed. I am going to compare the basic codal order to Machiavelli's comments on the "single ruler." Machiavelli does indeed point out that when a new regime takes over, its system of organization must be homogenous throughout the whole organism/society: "Whoever becomes the master of a city accustomed to freedom, and does not destroy it, may expect to be destroyed himself" (Machiavelli 1995, V, 16). Otherwise, "the memory of their ancient liberty does not and cannot let them rest; in their case the surest way is to wipe them out or to live there in person" (17). He continues, "Rarely, if ever, does it happen that a state, whether it be a republic, or a kingdom, is either well-ordered at the outself or radically transformed *vis-a-vis* its old institutions unless this be done by one person . . . wherefore the prudent organizer of a state whose intention is to govern not in his own interests but for the common good . . . should contrive to be alone in his authority" (Machiavelli 1983, I.9, 132). That is, a new codal order or metanarrative is a centralist force; it is dynamic codification and there should only be one such code, one such ruler. But consider Machiavelli's next comment: "though but one person suffices for the purpose of organization, what he has organized will not last long if it continues to rest on the shoulders of one man, but may well last if many remain in charge and many look to its maintenance" (I, 9, 132). Dynamic codification, that homogenous force of semiosis must never remain dominant but must interact with thermodynamic heterogeneity, which is developed by the secondary phase of interactive networks. Just so did Romulus, after establishing Rome, set up the senate, not as a transparent medium of "his" words but as a reflexive force, for all that Romulus "reserved to himself was the command of the army in time of war and the convoking of the Senate" (I, 9, 133).

"Self-organization is a prerequisite for evolvability. . . . It generates the kinds of structures that can benefit from natural selection. It generates structures that can evolve gradually, that are robust, for there is an inevitable relationship among spontaneous order, robustness, redundancy, gradualism, and correlated landscapes. . . . [T]hat which is self-organized and robust is what we are likely to see preeminently utilized by selection. There is no necessary and fundamental conflict between self-organization and selection. These two sources of order are natural partners" (Kauffman 1995, 188). In this sense, I am going to consider the self-organization of semiosis to be, ultimately, the basis of all that is ethical.

ETHICS AND THE METANARRATIVE

Alas, how mortals hold us gods responsible!
For they say that their misfortunes come from us. But they get their sufferings, beyond what is fated, by their own acts.

—Homer (Bk. I, lines 32–34)

We may come to our conclusion with a commitment to "sensible reality": our whole knowledge of the world is derived from the observation of external facts. However, this actual external physical, chemical, biological reality, as well as the means of our observation and their conceptual result, is a result of the codifications of semiosis. Semiosis is the basis of life; it permits energy to exist. Semiosis should not be thought of only within the hermeneutic themes of the symbolic textualization of reality, only within the analyses of "words about" reality, or "images of" reality. All that is real, which is to say, all that can be experienced by any organism whatsoever, is existent within the actions of semiosis. Semiosis is the codification of energy into spatiotemporal units; these units are signs, whether they are material or conceptual forms, whether they are primary or metaphoric. Semiosis is viewed by some—those who understand it only as a textual force—as a curse, an artifactual mist over the eyes of humanity. I quote Hayden White's analysis of the absurdist movement: "Heidegger defines language as man's most dangerous possession . . . while Jean Paulhan conceives language as 'betrayal' . . . Bataille views literature as the paradigm of 'transgression' . . . while Maurice Blanchot, as de Man tells us, conceives the 'reading process' to be located 'before or beyond the act of understanding'. . . . And Said writes that Derrida believes that writing 'participates constantly in the violence of each trace it makes'. . . . Mystification of the text results in the fetishism of writing and the narcissism of the reader" (1978, 265).[27] This is a clear description of a belief in the essential power of an a priori godhead that is alienated by a commodified codification, a "giant conspiracy" to hide an essentialist truth. Semiosis is viewed by others, those who understand it as the existential strategy of energy, as a supreme method of adaptation and evolution. How did semiosis come about? How could something so magnificent, with its infinite polyphonic capacities to encode, recode, dissolve, and encode energy into an always-interactive intricate, whole, ever emerge? Did it come about because of Adam and Eve, who broke the Saussurian bond of a finite purity; or because of Prometheus, who betrayed the gods and brought the artifactual to mankind; or was it rather Cadmus, who brought the letters of language to communicate those concepts? We know these separate beings are all as one. Energy is semiosic; we, as grains of sand, or the desert of sand, or a poem of sand, exist only as signs; we think only in signs; we communicate only in signs.

Semiosis is the codification of energy—any and all energy. Its power, therefore, is infinite. However, as codification, it is essentially a statement about the limitations and the restrictions it puts on its own power. The sign, *sema*, is a spatiotemporal entity: a finite, closed organization of energy that may last from one millisecond to thousands of years. The codal potentialities of semiosis that can transform energy into that *sema* are unlimited, but the actualization of a codal grammar is a limitation on that potentiality. Semiosis establishes a particular codal organization and, thus, permits only a semiosis that is bound within a particular codal regime. Remember Hephaistos, the artificer, he who was so clever with his nets. Energy, in order to exist, must remain *philos*, "near and dear" and faithful to the nets of codification. Codal order exists only within actions of *philos* to a particular semiotic regime; when and if it dissolves, the energy must quickly become encoded into another regime, enfolded within the horizons of another act of faith. Energy is therefore experienced within a commitment to a particular codal order, an ethics of being part of that order. This is what I mean by semiosis as an ethical action—a knowledge of the self as part of a codal order; a self-control and acceptance of the limitations of that order; and a willingness to live the fullness of one's life, within that order. Semiosis is faith.

Semiosis is a humbling experience. There is no such thing as "ultimate freedom," as an ultimate right to be anything or everything. If we are to speak of freedom to live, which means, to be semiosic, then within the very meaning of semiosis is the term "limitation" or "codification." A code is, by its nature, a limit on the agapastic desire of energy for "fullness of being." Peirce's analysis of pragmaticism is based on a "starting point" not of original or final purity, but of the "now," "the very state of mind in which you actually find yourself" (5.416). This current reality is a result of an on-going semiosis such that what we experience is a "connected set of experiments [that] constitutes a single collective experiment" (5.424); which is to say, current experience is a result of reflexive or accountable states of energy. "The rational meaning of every proposition lies in the future" (5.427). The viability of semiosis lies within an ongoing contextual reality; will the code "work" or not work? Semiosis must be pragmatically contextual to the very restrictions of semiosis, which states that energy can only exist within bonds. Therefore, *sophronein,* control, is a recognition not merely that one lives one's life within bonds but of the fact that life, to exist, requires a commitment to these bonds.

Similarly, Levi-Strauss states that "sacrifice recognizes the noncorrespondence between the discontinuous and the continuous, yet it also recognizes the necessary bond between them. This bond is embodied in the sacrificial victim. The victim fills the gap between the discontinuous and the continuous. But precisely because he fills it, he must be destroyed. And the world then reverts to its earlier state, in which distinctions are made according to the parallel series of the discontinuous and the continuous" (Calasso 1994, 212). The limit, the border, of the *sema* is the gap. The gap cannot be maintained as an intact reality, for that would isolate and entomb the signs of semiosis; neither can it be dissolved. It exists as a part of the particles or signs; it is the "wave" as the signs are the particles. It is the site of the infinite potentiality of agapasm. Semiosis, the production of signs of reality rather than reality itself, is our sacrifice to the maintenance of energy on this planet. As soon as we become encoded, we are a sacrifice, we are finite codal form, and, thus, we are an agential part of semiosis, we are that which permits energy to exist. Our self-knowledge must accept our reality, which is our codification, for what it is: a gift of life, not for us, but for energy. That is, finally, *noesis* (wisdom), and must lead to the disappearance of any sense of hubris (outrage at having been so used), and to a *sophia* (understanding and acceptance of the reality of semiosis).

If we understand power, not in the nominalist sense (as a commodity), but as the agapastic desire of energy to exist, then we must accept that power exists in everything without discrimination. One can be devoured by it; can dissolve into it, as a moth dissolves into the flame. This is the slave mentality, wherein one establishes power as a negative Other, with its agenda of domination. Equally, one can merge with it, and naively become a metaphor of it, foolishly thinking that one *is* power, rather than being a coded cell of this power. This is the naiveté of hubris: the man who considers that power has moved into him, that he is *habros,* luxuriating in the fullness of its might. Instead, power devours him—possibly not immediately, but inevitably. Against Darwin's simplicity of the stronger, Nietzsche says that "species do *not* grow more perfect: the weaker dominate the strong again and again—the reason being that they are the great majority, and they are also *cleverer.* . . . Darwin forgot the mind. . . . To acquire mind one must need mind—one loses it when one no longer needs it. He who possesses strength divests himself of mind. . . . One will see that under mind I include foresight, patience, dissimulation, great self-control, and all that is mimicry (this last includes a great part of what is called virtue)" (1968, 76). Rejecting the dyadic mechanisms of the unilevel architecture, that level of the one versus the other, semiosis introduces the triadic bilevel architecture, to bring in mediation, the mind, the action of reflexion.

The individual who is also an "ubermensche" operates within such a complex bileveled semiosis, within the borderline regime between the orderly and the chaotic, the dynamic and the thermodynamic; it is he who is aware of both types of codification, and yet who is *sophronein;* aware of the dangers of any excess of either code, the dangers of any merger of the two; and constantly active in maintaining a dialogue between the two. It is not easy; we must remember Peirce's comments that any fixation of belief, which is to say, any monologic authoritarianism created within a unilevel semiosis, is far more comfortable than the dialogics of a bilevel architectonics. Therefore, Nietzsche can write that "my humanity is a constant self-overcoming" (1969, 233), an overcoming of the urge to "give in" to the comfort of immanent, essentialist laws.

So too Jacques Monod, who rejects the position that "objective truth and the theory of values constitute eternally separate, mutually impenetrable domains" (1971,173) and instead writes, as we have earlier noted, that "the very definition of 'true' knowledge reposes in the final analysis upon an ethical postulate" (173). What does this mean? If we consider that the knowledge base of a society—or any semiosis, for that matter—is its metanarrative, its continuity, and its values are its immediate expressions of behavior, then are these two levels of reality meant to be kept forever separate? The answer is yes *and* no. "In an animist system the interpenetration of ethics and knowledge creates no conflict, since animism avoids any basic distinction between these two categories. . . . [However] the moment one makes objectivity the *conditio sine qua non* of true knowledge, a radical distinction, indispensable to the very search for truth, is established between the domain of ethics and of knowledge. Knowledge in itself is exclusive of all value judgment . . . whereas ethics, in essence nonobjective, is forever barred from the sphere of knowledge." However, "ethics and knowledge are inevitably linked in and through action. Action brings knowledge and values *simultaneously* into play, or into question" (174; italics in original). Action is semiosis; semiosis permits a dialogue between these two codifications, the subjective thermodynamics of value, and the objective dynamics of knowledge. Not a merger, but an active dialogue. He continues, "we shall therefore take the position that no discourse or action is to be considered meaningful, *authentic,* unless—or only insofar as—it makes explicit and preserves the distinction between the two categories it combines. Thus defined, the concept of authenticity becomes the common ground where ethics and knowledge meet again; where values and truth, associated but not interchangeable, reveal their full significance to the attentive man alive to their resonance. In return, *inauthentic* discourse, where the two categories are jumbled, can lead only to the most pernicious nonsense, to perhaps unwitting but nonetheless criminal lies" (175). The acceptance of a dialogic metanarrative, a socially developed interactive base of knowledge, provides us with a capacity for reflexion, for objectivity, and avoids the mechanical necessitarianism of the unilevel architecture, that tenacious clarity of the Cartesian frame. Therefore, Monod continues that "true knowledge is ignorant of values, but it cannot be grounded elsewhere than upon a value judgment, or rather upon an *axiomatic* value. It is obvious that the positing of the principle of objectivity as the condition of true knowledge *constitutes an ethical choice and not a judgment arrived at from knowledge, since, according to the postulate's own terms, there cannot have been any 'true' knowledge prior to this arbitral choice*" (176; italics in original).

As a codal construct, conceived within the passions of the will, expressed within the restrictions of codes, the metanarrative is an aesthetic drama, a poetic construction of both the codes and the users of the codes. *Poieo* is "to compose, to construct," in the sense of "doing something to someone." Its synonym, *drao,* means "to do, perform," "within the world of tragedy but also 'sacrifice, perform ritual' within the 'real world,' the outer world that frames the world of tragedy" (Nagy 1990b, 387). "What is pathos or *action experienced* by the hero within the world of tragedy is drama, that is, *sacrifice and the performance of ritual,* from the standpoint of the outer world that frames it. This outer world is constituted by the audience of the theater, who become engaged in the drama and who thereby participate in the inner world that is the pathos of the hero" (Nagy 1990b, 388; emphasis in original). The metanarrative is a victory of dialogue over the monologue, of life over death. It is within this sense of its nature as an artifact that the pragmatic metanarrative exists within a commitment, an acceptance, of its nature as an action of semiosis.

"All men by nature desire understanding," the famous first line of Aristotle's *Metaphysics,* is clear. And "unless man have a natural bent in accordance with nature's, he has no chance of understanding nature at all" (Peirce 6.477). We are all, naturally, signs; we are all codifications of energy. Within the bileveled frame, energy has the power of reflexion—the power, as Perceval finally understood, of questioning, of an endless opening up of the Self to the Other, and the potentialities of future codification. Semiosis, the transformation of energy, within the action of reflexion, is the basis of all life.

NOTES

CHAPTER 1

1. Charles S. Peirce references from the Collected Papers are abbreviated as volume and paragraph numbers (separated by a point) according to the custom that has been established in this matter among users of the Collection.
2. I will frequently refer to "semiotic" as "semiosic," by which I suggest that action is an essential component of semiosis.
3. "From its white tip/a drop of crimson blood would drip/and run along the white shaft and/drip down upon the squire's hand" (Cline 1985: lines 3196–3200); "a maiden/who bore a grail, with both hands laden" (lines 3219–3220).
4. References to Aristotle will include the title of the work, book and chapter number (if applicable), and line references.
5. I use the term "text" with intent, to suggest both the authored and authoritative functions of this communitas level.
6. By "nodes," I refer to sites or phases of synaptic interaction in which different codalities of energy meet and are transformed (coded) into other codalities. These nodes and nodal actions will be further discussed throughout this book.
7. Self-organization will be discussed in chapter 7.
8. Mathematically, contrast axiomatic set theory with naive set theory: the former is a set of uninterpreted axioms, the latter is an articulated body of given knowledge. Structuralism can be understood within naive set theory, as a formal set of rules with a specific interpretation.
9. The designation W followed by volume and page numbers with a period in between abbreviates the ongoing *Writings of Charles S. Peirce: A Chronological Edition* under the general editorship of M. Fisch and the direction of Christian Kloesel, Indiana University Press.
10. This linear algorithmic accumulation of symbols operates by inductive procedures, which are based around the cumulation of particular premises that lack a mediating bond.
11. Unlike those of Vico, Plato's triadic divisions do not dialogically interact but exist in an algorithmic hierarchy; this led to a knowledge operating within a cumulative unilinear frame. See later discussions on a mediative semiosis as outlined by Aristotle, Aquinas, and Peirce.

12. The commodification, marketing, and forced consumption of a colonist's metanarrative has two results. First, it will eventually destroy the home country's long-term capacity to be semiotic (to transform energy into signs), because its metanarrative has become a specific commodity rather than a generality of belief and behavior. Second, it will destroy the host country's capacity to be semiotic because its original metanarrative has been destroyed and the new commodified metanarrative cannot function as such but renders the host society to a state of constant consumer-dependency. Both societies, if they are to remain in contact, must develop a new and shared metanarrative; that is, a mediation level that is not only general enough to permit common interaction but that is broad enough to accommodate the specific articulations of a reality that is specific to each country's geographic and historic identity. This whole process of commodification of the metanarrative, loss of semiotic power, and generation of a new metanarrative will take a minimum of three generations.

13. I am going to use the term "reflexion" throughout this text rather than "reflection" to better explain the action of mediation. Reflexion suggests an analysis of *relationships* between members of a domain; reflection is simply a reversal of an axis direction and has no implication of analysis or of relationships. (See *Harper Collins Dictionary of Mathematics* 1991, 498–499).

14. See his argument (1941) against descriptive "knowledge: in 1941, *Posterior Analytics,* Bk. I, and *Metaphysics,* Bk. VI.

15. This was the error of the Marxist analysis of two classes as the catalystic source of change and development. These two classes are both articulated results of codification; not only are they closed "signs," but their identities are bound to each other such that they are one sign-action. Setting them up in a binary Manichean confrontation is a "false" method of trying to activate energy. The result of such a binary frame is the destruction or decodification of either or both signs, the obliteration of both forms of Otherness; it does not produce a new sign. The real source of transformative (and not simply reproductive) semiosis is the interaction of two different codal actions; this will be discussed in chapter 3.

CHAPTER 2

1. Peirce's comments on the fixation of one's belief by tenacity or a priori essentialism are pertinent here (5.358–387).
2. This is similar to the Christian separation of the soul from the body and its nature as eternal or "pure."
3. Peirce's paper "The Spirit of Cartesianism," 1868, should be read for his rebuttal of the Cartesian assumptions. His conclusion regarding resting the knowledge base of a society/species solely upon individual opinion is

the quotation " . . . proud man, Most ignorant of what he's most assured, /His glassy essence" (5.317). See also Plato's rejection of *doxa,* or personal "cave" certainties, as the basis for knowledge.
4. I refer to the late scholastic as "degenerate" because it had merged its original bilevel frame into a unilevel semiosis and had therefore, commodified both "that which it accessed" and its "particular agents of access." It had commodified truth into a commodity as owned by the church, and its agents into the bankers of that truth.
5. Historical "developments" would be understood as mythologizing and obscuring the pure essentiality of truth. One can only recall Plato's rejection of art and poetry as obscuring and falsifying truth, and Saussure's rigid separation of the diachronic (historical relations or bonds) and synchronic (current bonds) analyses of language.
6. This is an idyllic and incorrect view of indigenous societies, who also established symbolic signs of measurement of value, such as shells, artifacts, songs, dances and other forms of ritual behavior that represented the transformation of energy into finite signs of power, which even accumulated value over time.
7. Internal consistency is a decisive factor in the essential purity of the innate truths of the entity, and experimental verification is the existential existence of the entity. The definition of purity depends on whether one considers that access to its essence resides in the conceptual or the sensual nodes of the individual, and therefore, whether purity is defined as a rational or an emotive force.
8. The separation of church and state is based around this problem, a recognition that the *true* and the *just* should not be merged but should exist in a dialogic interaction with each other.
9. Rejection of such a "mediatory framework" identifies political parties as "republican, conservative;" the mediatory framework that is rejected is the discursive dialogue of the community, and decisions based on that communal reflexion.
10. Popper (1972) argues that Plato's "Forms or Ideas constitute a third world *sui generis.* Admittedly, they are virtual or possible *objects* of thought—*intelligibilia.* Yet for Plato, these *intelligibilia* are as objective as the *visibilia* which are physical bodies: virtual or possible objects of sight. Thus Platonism goes beyond the duality of body and mind. It introduces a tripartite world, or, as I prefer to say, a third world" (154). I would disagree with this, for Plato's Forms function as original intentionality rather than mediation, and thus exist on a unilevel order of thought.
11. Framework analysis is understood as 'sets of categories' through which experience is organized. Godlove (1989) points out "the two central features of the framework model as it appears in modern literature: first, the distinction between incoming neutral sensation and systems of organizing . . .

categories; and, second, the idea that we must view the world through one or another of these noetic lattices" (4). This is an existential codifying structure on a unilevel frame, within the individual perspective, and not an unconscious interactive codal action operative within a bileveled architectural frame.

12. "You could not ask why, from the peak/ of the white lance's point, that drop/ of blood came springing from its top/ and when you saw the grail, in turn, / you did not ask or try to learn/ what nobleman was being served" (Cline 1985, lines 4656–61).

13. We can think of totalitarian states, in which the operative stabilizing force of the generalizing level, the habits of the communitas—which should always be a mediating, dialogical and reflexive interaction—has been replaced by various forms of closed and monological laws.

14. To produce a mimetic *copy* is not semiosis but is a mechanical action. The production of a semiosic sign is possible only within a dialogic interaction of different forms of energy; the resultant "sign" is a transformation of various forms of energy—and most certainly, is never a copy. An authoritarian monologue insists on mimetic copies of its originals.

15. Other nominalists focus around the sensual node and define its codifications as the pure source of truth; these are primarily *group-advocacy* rights agencies such as feminist, religious, ethnic and other "closed-identity" or homogenous-style groups.

16. See discussion of dynamic codification in chapter 3.

17. The absence of the "signatory" and the "referent" puts Writing into some seemingly mediative gap between these two absences; however, since it is an a priori rather than a constructed habit, and since it functions in the absence of the two nodal points of the sensual and the conceptual, Writing becomes a mystic and essentialist, rather than a mediative and reflexive, force.

18. Aristotle's metaphysics is a bilevel architecture.

19. As I have previously remarked, the group cannot think; only individuals are engaged in the semiosic experience.

20. Again, this statement is made within a unileveled architecture, in which one nodal means of codification is oppositional to the other; one node is "valid" and the other must be hidden, subdued.

21. The aesthetic will be examined under the theme of "poesis" and "desire" in chapter 7.

22. "About the lance, why it was bleeding/ about the grail, whom they were feeding" (Cline 1985, lines 3399, 3400).

23. Besides the well-known philosophical and religious dualisms, we can see this expressed within political regimes, which must also deal with the realities of finiteness and continuity. "The King has two Capacities, for he has two Bodies, the one whereof is a First Body natural . . . and in this he

is subject to Passions and Death as other Men are; the other is a Body politic, and the Members thereof are his Subjects, and he and his Subjects together compose the Corporation . . . and he is incorporated with them, and they with him, and he is the Head, and they are the Members." (Sixteenth Century, in Plowden's Reports; in Kantorowicz 1957a, 11).

CHAPTER 3

1. "You saw the time and place were right/for asking, yet were taciturn. You had a perfect chance to learn/but kept still in an evil hour "(Cline 1985, lines 4666–4669).
2. I again caution that the transformation of these dynamic axioms into articulated codes, or measurements, is a unileveled error: it ignores or denigrates the necessary interaction of thermodynamic energy.
3. One can presumably revert to a less-developed state of social evolution.
4. Knowledge in this case is understood as increased specificity of description.
5. The source of truth in a unileveled frame is located within a number of single and often unrelated sources—whether a priori or a posteriori—and thus becomes a descriptive pattern for a mimetic reality, rather than a more open potentiality-of-becoming.
6. See discussion on the relationship of power and purity in Nagy 1990b, 306–308, 366–369.
7. See also discussion in Brooks and Wiley 1988, 357.
8. Consider a newborn child, who must be nurtured by other artifacts/signs, within a knowledge-regime, if it is to survive.
9. It need not do so directly: it can bond with other thermodynamic codal formats if they happen to be linked with dynamic codification; these would be "intervening" codes. The child does not bond with another child, but with the parent, a more stable sign-unit operating within a dynamic codal format.
10. The sensuality of Firstness links with the general axioms of Thirdness and the conceptual particularities of Secondness, to produce the particular sign, a spatiotemporal reality operating within the codal realm of Secondness. See further discussion in chapter 4.
11. See Nagy's discussion of the etymology of the Latin *focus*, 1990a, 160–180. I do not consider the "pluralism"—the constant deconstruction of stasis, the avoidance of systemic forms, which are indicative of deconstructionism—to be supportive of thermodynamic codification. Rather, this is an admission of the failure to make contact with dynamic intentionality (a result of the use of a unilevel architectonics), and a resultant isolation of codification, both dynamic and thermodynamic, into a state of "anomie."
12. I would consider this a form of structuralism: the *system* of natural selection, rather than operating as a generalizing and network-establishing

codal force, has become formalized into a reified body of knowledge, a static and authoritative metalanguage rather than a mediating metanarrative.
13. These can be understood as Peircean Firstness, Thirdness, and Secondness; or Sensual node, Metanarrative node, and Conceptual node. The semiosic movement of codification is from Firstness, via the mediative generalizations of the syntactic logic of Thirdness, to the specific articulation of the single artifact or sign.
14. Recall Saussurre's insistence on the separation of diachronic and synchronic modes.
15. This interaction will be further discussed in chapter 5.
16. Nodes can be understood as cluster points, points of data accumulation where different codal forms intersect, recodify and thus transform their codes and energies.
17. This artifactual external source may be accessed by intuition or mechanical means.
18. Networks will be further discussed in chapter 5.
19. Level should be understood within the theme of hierarchies of organization of the genre's network, which are developed as the result of the incorporation of irreversible (thermodynamic) processes within the codal formats of dynamic processes. The result of network development is a semiotic ensemble, a complex architectural construct.
20. Other analyses will reverse the meaning of the two: postmodern analysis sees the social as static and anti-progressive, and the individual as free but not necessarily also developmental.
21. See later discussion on cyclic or "recurrent Firstness."
22. These thinkers suggest that truth is universal and that the human mind and/or senses can access these truths in their purity. As such, the individual is a passive receiver and not a social mediator; thermodynamic energy is not a means of increasing the codification of energy but is understood as errant and loose energy whose very existence must be suppressed. For a discussion of the categories, see *Collected Papers,* Volumes V and VI, especially Peirce's lectures on pragmatism (1903), architectonics (1891), and necessity (1892).

CHAPTER 4

1. I will use the term "aesthetic" to refer to the human creation of our metanarratives. These metanarratives are not manufactured by systemic actions within systemic structures (the factory method) but are "poetic" actions, a union of thermodynamic spuriousness with the dynamic logic of a people.
2. This spider's web is a good visual image, when we consider that codification must set up interactional networks within which a variety of nodal

points (sites of interaction of different energies) transform and recodify the energies that, in their nature as string-potentialities, intersect at these sites.
3. References to the work of Vico are by paragraph number.
4. See Peirce's article "Fixation of Belief," (1877), 5.358–5.387.
5. Popper considers that Plato's Forms constitute a third world; however, I reject this, because they are unavailable for dialogic interaction and change. They must be considered asocial and essentialist a priori essences. Penrose is also making the same error (see discussion in *Three Worlds and Three Mysteries* 1995, 411–421) although I believe both are simply using a mistaken image, and are instead discussing an axiomatic mediative logic.
6. We must remember that the sign in Secondness is a result of the semiotic transformation of codal energies from two other nodes; Firstness and Thirdness. Postmodernism rejects these nodes and confines semiosis within one nodal point, Secondness, which produces discrete particles. However, since these particles are isolated from interaction with any other codification and any other source of energy, they are aberrant, "wild" and completely entropic.
7. Do you know what we must withstand/if the king cannot hold his land/and for his wounds obtain no cure?" (Cline 1985, lines 4675–7 . . . [all these calamities] you will be the one to blame" (line 4683).
8. Compare Duns Scotus's *hic et nunc*.
9. See Aristotle's analysis of this and his rejection of the substantial reality of the Platonic Form. (*Metaphysics*. Bk. VII: Ch.11–15).
10. A metalogue is an authoritative monologue expressed within individual signs or structures.
11. I understand the metaphor, not as a simile, but as a transformative codification of a number of codified energies that meet at a nodal point. Therefore, the metaphor is a new codification that is yet linked by codal ties with previous codifications. Metaphoric codification is therefore indexical, as Peirce has pointed out.
12. A comparison with Popper's four aspects of language can also be made with St. Bonaventure's "syllogism of sin," which consists of four steps. "The first step of the right foot is awareness of the sin, the second, that of the left foot, is desire, the third, of the right foot, deliberation, and the fourth, of the left foot, choice." (Sermones: dominica tertia in Qaudragesima II; Opera Omnia Quaracchi 1901, IX, 225. In Freccero 1986, 42).

CHAPTER 5

1. Compare this with the concept of "punctuated equilibrium," with long periods of stasis and short intervening, highly interactional phases of change.

2. It is interesting to note Plato's insistence on the small population of the polis; approximately 5,000 citizens, operating within strictly regulated formalized hierachies; both these facets of a one-dimensional semiosis would permit a long-term continuity of behavior if the isolation of the regime is maintained.
3. D'Arcy Thompson calls similar nodes "points of arrest," a "locus of no growth" (1966, 278–80), at which a single growth direction is halted; changes may occur at this node which depart from the original stream of growth.
4. Potentiality and actuality are, following Aristotle, and contradicting postmodern physics, *not* merged, but completely separate yet interactive states of energy.
5. The other strings within this contact are also recodifying.
6. *Polymer* means a "chemical compound."
7. See for example, discussion by Susan Petrilli, "Dialogism and Interpretation in the study of signs." Semiotica 97–1/2 1993; 103–118; the "decodification semiotics" (Rossi-Landi 1992); and "equal exchange" (Ponzio 1990, 1993).
8. This assumption that the individual entity is completely independent, self-referential, and in control of its interactions is a one-dimensional concept of the sign/entity, and ignores its interactional semiosic bonds with the collective and interactional semiosic processes.
9. "Accentuation" can be understood as the code, "articulation" can be understood as the intentionality of meaning.
10. The Peircean terms of object/representamen/interpretant have frequently been presented in such a linear triangle. This is a serious mistake, suggesting as it does that one moves in a serial path from one 'node' to the next. Rather, the Peircean semiosis is prismatic; all correlates operate together.
11. Obviously, communication theories are based around dynamic codification; thermodynamic deviations would be violently rejected as anathema to communication.
12. This concern with the polluting effects of the body, or medium, is a key factor of dualistic theories that *lack* a metanarrative (Plato, Descartes) and attempt to retain the purity of the original sign; and monadic theories that lack otherness and whose entities therefore exist as strings-of-intentionality rather than actual particles, as ambiguous abstractions whose identities remain hidden but 'authorized' by various theistic and mystic powers.
13. There is also Aristotle's analysis of Homer as "the great teacher of other poets in the art of telling lies *comme il faut*. This technique is a matter of false inference" (*Poetics*, 1460a).
14. The concept of Purity, an original meaning, is valid here whether the "original" exists in its material/conceptual essence or not. The non-existence of a cat is as pure a meaning as the existence of a cat.

15. For further discussion of these themes, within different contexts, see: C. W. Spinks 1991; Susan Petrilli 1993.
16. These three ages of the cognitive act are similar to Peirce's three phases of semiosis: Firstness, Secondness, and Thirdness. Firstness would be comparable to the age of the gods; Thirdness to heroes, and Secondness to the particularities of Mankind. We could also compare Vico's three ages with Plato's three faculties of the soul: Appetite, Spirit, and Rational.
17. This was also done by Saussure and is the basis of theories of formal metalanguages.
18. Although I stand by my understanding of Plato as a unileveled nominalist, he has a plethora of triadic relationships. The Soul is understood to consist of the sensual, spirit, and rational; the First Body consists of the belly, chest, and head; the State is a hierarchy of the Rulers, Auxiliaries, and Workers; and Desire consists of appetite or greed for wealth, honours, and wisdom. The difference between the Platonic and the other mentioned triads is that the latter are interactive prisms and the Platonic is either a singular or an algorithmic or serial relationship.

CHAPTER 6

1. This desire is not necessarily for the Other, but can be for the Self, since the synaptic site puts energy into a state of potential codal deconstruction. One can desire one's own codal stasis and not merely the nature of the Other. Hence, all organisms have "defence" mechanisms to protect this self-integrity when they feel threatened by the intrusions of others.
2. See Deely's analysis (1982) of the "barren period" of semiosic analysis from the fifteenth through nineteenth century, which removed the semiosic mediation of the bileveled frame from the cognitive experience.
3. Of course, we know that this is not the case: "pygmies" or San/Dobe !Kung/Ju-Ohansi function within symbolic or ritualistic regimes that provide them with a rule of law for all nodal phases in their lives: birth, marriage, problematic situations, fights, death. Small-population societies may be less symbolically complex than large-population societies, but, as Peirce continues: "We have no power of thinking without signs" (5.265).
4. The natural symbols or restrictive codes can be compared with Peirce's fixation of belief by a priori means.
5. The nodal phase, whether slight or large, momentary or carnival, is still operating within semiosis: it is most definitely not a state of free energy. However, it operates within an open, general, and less restrictive semiosis than the closed nature of the actual sign; that is its function—to permit the semiosic transformation of energy within interactional and more expansive generalizing codification.

6. A full decontextualization would be complete dissolution of the sign; partial decontextualization means that many of its hierarchially linked network of meanings are stripped away. The peasant moves out of the sign-state of being a peasant and bonded within many social networks, and moves into the sign-state of a more general and less specific "human-being." This would compare with Douglas's movement from a restrictive ritual to an elaborated ritual. To move out of this next state of being a member of the wider human community would be pathological—which is why trance-states, whether induced by drugs or other means, are normally carefully controlled in indigenous societies. The individual must not move outside the deeper awareness of being a member of a commonality (no matter which commonality); if such were to happen, he would be rendered insane.
7. Compare all initiation rites or training periods, such as those in the army and the marines, which all "recodify" the individual and insert him into a new codal regime.
8. These terms are the same as those used by David Bohm (1981).
9. The commodification of both will also set them up in binary conflict—the meaning versus the medium—and will see either as "conspiring" to betray the integrity of the other.

CHAPTER 7

1. As previously discussed, modernism did use the dynamic codification of the community but made the error of defining it not as part of the individual's semiosic architecture, but as an objective reality, whose powers of interaction were essentialist and monologic, even if, in part, controlled by the technological skill of the individual.
2. Whom does the Grail serve? . . . But Perceval, unlike the other knights . . . [said that he would do nothing other than search] . . . until he learned about the grail/and whom they served with it, nor fail/for any suffering or mischance/until he found the bleeding lance,/until at last the truth was said/ and he discovered why it bled" (Cline 1985, lines 4728–4740).
3. In Greek, the word *entropy* is related to a number of terms that involve a transforming relationship with Otherness. Hence it refers to rubbing in unguents, to mixing in a third part; a turning towards, a respect or reproach to someone else; and even the concept of tricks and artifice in the interaction.
4. This should be emphasized: the chance-driven appearance of a basic dynamic code may theoretically be "open and free," but both its emergence and its actualization—its actual success in becoming a semiosic reality—are operative within the codal interactions of adjacent networks. Otherness plays a vital role in both the emergence and in the existentiality of the desires of energy.

5. Peircean pragmaticism does not mean "practical, the practicalities of current action," which is a debasement of the term; it means that there is a focus on a scholastic realism, which is to say, that our interactions with objective reality operate via a reflexive metanarrative. Pragmaticism emphasizes the continuity of this metanarrative and its ongoing, future accountability to objective reality, which means that "thought is what it is, only by virtue of its addressing a future thought" (Peirce 5.316).
6. This is not similar to uncoded chaos; it is simple codification: energy cannot exist unless encoded.
7. The theory of the infallible (God, Form) of the unilevel architecture is based on the completeness of its a priori essentialism, and therefore must reject evolution or adaptive change.
8. A regime without stability, that cannot produce iterative signs, is chaotic and will collapse within a generation. That is, a regime cannot only produce new signs; this uncertainty is not only too "expensive" with its lack of secondary networks of codification, its insistence that semiosis be carried out only within primary actions (semiosis without deictic or elenctic differentiation), but it is also too dangerous for energy as it provides no certainty of a continuity of semiosis.
9. See Peirce's study of Synechism, and the ideas of continuity and evolutionary love (1893, 1898, 1903); Collected Papers, Volume VI.
10. The idea of natural selection, which 'sifts through existent signs (whether formed haphazardly or within a continuum), in a post hoc manner, ignores the necessity of a primary codal ordering which moves into semiosis before the secondary codal specifications, which latter result in the actual spatiotemporal sign. (See Kauffman, 1993, 1995).
11. This struggle between anancastic and tychastic evolution recalls the homoousios/homoiousios controversy, or the Athanasian/Arian conflict, of fourth-century christianity.
12. The Greek term *klina* refers to slopes, bending, resting against something else; this sense of a relationship to a more stable Other includes its meaning as "moving from the right course."
13. Communication concerns itself with the single sign, or with a "package" of single signs, and has nothing to do with semiosis.
14. One way to deny the need for flexible adaptative strategies is to suggest that all differentiation is a priori established by the original Intentionality—of God or Platonic Form.
15. I will here note again that the deconstructionism of postmodernism includes only decodification and does not include—indeed, seeks to exclude/confine—the agapastic desire for the bonding actions of codification. It therefore insists on confining energy to the synaptic cleft or "gap" site, a permanent state of uncodified chaos. This is highly entropic to energy, resulting in a constant depletion and loss of energy to

simple codes; deconstruction therefore results in simplicity rather than complexity of knowledge (which is why it focuses on emotive and enveloping "love" and excludes critical reflexion). Further, maintaining energy in this state of non-codification actually requires a great deal of energy to prevent bonding, hierarchical networks and the development of codification beyond the most immediate and non-reflexive. Energy, instead of forming systems of knowledge, is used to maintain simple or "primitive" regimes. This state is ultimately self-destructive.

16. A monologic essentialism is basically asemiotic and will lead to the death of energy. The Platonic polis was set up to operate as a formal system of closed signs; any semiosic or dialogic interaction of these signs was minimized. Such a regime was essentially non-evolutionary and ultimately, completely entropic.

17. Since we "think only in signs," then knowledge is based around a reflexion on these signs; however, the agapastic interaction is not that knowledge but simply a first phase, a sensual and emotional bonding of the shared general codes between the two nodal sites of Self and Other. This is Vico's *mythos,* Plato's *thymos.* This is a prerequisite for true knowledge (see Plato's highest form: knowledge of the Forms; Popper's Argument; Aristotle's bonding of patient and agent)—but is not, itself, knowledge.

18. See Aristotle's analysis of this in *De.Gen.* Bk. I: Ch.7.

19. This newly freed energy need not be transformed into one merged sign, or into two signs—that is, not simply into newer versions of their old—but can be easily transformed into any number of completely different semiosic tropes.

20. Essentialist or unilevel regimes, bound as they are within the isolation and oppositional rigidity of their "state of Secondness," their nominalism, reject this phase of desire. Their architecture separates knowledge from experience so thoroughly that their semiosis is completely monological and, ultimately, finite.

21. As previously discussed, this will be a random yet interaction-driven codal formation that is immediately responsive and responsible to the surrounding codal activities.

22. That is, they are susceptible to, and capable of, dynamic codification (stasis) as well as the excitations of thermodynamic forces (randomness).

23. The butterfly effect should not be, as it is in common parlance, transformed into a romantic image of the "weak affecting the strong." This is a complete error; such an effect could only happen within a regime that was already in a state of chaos, which had already lost its dynamic codal operations and was thus, as lacking a power-base, highly susceptible to all fluctuations. A stable codification is immune to butterflies—both from within and from neighboring regimes.

24. Instantaneous collapse of a basic order may, in a simple biological order, seem "instant," but the collapse of a social regime within the span of a short human generation is equally instantaneous.
25. Such an isolate or specialized semiosis is not inherently dysfunctional; it might be quite correct for the entire system of which it is a part: A bee is therefore a part of a whole ecological process that includes flowers, birds, and mammals. The liver, the heart—both are parts of a whole organism and are meant to operate in a specialized or "isolate" semiosis. All such specializations increase the complexity and, therefore, viability of semiosis.
26. In the modern, global "computer-society," complexity or a borderline state may actually be reduced because the seemingly diverse fluctuations from the multitude of sites are rendered non-affective (to stability) because they move through the system as commodified or "frozen" particles and are not accessible for semiosic transformation. They increase rather than decrease homogeneity. This phase may last only until a global regime is more established.
27. It should be emphasized that the "absurdist movement" as described by White is very different from the "absurd man" as described by Camus; the latter operates very well within the ethical metanarrative that I am describing.

BIBLIOGRAPHY

Abilard, P. 1978. *Sicetron.* Ed. B. Boyer and R. McKeon. University of Chicago Press.

Aeschylus. *Prometheus Bound.* Trans. D. Grene. In *The Complete Greek Tragedies.* Edited by D. Grene and R. Lattimore. Chicago: University of Chicago Press, 1959.

Aristotle. 1941. *The Basic Works of Aristotle.* Ed. R. McKeon. New York: Random House.

Augustine. 1948. *Basic Writings of St. Augustine.* Ed. W. J. Oates. New York: Random House

Bakhtin, M. 1981. *The Dialogic Imagination.* Austin: University of Texas Press.

———.1984a. *Problems of Dostoevsky's Poetics.* Minneapolis: University of Minnesota Press.

———.1984b. *Rabelais and His World.* Bloomington: Indiana University Press.

———. 1990. *Art and Answerability.* Ed. M. Holquist and V. Liapunov. Austin: University of Texas Press.

Barthes, R. 1972. *Mythologies.* London: Jonathan Cape.

———.1986. *The Rustle of Language.* Oxford: Basil Blackwell.

Bateson, G. 1972. *Steps To an Ecology of Mind.* New York: Ballantine.

Baudrillard, J. 1992. *The Ecstasy of Communication.* In C. Jencks. *The Postmodern Reader,* 151–157. New York: St. Martin's Press.

Bernstein, B. 1971. *Class, Codes and Control.* London: Routledge and Kegan Paul.

Bible. King James Version.

Boas, F. 1919. *The Mind of Primitive Man.* New York: MacMillan.

Bohm, D. 1981. *Wholeness and The Implicate Order.* London: Routledge and Kegan Paul.

Borowski, E. and J. Borwein. 1991. *Harper Collins Dictionary of Mathematics.* New York: Harper Perennial

Breal, M.1991. *The Beginnings of Semantics: Essays, Lectures and Review.* Trans. George Wolf. London: Duckworth.

Brooks, D.R., and E. O. Wiley. 1988. *Evolution as Entropy.* 2nd ed. Chicago: University of Chicago Press.

Calasso, R. 1993. *The Marriage of Cadmus and Harmony.* New York: Alfred Knopf.

———.1994. *The Ruin of Kasch.* Cambridge: Belknap Press of Harvard University Press.

Camus, A. 1955. *The Myth of Sisyphus and Other Essays.* New York: Vintage.

Chomsky, N. 1995 "Language and Nature." *Mind* 104.413. (January):1–61.

Chretien de Troyes. 1990 *Le Conte Du Graal.* Trans. C. Mela. Paris: Librairie Generale Francaise.
Cline, Ruth. 1985. *Perceval, or The Story of the Grail.* Athens: University of Georgia Press.
Coletta, W. J. 1993. "The Semiosis of Nature: Towards an Ecology of Metaphor and a Biology of Mathematics." *The American Journal of Semiotics* 10, nos. 3–4: 223–244.
Corrigan, R. Ed. 1990. *Classical Greek and Roman Tragedy: Eight Plays.* New York: Applause Theatre Books.
Dante, A. 1993. *The Divine Comedy.* Trans.D. Higgins and C. H. Sisson. Oxford: Oxford University Press.
Darwin, C. 1963. *The Origin of Species.* New York: Washington Square Press.
Davies, P. & J. Brown. Eds. 1988. *Superstrings: A Theory of Everything?* Cambridge: Cambridge University Press.
Deely, J. 1982. *Introducing Semiotic: Its History and Doctrine.* Bloomington: Indiana University
Deleuze, G. 1983. *Nietzsche and Philosophy.* Trans. H. Tomlinson. New York: Columbia University Press.
De Man, P. 1979. *Allegories of Reading.* New Haven & London: Yale University Press.
———.1983. *Blindness and Insight.* Minneapolis: University of Minnesota Press.
Derrida, J. 1976. *Of Grammatology.* Baltimore: Johns Hopkins University Press.
———.1988. *Limited Inc* Evanston, IL: Northwestern University Press.
Descartes, R. 1912. *A Discourse on Method.* London: Dent & Sons.
———. *The Philosophical Writings of Descartes. Vol III. The Correspondence.* Trans. J. Cottingham, R. Stoothoff, D. Murdoch, A. Kenny. Cambridge: Cambridge University Press.
———.1962. *The Meditations and Selections from the Principles.* Trans. J. Veitch. La Salle, IL: Open Court.
de Tocqueville, A. (1835) 1956. *Democracy in America.* Ed. R. Heffner. New York: Mentor.
Douglas, M. 1973. *Natural Symbols.* New York: Vintage
John Duns Scotus.(circa 1266–1308). 1965. Eds. John K. Ryan & Bernardine M. Bonansea. Washington, DC: The Catholic University of America Press.
Eco, U. 'Postmodernism, Irony, the Enjoyable." In Brooker, P. ed. 1992. *Modernism/Postmodernism.* London, New York: Longman, 225–228.
———. 1976. *A Theory of Semiotics.* Bloomington: Indiana University Press.
Eldredge, N. 1985. *Time Frames: The Rethinking of Darwinian Evolution and the Theory of Punctuated Equilibrium.* New York: Simon and Schuster.
Eldredge, N. and S. J. Gould. 1972. "Punctuated Equilibria: An Alternative to Phyletic Gradualism." In T.J.M. Schopf, ed. *Models in Paleobiology.* 82–115; reprinted in Eldredge, 1985, 193–223. San Francisco: Freeman, Cooper and Co.
Eliot, T.S. 1954. *Selected Poems.* London: Faber and Faber.

The Epic of Gilgamesh. Trans. M. Kovacs. Standford, CA: Stanford University Press, 1985.
Euripides. "The Bacchae." *Euripides. V.* 1959. Trans. W. Arrowsmith. Eds. D. Grene and R. Lattimore. Chicago: University of Chicago Press.
Freccero, J. 1986. Dante: The Poetics of Conversion. Ed. R. Jacoff. Cambridge: Harvard University Press.
Gilgamesh. Trans. J. Gardner and J. Maier. New York: Knopf Press, 1984.
Godlove, T. F. Jr. 1989. *Religion, Interpretation and Diversity of Belief: The Framework Model from Kant to Durkheim to Davidson.* Cambridge: Cambridge University Press.
Grene, D. and R. Lattimore. Eds. 1959. *The Complete Greek Tragedies.* Chicago: University of Chicago Press.
Hassan, I. 1987. *The Postmodern Turn: Essays in Postmodern Theory and Culture.* Columbus: Ohio State University Press.
Harries-Jones, P. 1995. *A Recursive Vision: Ecological Understanding and Gregory Bateson.* Toronto: University of Toronto Press.
Haren, M. 1992. *Medieval Thought:* 2nd ed. Toronto: University of Toronto Press.
Hegel. 1929. *Selections.* Ed. J. Loewenberg. New York: Scribner's Sons.
Holm, J. and J. Bowker, Eds. 1994. *Rites of Passage.* New York: Pinter.
Homer. 1951. *The Iliad of Homer.* Trans. R. Lattimore. Chicago: University of Chicago Press.
———. 1965. *The Odyssey.* Trans. Richard Lattimore. New York: Harper and Row.
Jameson, R. 1981. *The Political Unconscious.* Ithaca, NY: Cornell University Press.
Jacob, F. 1973. The *Logic of Life: A History of Heredity.* Trans. B. Spillman. Princeton, N.J: Princeton University Press.
———. 1982, 1994. *The Possible and the Actual.* Seattle: University of Washington Press.
Kantorowicz, E. 1957a. *The King's Two Bodies: A Study in Medieval Political Theology.* Princeton, NJ: Princeton University Press.
———. 1957b. *Frederick the Second,* 1194–1250. New York: Ungar.
Kauffman, S. 1993. *The Origins of Order: Self Organization and Selection in Evolution.* New York, Oxford: Oxford University Press.
———. 1995. *At Home in the Universe: The Search for Laws of Self-Organization and Complexity.* New York, Oxford: Oxford University Press.
Kaufmann, W. 1974. *Nietzsche.* 4th ed. Princeton, NJ: Princeton University Press.
Lacan, J. 1977. *Ecrits: A Selection.* Trans. Alan Sheridan. New York: Norton.
Lee, R. 1984. *The Dobe !Kung.* New York: Holt, Rinehart and Winston.
Lukacs, G. 1963. *The Meaning of Contemporary Realism.* Trans. N. and N. Mander. London: Merlin.
Lyotard, J-F. 1984. *The Postmodern Condition: a Report on Knowledge.* Trans. G. Bennington and B. Massumi. Minneapolis: University of Minnesota Press.
Machiavelli, N. 1983. *The Discourses.* Trans. L. Walker. Harmondsworth, Eng: Penguin.

———. 1995. *The Prince*. Trans. G. Bull. Harmondsworth, Eng: Penguin.
Marx, K.1971. *The Grundrisse*. Ed. and trans. D. McLellan. New York: Harper & Row.
Monod, J. 1971. *Chance and Necessity*. New York: Knopf.
Motz, L & J. Weaver. 1995. *The Story of Mathematics*. New York: Avon Press.
Nagy, G. 1979. *The Best of the Achaeans: Concepts of the Hero in Archaic Greek Poetry*. Baltimore, MD: The Johns Hopkins University Press.

———. 1990a. *Greek Mythology and Poetics*. Ithaca and London: Cornell University Press.

———. 1990b. *Pindar's Homer: The Lyric Possession of an Epic Past*. Baltimore, MD: The Johns Hopkins University Press.

Nicolis, G., and I. Prigogine. 1989. *Exploring Complexity*. New York: Freeman.
Nietzsche, F. 1956. *The Birth of Tragedy and The Geneology of Morals*. Trans. F. Golffing. New York: Doubleday.

———. 1961. *Thus Spoke Zarathustra*. Harmondsworth, Eng: Penguin.

———. 1966. *Beyond Good and Evil*. Trans. W. Kaufmann. New York: Vintage/Random House.

———. 1968. *Twilight of the Idols / The Anti-Christ*. Trans. R. Hollingdale. Harmondsworth, Eng: Penguin.

———. 1969. *On the Geneology of Morals/ Ecco Homo*. Trans. W. Kaufmann. New York: Random House.

Ogden, C. and I. Richards. 1936. *The Meaning of Meaning*. New York: Harcourt Brace.
Olschki, Leonardo (1961) 1966. *The Grail Caste and its Mysteries*. Manchester: University of Manchester Press.
Pappas, N. 1995. *Plato and the Republic*. New York: Routledge.
Parry, D. 1991. "The Centrality of the Aesthetic in Vico and Nietzsche." *New Vico Studies* 9:(1991): 24–42. Atlantic Highlands, NJ: Humanities Press.
Peirce, C. S. 1931–1935. *Collected Papers*. Vols. 1–6 Eds. C. Hartshorne and P. Weiss, Vols. 7–8 Ed. A. Burks. Cambridge, MD: Harvard University Press.
Peirce, Ch. S. *Writings of Charles S. Peirce: A Chronological Edition*. Vol.4 1890–1884, Vol. 5 1884–1886. Ed. Ch. Kloesel. Bloomington: Indiana University Press.
Penrose, R. 1990. *The Emperor's New Mind*. New York: Vintage.
Petrilli, S. 1993. "Dialogism and Interpretation in the Study of Signs. *Semiotica* Vol. 97, 1/2 1993. 103–118.
Pindar. 1976. *The Odes of Pindar*. 2nd ed. Trans. R. Lattimore. Chicago: University of Chicago Press.
Plato. 1976. *Meno*. Trans. G. Grube. Indianapolis, IN: Hackett.

———. 1935. *The Republic* Vols. I and II. Trans. P. Shorey. Cambridge, MA: Harvard University Press.

Poirier, R. 1971. *The Performing Self*. New York: Oxford University Press.

Ponzio, A. 1990. *Man as a Sign: Essays on the Philosophy of Language.* Trans. and ed. S. Petrilli. Berlin, New York: Mouton de Gruyter.

———. 1993. *Signs, Dialogue and Ideology.* Trans. and ed. by S. Petrilli. Amsterdam, Philadelphia: J. Benjamins.

Popper, K. 1950. *The Open Society and its Enemies.* Princeton, NJ: Princeton University Press.

———. *Objective Knowledge: An Evolutionary Approach.* London: Oxford University Press.

Prigogine, Ilya and I. Stengers. 1984. *Order out of Chaos: Man's New Dialogue with Nature.* New York: Bantam.

Rossi-Landi, F. 1992. *Between Signs and Non-Signs.* Ed. with an introduction by S. Petrilli. Amsterdam, Philadelphia: J. Benjamins.

Sachs, M. 1988. *Einstein versus Bohr.* La Salle, Il: Open Court.

Said, E. 1979. *Orientalism.* New York: Vintage.

De Saussure, F. 1964. *Course in General Linguistics.* London: Peter Owen.

Shannon, C. and W. Weaver. 1964. *The Mathematical Theory of Communication.* Urbana: University of Illinois Press.

Sheldrake, R. 1981. *A New Science of Life.* Los Angelos: Tarcher.

Solodow, J. B. 1988. *The World of Ovid's Metamorphoses.* Chapel Hill, London: University of North Carolina Press.

Sophocles. *Oedipus the King.* Trans. D. Grene. In Sophocles I. 1954. D. Grene and R. Lattimore, Eds. Chicago: University of Chicago Press.

———. *Antigone.* Trans. E. Wyckoff. In Sophocles I. 1954. D. Grene and R. Lattimore, Eds. Chicago: University of Chicago Press.

Spinks, C. W. 1991. *Peirce and Triadomania: A Walk in the Semiotic Wilderness.* Berlin, New York: Mouton de Gruyter.

The Song of Roland: The Oxford Text. 1972. Trans. D.D.R. Owen. London: Allen and Unwin.

Thompson, D. 1966. *On Growth and Form.* Cambridge: University of Cambridge Press.

Trypanis, C. Ed. 1971. *The Penguin Book of Greek Verse.* Harmondsworth, Eng: Penguin.

Turner, V. 1969 *The Ritual Process.* Chicago: Aldine.

Verene, D.P. 1981. *Vico's Science of Imagination.* Ithaca and London: Cornell University Press.

Vico, G. 1948. *The New Science.* Trans. from the 3rd ed. (1744) by T. G. Bergin and H. H. Fisch. Ithaca, NY: Cornell University Press.

Virgil. 1990. *The Aeneid.* Trans. R. Fitzgerald. New York: Vintage.

Voloshinov, V. N. 1973. *Marxism and the Philosophy of Language.* Trans. L. Matejka and I. R. Titunik. Cambridge, MA: Harvard University Press.

White, H. 1978 *Tropics of Discourse.* Baltimore, MD: Johns Hopkins University Press.

———. 1973 *Metahistory.* Baltimore, MD: The Johns Hopkins University Press.

INDEX

Aristotle, 5, 6, 11, 39, 43, 49, 50, 55, 57, 58, 73, 75, 80, 81, 82, 109, 100, 110, 114, 115, 128, 139, 140, 141, 142, 146, 148, 152, 154, 180, 184, 186, 189, 190
Aeschylus, 44, 45, 56
Bakhtin, M., 86, 95, 103, 125, 126, 127, 128, 129, 131, 133, 138, 154, 155
Barthes, R., 37, 53, 104, 105, 132–133
Baudrillard, J., 38, 39
Bateson, G., 28, 56
Bilevel 5, 6, 11, 13–14, 15, 26, 30, 33, 38, 40, 42, 43, 44, 55, 64, 87, 91, 93, 94, 97, 107, 119, 120, 127, 129–132, 179, 185, 186
Boas, F., 36
Breal, M., 82, 83, 84, 85, 86, 109, 110, 111
Brooks, D. R., and Wiley, E. O., 49, 50, 51, 59, 61, 83, 187
Calasso, R., 8, 23, 24, 25, 34, 37, 45, 51, 54, 55, 63, 68, 125, 129, 130, 140, 145, 153, 154, 156, 157, 158, 162
Cartesian, *See* Descartes
Camus, A., 40, 58, 91, 94, 145, 195
Codes, Codification, 33, 49–88, 91, 109–115, 132–134, 139–141, 152–153
Coletta, W. J., 161
Commodification, 19–25, 33, 35, 37, 38, 63, 108, 132, 192
Communication, 106–109
Communal, Communitas, 15, 40, 41, 44, 56, 62, 73, 186
Complexity, 22, 93–97, 112, 125, 144
Darwin, C. (Darwinism), 10, 53, 61, 124, 148, 151, 158, 160, 162, 178
Deconstruction, deconstructionism, 34, 41, 104, 105, 108, 124, 168, 193, 194
De Man, P., 28, 108
Democracy, 52
Derrida, J., 34, 35, 39, 40, 106, 149, 150, 176
Descartes, R. (Cartesianism), 9, 15, 16, 17, 18, 19, 22, 26, 27, 29, 30, 35, 63, 149, 184
Desire, 139, 147–163
  Agapastic desire, 153–158, 193, 194
  Tychastic desire, 158–160, 193

Anancastic desire, 160–162, 193
De Tocqueville, A., 9, 18, 25, 26, 29, 30, 52, 64
Dialogue, 28, 33, 42, 55, 61, 62, 65, 66, 67, 78, 86, 87, 112, 127, 128, 159, 173
Douglas, M., 120, 121, 122, 128
Dunamis, dynamic, 39, 137
Dyad, dyadic, 5, 10, 21, 30, 37, 40, 43, 45, 79, 98–101, 104
Dynamic codification, 8, 46, 50–57, 59, 60, 62, 64, 65, 67, 68, 71, 86, 87, 91, 93, 96, 97, 98, 107, 117, 119, 127, 131–132, 137, 144–145, 168, 187, 192, 194
Eco, U., 32, 104, 107
Eros, 39
Erotesis, (*see also* Desire), 39, 42
Essentialism, 4, 20, 23, 25, 33, 34, 35, 66, 79, 149, 194
Ethics (*see also* pragmaticism), 56, 79, 131, 176–181
Euripides, 52, 60, 61, 69, 77, 78, 105
Evolution, 117, 130, 137–175
False-Memory, 108
Far-from-equilibrium, borderline, 71, 103, 115, 127, 169–174, 195
Firstness, 27, 39, 44, 73, 79, 81, 87, 100–101, 107, 111, 114, 143, 145, 157, 188
Framework (*see also* Structuralism), 27, 185
Genre, 127–128
Hassan, I., 36, 37, 38, 39, 41
Hero, Heroes, 19, 72, 80, 127, 157
Hierarchies, 35, 62, 83–84, 91, 109–115, 123, 188
Hegel, Hegelian, 9, 26, 34, 53, 63, 66, 101, 123
Hesiod, 32, 118
Homer, 13, 33, 42, 45, 57, 67, 95, 118, 129, 158, 176
Hubris, 7, 28, 94, 178
Information, 91, 98
Intentionality (*see also* Desire), 101–106, 117
Jacob, F., 84, 95, 117, 126, 144, 164
Jameson, R., 10, 33
Kauffman, S., 53, 67, 71, 80, 83, 84, 85, 86, 88, 93, 97, 102, 103, 115, 121, 122, 132, 147,

148, 158, 162, 163, 164–166, 168, 175, 193
Lacan, J., 35, 138, 157
Levi-Strauss, C., 34, 53, 178
Lyotard, J-F., 9, 10, 21, 24, 25, 31, 32, 36, 38, 39, 41, 148, 149, 150
Machiavelli, N., 36, 56, 67, 71, 75, 145, 175
Marx, K. (Marxism), 14, 19, 22, 23, 25, 33, 53, 65, 66
Mediation (*see also* Thirdness, Metanarrative), 5, 11–12, 15, 16, 27, 38, 40, 43, 44, 45, 66, 73, 80, 91, 138, 142
Metanarrative, 5–15, 20–21, 30, 38–44, 55, 67, 72–77, 80–82, 84–86, 91, 109, 121, 137–181, 184
Metalanguage, 19, 22, 31, 35, 81
Modernism, 9, 10, 13, 15–19, 23–28, 31–35, 38, 40, 41, 54, 66, 78, 79, 93, 138, 149, 192
Monod, J., 58, 84, 132, 139, 179, 180
Morphogenetic field, 126–127
Mountain, 3, 4, 9, 13, 19, 22, 28, 43, 45, 57, 59, 79, 133, 153, 169
Nagy, G., 20, 52, 59, 60, 62, 78, 81, 92, 118, 129, 146, 154, 180, 187
Natural Selection (*see also* Darwin, Darwinism), 53
Networks, 64, 72, 84, 102–103, 139, 160–161
Newton, I. (Newtonian), 10, 50, 60, 68
Nietzsche, F., 57, 58, 71, 91, 113, 145, 150, 151, 169, 178, 179
Nodes, synaptic sites, 27, 55, 62, 63, 92, 98, 99, 107, 117, 118, 124, 128, 131, 138, 189
Nominalism, 9, 15–29, 31, 37, 41, 66, 76–77, 79, 82, 87, 106, 186
Peirce, C. S., 3, 5, 6, 8, 9, 11, 19, 21, 22, 25, 26, 27, 28, 29, 40, 42, 44, 45, 51, 52, 54, 57, 58, 60, 62, 64, 68, 71, 72, 73, 75, 76, 77, 80, 81, 82, 87, 96, 98, 100–101, 109, 110, 115, 117, 118, 121, 127, 130, 133, 134, 139, 140, 141, 142, 144, 146, 147, 148, 149, 152, 154, 155, 156, 157, 160, 161, 164, 167, 173, 177, 179, 180, 183, 184, 188, 189, 190, 191, 192, 193
Penrose, R., 50, 56, 61, 64, 65, 82, 96, 189
Plato (Platonism), 12, 17, 18, 24, 27, 39, 77, 98, 107, 112, 114, 115, 142, 143, 149, 151, 155, 168, 185, 190, 193
Popper, K., 28, 29, 73–74, 75, 76–78, 81, 87, 114, 131, 185, 189

Postmodern, 9, 10, 13, 22, 32–33, 34, 35, 36, 37, 38, 40, 41, 42, 54, 79, 149
Pragmatism (*see also* ethics), 173, 177
Prigogine, I., Prigogine and Stengers, I., 46, 49, 50, 51, 52, 54, 55, 56, 58, 59, 60, 61, 64, 65, 66, 67, 68, 163, 164, 166, 165, 167, 170, 171, 172, 174
Purity, 4, 15–20, 22–41, 54–55, 65, 106, 107, 108, 128, 148, 150, 185
Reflexive (*see also* metanarrative), 26, 40, 44, 45, 55, 62, 67, 97, 184
Ritual, 52, 53, 67, 117–134
    Iterative, 119–123
    Evolutionary, 123–126
    Lyric, 126–134
Saussure, F. (Saussurian), 27, 30, 33, 40, 66, 86, 99, 105, 106, 124, 132–133
Secondness, 27, 40, 63, 74, 79, 80, 81, 96, 99, 100–101, 106, 107, 108, 138, 189
Self-Organization, 175
Sema, 42, 44, 49, 62, 78, 79, 80, 92, 95, 156, 177
Sensual and Conceptual, 15–17, 30–31, 33, 35, 42, 62, 63, 76
Sign, 3, 8, 10, 12, 22, 26, 27, 28, 30, 40, 42, 49, 50, 73, 80–87, 99–105, 113, 125, 132–133
Sophocles, 55, 69, 78, 153
Structuralism, 21, 22, 27, 34, 35, 37, 41, 53, 778, 105, 106, 132, 133, 185, 187

Thermodynamic, 46, 50, 55, 57–60, 61, 62, 64, 67, 68, 71, 86, 87–93, 97, 98, 107, 118, 131–132, 137, 138, 168, 187, 194
Thirdness, 6, 11, 27, 43, 51, 62, 73–74, 79, 81, 109
Third Man, 86
Triadic, 5, 40, 63, 73, 97, 98–101, 108, 147

Unilevel, 5, 13, 15–31, 33, 37, 39, 41, 44, 45, 61, 63, 66, 76–77, 87, 92,107, 121–122, 124, 138, 149, 186, 187, 194

Vico, G., 12, 18, 39, 43, 51, 74, 75, 76, 78, 111, 112, 114, 141, 145, 157, 158, 191
Virgil, 4, 60, 117, 160

Water, 4, 9, 13, 34, 35, 43, 57, 69